# The People and Promise of California

# OTHER TITLES IN THE LONGMAN TOPICS READER SERIES

# The People and Promise of California

MONA FIELD
*Glendale Community College*

BRIAN KENNEDY
*Pasadena City College*

PEARSON
Longman

New York   San Francisco   Boston
London   Toronto   Sydney   Tokyo   Singapore   Madrid
Mexico City   Munich   Paris   Cape Town   Hong Kong   Montreal

Senior Vice President and Publisher: Joseph Opiela
Executive Editor: Lynn Huddon
Senior Sponsoring Editor: Virginia L. Blanford
Senior Marketing Manager: Sandra McGuire
Production Manager: Savoula Amanatidis
Project Coordination, Text Design, and Electronic Page Makeup:
    GGS Book Services, Inc.
Cover Design Manager: Wendy Ann Fredericks
Cover Photo: Copyright © David Young-Wolff/PhotoEdit
Senior Manufacturing Buyer: Dennis Para
Printer and Binder: R. R. Donnelley and Sons Company—
    Harrisonburg
Cover Printer: Phoenix Color Corporation

For permission to use copyrighted material, grateful
acknowledgment is made to the copyright holders on pp. 269–272,
which are hereby made part of this copyright page.

**Library of Congress Cataloging-in-Publication Data**

Field, Mona.
    The people and promise of California / Mona Field, Brian Kennedy.
        p. cm.—(A Longman topics reader)
    ISBN-13: 978-0-321-43489-0
    ISBN-10: 0-321-43489-7
    1. California—Social conditions.   2. Social change—California.
3. Social problems—California.   4. California—Economic conditions.
5. California—Ethnic relations.   6. California—Study and teaching
(Higher)  I. Kennedy, Brian, Ph. D. II. Title.
    HN79.C2F54 2008
    307.209794—dc22                                    2007025936

Copyright © 2008 by Pearson Education, Inc.

All rights reserved. No part of this publication may be reproduced,
stored in a retrieval system, or transmitted, in any form or by any
means, electronic, mechanical, photocopying, recording, or
otherwise, without the prior written permission of the publisher.
Printed in the United States.

Please visit us at www.ablongman.com

ISBN-13: 978-0-321-43489-0
ISBN-10: 0-321-43489-7

 2 3 4 5 6 7 8 9 10—DOH—10 09 08 07

before a Congressional committee. Following his statement, Michael Mills provides historical background on the blacklisting of the era.

California. You may think that you know the place, and if you've had a chance to live in or visit the state for any length of time, you probably do know a part of it. But as you read the selections collected here, the Golden State that emerges will surprise you, no matter how many of its facets you've explored or been exposed to through film, TV, or music.

To the world, the state is portrayed in somewhat uncomplicated images through film and TV. Though that portrayal has shifted from 1960s sunshine and surf (think *Beach Blanket Bingo*—1965) to a more violent view of late (think *Crash*—2005), the core message is the same: California is where it's at. This is where life is lived large. But living large has as many definitions as there are lifestyles in the place which invented the very idea of having—by choice—a way of living particular to each person. In reading this book, you'll find out that no one image can encompass the vastness of California.

Big enough to be a country of its own, with an economy taken by various estimates to be the fifth, sixth, or eighth largest in the world, California offers the promise of opportunity and freedom. For nearly two centuries now, people have ventured to California to pursue a dream. In the early days, they were lured by the possibility of striking it rich—that was what propelled the Gold Rushers of the 19th century. Today, the same hope of making it big motivates a different set of dreamers. What all of these seekers have found, along with the chance to better themselves, is complexity—many people, cultures, lifestyles, and geographies make up life in the state.

Maybe part of what makes the place so interesting is the fact that no matter what it is, California is not static. It is continually being redefined by its changing population, each wave of which arrives with a different version of a familiar dream. Sometimes, however, these promises of a better life come with a nasty flip side. From overcrowded and poorly funded schools to somewhat bizarre politics to growth which destroys the natural environment, there's enough going on to keep the most energetic activist busy working for improvement.

We called this book *The People and Promise of California* hoping to indicate the intimate way in which Californians are tied to the hopes that their state engenders. California has always offered a promise to newcomers. In the past, it was the urge to come and get rich through digging or panning for gold. In the present, it is the hope of superstardom in the movie industry or as a computer whiz with the latest version of technology which the rest of the world will embrace—and pay big bucks for. For some, the dream is not so big. A simple house in a quiet neighborhood and the pleasure of seeing children attain a university education in the field they choose to pursue is enough.

But if the state holds out a promise, it also represents a challenge, almost like a puzzle. Every newcomer manifests another set of needs which must be accommodated in a place which has seemed for years to have been stretched to its limits in its ability to provide. Thus there are many who make it their job to sort out the problems that growth, success, and the allure of a perfect climate and endless possibilities for self-invention offer.

Still others see these challenges as overwhelming, and either move away, or remain in the state but seek "another California." The alternatives they invent range from dropping out to farm illegal drugs in the rural parts of the state, to living on the streets of the cities, to spending time in trailers near the Salton Sea. You'll meet all of these people through the selections in this book, and more.

California. There are so many lives to be lived here that one book couldn't possibly explore them all. We've attempted in the space available to cover as many possibilities as we could, not settling for clichés about the place, but not leaving behind the traditional ideas of what California is, either.

As you read, consider the promises which this myriad of cultures and people offers to you. Maybe you'll discover new ways to approach your life in California. Maybe if you're not living here now, you'll find out that this dream-place is worth a try. Or maybe you'll just become a more informed individual through having considered the state from so many points of view. Whatever the case, we hope you enjoy the journey.

## ACKNOWLEDGMENTS

Brian would like to thank Gabriela for her patience and understanding of the importance of this project, and his dad, who has always been his biggest supporter. Mona would like to dedicate this book to her very own California girls, Nadine and Tania, and to Martin, who came west to California and never looked back. In addition, the authors would like to acknowledge the following manuscript reviewers: Melissa D. Aaron, California State Polytechnic University; Corey Cook, University of San Francisco; Beth Gillis-Smith, Moorpark College; Janette Lewis, UCLA; Dave McCuan, Sonoma State University.

# The Lure and Letdown of California

The gold nugget. The railway spike. The orange. The Hollywood sign. The computer chip. The stem cell. What do these have to do with one another? Each, in successive historic periods, has been the image which has lured people to California. But it does not necessarily follow that each has appealed to the same group of potential newcomers, because the images call for dreamers with much different sets of skills, and they promise a variety of placements on the social/labor ladder. What unites them, however, is their promise of a better life.

It might be said that this promise reflects the American dream more than the California dream, but the two are different. The former holds out the chance for independence, but its abiding image is domestic: the suburban house with white picket fence, two kids, and a dog. Dreamers who venture to the Golden State, by contrast, do so with much larger ambitions. They want to hit it big, transcend their past in the magical way that can take someone from muscleman to govern(at)or in one generation.

The California dream is as big and bright as the screen at a stadium-style movie theater. It's about money as well as notoriety. It's about excess. And, of course, it's tied to the climate. Sun, beaches, redwoods, mountains. From 60s surfer films, to the *Karate Kid* of the 1980s, through *Sideways*, these are the backdrops for the dream as "Hollywood" spreads it to the far ends of the world.

The urge to come to California stretches at least back to the Gold Rush, when it seemed like all a person had to do was dig around a little and get rich. Many of today's dreamers come to the Golden State hoping to make their fortunes in showbiz or computers. But these days, the lure is not the same for all of California's newcomers. Recent versions of the dream see people arriving in

California not to get rich, but to escape an oppressive economic or political situation at home. They may not be seeking sunshine, but simply the chance to better their economic situation. This too is part of the California dream, though the fact that many such immigrants come to the state illegally creates tension and controversy among the population already there.

The essays in this chapter all deal with the dream. First, the dream is defined in the selection by Kevin Starr. While he does not set out to be a cheerleader for the lure of the state, Starr helps us to understand the peculiar pull of California as he describes the mindset which makes California the locus of people's hopes.

Filling in some historical background are Lewis Lapham and Henry George. Lapham puts the dream into both historical context and perspective vis-à-vis the American dream, and George provides a voice from the past. He shows us that fears that the state is getting too crowded to accommodate new dreamers are not new, but that people have been worried about rapid growth in California for over 100 years.

Douglas Fischer takes a slightly more edgy tone as he explains the quirkiness of the state and also brings the dream into a more radically contemporary perspective. Chris Moran complements him by giving an example of one person's dream, how it was challenged, but how it came true in the end—if not quite in the storybook, happily-ever-after way.

DJ Waldie, Robert Lees, and Joel Kotkin and William Frey indicate the flip side of the dream. For Waldie, California is not a desperately sought destination. Rather, it's just where he's lived all his life. For Lees, the promise of a prototypically California career writing movie scripts turned into a nightmare as he was forced to answer for alleged "Un-American activities" before a Congressional panel. Kotkin and Frey talk about people who have perhaps lived in the state a long time, but who can no longer make their dreams work in what these authors label the "first" and "second" Californias. Where they end up is the "third California," which then must take on dream-like aspects, whether the fit is comfortable or not.

As you read, ask yourself whether you agree or disagree with these formulations of the dream. If you're a new Californian, did you or your family come to the state in response to a similar call? If you've lived in California all your life, have you ever thought of California as a dream-place, as so many do? Perhaps you're not from California at all. Do you see it as a dream destination?

Whether native, newcomer, or onlooker from a distance, given the reality of growth, with Starr predicting the population of the state to go from 36 million to 55 within the next generation, do you feel that this is a place which can sustain your dreams as you move from college into the next phases of your life, or will you "seek your fortune," to quote the old phrase, somewhere else?

---

# A Nation-State
## KEVIN STARR

*Kevin Starr is University Professor at the University of Southern California in Los Angeles. He received his PhD from Harvard University. A former Guggenheim Fellowship recipient, Starr served as the state librarian of California from 1994 until 2004. He now claims both LA and San Francisco as his home turf. His epic 7-volume work,* Americans and the California Dream, *published over a period of three decades, will define the development of the state for the generations of historians and students who come after him.*

———————— ✦ ————————

Where did it come from—this nation-state, this world commonwealth, this California? How did an American state, one in fifty, rise to such global stature, with its $1.5 trillion economy making it, as of 2005, the fifth-ranked economy on the planet? Never before in human history, it could be argued, had such a diverse population assembled itself so rapidly under one political system. By 2004, the Los Angeles Unified School District alone was reporting some ninety-two languages in use in its student population. The city itself, meanwhile, had become the second largest Mexican city on the planet and a ranking Korean, Iranian, Armenian, and Ethiopian metropolis. With a population of thirty-six million in 2004, California contained 12.5 percent of the population of the United States as of Census 2000. Metropolitan Los Angeles was the second largest urban region in the nation, the San Francisco Bay Area the fourth. If the five-county Los Angeles metropolitan region alone were a separate state, its 20.6 million people would make it the fourth largest state in the country.

Where had these people come from? And why were they here? What forces of war and peace, of economics, what shifts of demography and social aspiration had caused the population of California to shoot up from seven million in 1940, to seventeen million in 1962 (when California surpassed New York as the most populous state in the nation), to nineteen million by the mid-1960s when immigration laws were reformed, allowing for new migration from Asia, Africa, Latin America, and the Middle East? Sponsored by Spain and Mexico in its colonial and early frontier eras, California—with 32.4 percent of its population Latino as of 2000—was in the process of becoming the most important center of Mexican culture and society outside Mexico itself. Facing the Asia-Pacific Basin, California was likewise becoming an epicenter of Asian American civilization, with nearly 11 percent of its population of Asian origin and San Francisco on the verge of becoming the first prominent American city with an Asian American majority.

Here was an American state that by the twenty-first century had become a world force in terms of people, trade and commerce, tourism, and technology, and, more subtly, a state possessed of a certain glamor, a magic even, rich with the possibilities of a better life. Here was a crossroads commonwealth. By the millennium, California was exporting some $1.7 billion in goods worldwide—mostly to Mexico, Japan, Canada, Taiwan, South Korea, the United Kingdom, the Netherlands, and mainland China, its leading trading partners (in that order), but also to twenty-six other ranking trading partners as well. The Port of Los Angeles-Long Beach on San Pedro Bay was the busiest port in the nation and one of the ranking ports of the world. Five million overseas visitors were pouring into California each year by the late 1990s, and the travel and tourism economy of the state was generating more than $75 billion annually from domestic and international travelers and employing more than a million Californians before the terrorist attacks of 9/11. What did the non-business travelers come to see? Disneyland in Anaheim, first of all, and Universal Studios in Hollywood, followed by an array of amusement parks and outdoor attractions including the Golden Gate National Recreation Area and Yosemite National Park.

These dual attractions—the entertainment industry and natural beauty—virtually define the state. In the early twentieth century, California had won the contest over the best site for the emergent motion picture industry. And this in turn established a matrix for the development of other new entertainment media—radio, records, television, video, CDs, DVDs—that were to follow. The main reason California was attracting so many visitors, foreign and domestic, was that California had long since been presenting itself to them via the various entertainment media as a land of enchantment and dreams. Much of the world tended to perceive the United States itself as, somehow, California, thanks to television programs such as *Baywatch*, which broadcast to millions a Day-Glo version of life on the sunny beaches of the Golden State.

At times, California seemed imprisoned in a myth of itself as an enchanted and transformed place: a myth that, in one way or another, had its origins in the Spanish colonial era. The very acceleration of California into an American commonwealth had been the result of a gold rush, with all that such beginnings implied for the perception of California as a place where human beings might break through the constraints of day-to-day life and come into possession of something immeasurably better. Such a utopian expectation also brought with it, when things did not go well—when California was wracked by earthquake, fire, and flood; when its prisons filled to overflowing; when its economy went into sudden collapse; when its politics grew dysfunctional; or merely when Californians experienced the inevitable human tragedies, shocks, and setbacks they had come to California to escape—the common complaint that California had been hyped beyond recognition: that for all its media-driven pretenses to glitz and glamor, California was, all things considered, just another American place, and sometimes even worse than that.

Still, it had to be admitted—even in bad times—that California *noir*, as disappointing as it might be, could not negate the cumulative achievement of California as a fused instance of American and global cultures. Here, among other things, nature had been supplemented and heroically rearranged so as to make possible a population of thirty-six million—an estimated fifty-five million by 2040—which natural conditions alone could never have supported. Not since ancient Rome or the creation of Holland had any society comparably subdued, appropriated, and rearranged its water resources. Or used this water-related infrastructure, including hydroelectricity, to establish—again, so swiftly—the foundations for a mass society at once agricultural and industrialized. Or created such extensive cities and suburbs in such short order. Or linked these built environments in an equally rapid time with highways, freeways, and bridges of comparable magnitude.

California emerged as a society with a special capacity for technology. In the nineteenth century, the locally invented Pelton turbine increased water-driven power sixfold. Pioneered in California by the heavier-than-air glider flights of John Montgomery in 1883, aviation was localized in California a few short years after Kitty

Hawk, and the great names of California aviation—Lockheed, Curtis, Douglas, Northrop—became synonymous with the very planes they designed and built. In the 1930s and early 1940s, California played more than its part in the release of atomic energy. In what later would be designated the Silicon Valley, the semiconductor was invented, and from this came the digital revolution, including the Internet, also perfected in California. The millennium found California on the cutting edge of yet another revolution: biotechnology.

The great universities and research institutes of California were the cause and the result of this aptitude for science and technology. It began in the American frontier era with the technology of mining, which led to the establishment of an academy of science and a state geological survey. And then, when barely out of its frontier phase, California turned to the purest science of them all—astronomy—with the construction of the first of three world-leading astronomical observatories. From this arose a scientific community that demanded—and achieved—some of the best universities and research institutes in the nation.

The very same society that was ordering and rearranging its environment through technology was also learning to revere nature as its primary symbol of social identity. From the beginning, American California was at once what human beings had made of it and what they had found there in the first place: a region of magnitude and beauty, encompassing all the topography, climate, and life zones of the planet (with the exception of the tropical), from the seashore to the desert, from the Great Central Valley at its center to the snowcapped Sierra peaks guarding its eastern flank. From the beginning, American California was caught in a paradox of reverent awe and exploitative use. As early as 1860, the state had urged the setting aside of the Yosemite Valley not just because it was so grand and so beautiful, but because its very grandeur and beauty established the expectation of what California should become in its social and moral existence. A streak of nature worship—sometimes mawkish and sentimental, sometimes neopagan in its intensity, and, toward the millennium, frequently Zen-like in its clarity and repose—runs through the imaginative, intellectual, and moral history of California as a fixed reference point of social identity. A society that had consumed nature so wantonly, so ferociously, was, paradoxically, nature's most ardent advocate.

California is an American story that from the beginning has been a global story as well. Despite its quasi-autonomous existence—the power of its economy on the world stage, the overseas offices maintained by the state government to promote international trade, the continuous diplomacy demanded by its worldwide investments—California remains an American place, perhaps the most American of American places, prophesying the growing diversity of the United States. In the mid-nineteenth century, the American people, operating through their federal government, brought American California into being. By the millennium, the national importance of California had become far more than the fifty-three Californians who sat in the House of Representatives or the two women who sat in the United States Senate. California had long since become one of the prisms through which the American people, for better and for worse, could glimpse their future. It had also become not the exclusive, but a compelling way for this future to be brought into existence. California, noted Wallace Stegner, is like the rest of the United States—only more so. How California came to be such a representative American place, what has been gained and what has been lost, is the theme of the brief chronicle.

## Questions for Discussion

1. Starr defines California as a "nation-state." He supports the use of the term with data on population and the economy. Do his numbers form a compelling argument? What other, less tangible, factors which make California a nation-state are discussed? Does the essay explain, or simply imply, the difference between that and a "state" in the familiar sense?

2. Starr claims that California attracts newcomers through its natural beauty and resources **and** because it ceaselessly promotes itself. What elements of California's history does Starr attribute to such myth-making? How might this be traced to the California dream, which Starr mentions only in passing?

3. The essay indicates that California has been able to grow despite obstacles that should have limited it. However, that growth has created a paradoxical relationship between the people of the state and nature. What tensions has this relationship created?

## Ideas for Writing

1. Starr believes that the growth of technology is natural in the state, and is an asset. He gives the world-class university system as an example of technology's benefit for California. Write about whether you agree with his positive viewpoint or believe that there is another way to understand what technology has done or is doing to the state.

2. Starr makes mention of water resource use and misuse, but he doesn't elaborate. Do some further research on water issues, then write an essay in which you discuss whether you see water as a pivotal issue in the past and/or future of California. (Helpful hint: compare the excerpt from Wade Graham's "A Hundred Rivers Run Through It" in Chapter 4.)

# The Way West
## LEWIS LAPHAM

*Lewis Lapham was born in San Francisco but has lived most of his adult life in New York, where he edited* Harper's Magazine *for nearly thirty years. In 2006, he became Editor Emeritus and started* Lapham's Quarterly, *a journal focusing on history. In addition to his editorial duties, Lapham penned over 300 essays for the magazine as well as publishing 13 books. He also wrote and presented the six-part documentary series* America's Century, *broadcast on PBS in the US and Channel Four in England. His articles have also appeared in many leading magazines including* Life, Fortune, *and* Forbes.

———————————————— ✦ ————————————————

*No prudent man dared to be too certain of exactly who he was or what he was about; everyone had to be prepared to become someone else. To be ready for such perilous transmigrations was to become an American.*

-DANIEL BOORSTIN

On a flight from New York to San Francisco last November the plane crossed the North Platte River at an altitude of 35,000 feet over southern Wyoming, and because it was a clear day I could see the traces of what was once the Oregon Trail. The calendar was coming up on a new century, the man in the next seat sending coded messages to Silicon Valley on a laptop computer, and I found myself thinking about the mercurial character of the American frontier. The old European idea of the frontier suggested something heavy and permanent—a stone wall, a gun emplacement or a fortress, a range of mountains meant to hold in check the movement of peoples and the passage of time. But in the American West the frontier was always about the future, and the past came and went as quickly as an April snow.

When Thomas Jefferson signed the deed to the Louisiana Purchase of 1803, he assumed that the land would remain open to the settlements of virtue and ease for at least 500 years, and he thought that the extension in space would provide an alternative to, possibly an escape from, the development in time. If the virtuous republic kept moving, maybe it could let slip the burdens of history and outrun the decay that had rotted the monarchies of Europe.

The wooden carts and tented wagons on the Great Plains in the summer of 1846 formed an unbroken line, 642 miles long, from Independence, Missouri, to Fort Laramie, Wyoming, and the throng of emigrants (men, women, and small children) walked at the pace of their oxen and mules. Having invested their faith in the advertisements for a virtual reality on the far side of the horizon—"oats half an inch thick through the stalk and eight feet high . . . clover grows to five feet, covering the hills with natural hay"—the company of the about-to-be-blessed labored up the long slope to South Pass during the entire month of July. In the evenings they sang Methodist hymns, and beyond the circle of their campfires they listened to the voices of distant wolves and sometimes to the drunken screaming of the Teton Sioux.

American Airlines Flight 65 made good the same distance in fifteen minutes, the audio channels offering the voices of Celine Dion and Garth Brooks, the steward asking if I would like another glass of the Pinot Noir. The gentleman to my left, who looked to be thirty years old and part Asian, stored his computer in a leather briefcase and brought out a brochure, handsomely illustrated, that listed the prices for property on the beach at Aptos.

Most everybody leaving from points east over the course of the nineteenth century entered themselves in a race—a race for land, for gold, for grass, for water, for the fortune they were sure awaited them around the next bend in the river or fifty miles farther into the mountains. The wagon trains leaving for Oregon elected their treasurers for a period of no longer than four months, their commanding officer for twenty days. The promise of a fresh start in a new line of country glimmered on the horizon like the hope of tomorrow's rain, and the steamboats on the Mississippi and Ohio rivers frequently exploded because the passengers placed such a high value on speed that they pressed the captain to force his engines beyond the limits of the boilermaker's art.

The prizes fell to the individuals who were shifty and quick, and the rule in effect west of Kansas City was the rule of capture ("Boom and Bust," "Settle and Sell," "Get In, Get Rich, Get Out") that also expresses, then as now, the American proof of salvation.

If the American frontier was about nothing else, it was about the triumph of hope over experience, and if on the way to California or the Willamette Valley the travelers in the 1850s reported great numbers of dead horses and abandoned wagons on the trail, the echo of the hopes that so recently preceded them lingering in an empty chair or the scent of flowers on a new grave, they consoled one another with the telling of the great story about their impending admission to Paradise. They had a gift for confusing metaphysics with geography, which was why the land given to the Mormon faithful by the Angel Moroni (a.k.a. "The Kingdom of Deseret") happened to occupy the same map coordinates as the Utah Territory.

The itinerant chroniclers wandering through the nineteenth century trans-Mississippi West composed, ad hoc and intending nothing literary, the serial narrative of the American epic. Across the span of the century they made the passage from the states of wonder to the tasks of conquest to the tricks of memory. During the early years of the expedition the hazards of new fortune favored the wayward individual—the prospector and the fur trader willing to take a chance on the set of a stream or a scent in the wind, the bargeman poling up the Missouri River in the direction of what he noted in his log as "just a little beyond no place." The tone was pastoral, and the first generation of plainsmen took the trouble to learn the Indian languages and prided themselves on their capacity to distinguish between a Comanche and a Gros Ventre. Solitary adventurers subject to fanciful visions started out in one place and ended up in another, never quite knowing how they got there, drifting across the prairie with the tumbleweed until they lodged against a woman, a business opportunity, or a jail.

The land still open to "perilous transmigrations" welcomed the improvisations of William Larimer, born in Pennsylvania in 1809, trying a number of different enterprises (general store, freight service, horse trading, railroads) until he went broke in the depression of 1855 and moved west to the Nebraska Territory. Having lost a fortune making wrong guesses about the likely routes of the Ohio and Pennsylvania railroads, he once again speculated in the buying of prospective railroad lands. Once again, Larimer was misinformed, and after a cold winter on the Platte River, he moved to Omaha. He found the place unpromising, and two years later he moved on to Leavenworth, Kansas, where he soon heard rumors of gold in Colorado. He left immediately, and forty-seven days later he found two dozen cabins under construction on the west side of Cherry Creek. He spent one night in camp, but in the morning, still unsatisfied, he packed some blankets, crossed to the east side of the creek, set up four cottonwood poles, and named the place Denver.

As the course of progress and the pennants of civilization moved steadily west, the cavalry no longer inquired about the names of its enemies. The Indian tribes to whom President Andrew Jackson in 1830 granted the land west of the Mississippi "for as long as grass grows and rivers run" encountered the policy of General William Tecumseh Sherman, commanding the armies of the west in 1870 by way of a reward for his destruction of Atlanta, who framed the question of the Indians as a problem in subtraction, supposing they must be "exterminated." The beaver played out in the 1840s, the buffalo in the 1880s, and in the latter years of the century circumstances favored organized capital—the mining company, the land trust, the railroad monopoly looking for a safe bet on a sure thing. The story was over and told almost before anybody knew what to look for or why they had come so far, and by 1893, the year that Frederick Jackson Turner announced the closing of the frontier, Buffalo Bill Cody was presenting his Wild West Show at the Chicago World's Fair as a fabulous tale of an already mythical past.

But maybe not in California. Having been born in San Francisco in 1935, I never learned to draw too careful a distinction between history and myth. The changes brought to pass by the events of the last sixty-odd years have been many and various, but none of them seems to me more remarkable than what hasn't changed, which is the dreaming habit of mind, characteristic of the western emigration and still indigenous to California, that delights in metaphor and chooses to believe in what isn't there. The future comes and goes so quickly that one gets used to surprise entrances and sudden exits.

By the time American Airlines Flight 65 began its descent over the Sierra Nevada, I had counted five nationalities and four languages among the passengers seated in rows fourteen through twenty-one, and I remembered that John Charles Fremont (a.k.a. "The Great Pathfinder") had made a similar observation about the travelers accompanying him south into the San Joaquin Valley in 1843:

> Our cavalcade made a strange and grotesque appearance; and it was impossible to avoid reflecting upon our position and

composition in this remote solitude . . . still forced on south by a desert on one hand, and a mountain range on the other; guided by a civilized Indian, attended by two wild ones from the Sierra; a Chinook from the Columbia; and our own mixture of American, French, German—all armed; four or five languages heard at once; above a hundred horses and mules, half wild; American, Spanish, and Indian dresses and equipments intermingled—such was our composition.

Fremont's report of what he had seen on the way west (published in 1845 to best-selling public acclaim) prompted the exodus across the plains, many of the pioneers carrying copies of it to Fort Bridger and Soda Springs. As a boy of ten I read his book and wrote a school paper about his life, which still strikes me as a fantastic variation on Boorstin's theme of metamorphosis: half French, born a bastard in Savannah, Georgia, in 1813, commissioned as a lieutenant in the United States Army at the age of twenty-five, married (secretly in Washington) to the daughter of Senator Thomas Hart Benton, bound for Montana and the Wind River Range with Kit Carson in 1842, proclaimed governor of the "Bear Flag Republic" in California in 1846, arrested for mutiny in 1847 and found guilty by a court-martial in Washington, returned in 1849 to California (where he owned a gold mine and was elected to the Senate), nominated in 1856 as the first Republican candidate for the presidency of the United States, appointed major general in the Union Army by President Lincoln in 1861, defeated, in 1862, by Stonewall Jackson in a succession of battles in western Virginia, remanded in 1863 to a life of obscure failure, died bankrupt, in 1890, in a New York boarding house.

The discovery of gold at Sutter's Mill in 1848 confirmed Fremont's press release about Paradise regained, and like Athena springing full-blown from the head of Zeus, California emerged full-blown from the myth of Golconda. The fortune-bearing gravel ranged across an escarpment roughly 300 miles long and 50 miles wide, present at depths varying from a few inches to a few hundred feet, and for twenty years the miraculous sand offered the chance of sudden riches to anybody who cared to come and dig. The Gold Rush emptied San Francisco of two-thirds of its population. Merchants closed their doors on four hours' notice; bartenders quit their saloons before dark. An entire military command deserted its post, the men selling their rifles and horses in order to buy mining equipment and mules, and by the spring of 1849 some 200 ships had been abandoned in San Francisco Bay, the captains and crews gone off to the gold fields with the passengers, who had paid as much as $400 for the voyage around Cape Horn.

Because the Gold Rush attracted prospectors from everywhere in the world, not only Americans from "out East" but also Frenchmen, Chinese, Mexicans, Dutchmen, and Swedes, and because they arrived at more or less the same moment, everybody got off to a more or less even start in a new line of country, a country without an established social order, without government, without law, tradition, system, prior claimants. The volatility of the abruptly formed mass produced what the late Carey McWilliams postulated as the equation "gold-equals-energy," which in turn promoted the all but instantaneous creation of something new under the sun. Citing the testimony of Bayard Taylor, an early traveler in San Francisco who likened the city to "the magic seed of the Indian juggler, which grew, blossomed and bore fruit before the eyes of his spectators," McWilliams observed that "in California the lights went on all at once, in a blaze, and they have never been dimmed."

By 1864 the Californians had taken $100 million of gold from the public domain without paying a dollar in taxes, and with their newfound wealth they made a commercial empire—iron foundries, shipping companies, eventually banks and railroads—that owed nothing of its existence to old ideas, settled monopolies, eastern money. The motley character of their society, which was plural, cosmopolitan, tolerant, and unstable, guaranteed a freedom of movement and encouraged, or at least didn't frown upon, the freedom of thought.

It is no accident that California over the last 150 years has provided the country with so many of its new directions, most recently in the entertainment and computer industries but also by way of its enthusiasm for land swindles, environmental ballot initiatives, sexual experiment, aircraft design, and hybrid vegetables. Nor is it surprising that the state continues to attract adventurous spirits from all points of both the moral and geopolitical compass. The belief that wealth follows from a run of luck fosters among the Californians (in Silicon Valley in 1999 as in the Sacramento Valley in 1849) a willingness to deal the cards, take the chance, entertain the proposition from the gentleman wearing the mismatched boots or the lady with the parrot.

When I was a child in San Francisco the country was at war with Germany and Japan, and I can still see the naval armada, aircraft carriers as well as battleships, riding at anchor in the bay; the civilians in the streets dressed like the characters in a story by

Raymond Chandler (the men in hats, the women wearing fur); Alan Ladd was in love with Veronica Lake; a computer was a giant robot in a science-fiction novel, San Jose somewhere vaguely south on El Camino Real, a dusty farm town where Mexicans wrapped in blankets dozed in the shade of the eucalyptus trees, and if Herb Caen had been asked to guess what was meant by the word "silicon," he most likely would have said something about an insect repellent or a Chinese tailor who had figured a new way to make silk shirts.

But it comes as no surprise that what was once the busiest port on the Pacific Coast, famous for building ships and handling the heavy cargoes of a distant war, now draws its principal income from the virtual reality made for the tourist trade and the airy illusions that account for the success of the Gap. Like the fortune-bearing gravel found at Sutter's Mill, the microchips mined from an even more miraculous sand make possible another set of magic equations; once again the frontier escapes into the lightness of air, the way into the future a projection in space and time "just a little beyond no place."

## Questions for Discussion

1. Lapham makes a crucial distinction between the American dream and the California dream, suggesting that one has space as its abiding metaphor, the other, time. The focus on time, he suggests, keeps the California dream alive. How does he make this argument?
2. What type of person did it take to pursue the original California dream—the hope for Gold Rush riches—according to Lapham? Why is Charles Fremont a good example of this kind of person?
3. What form does the California dream take today, according to the article? Who is the typical contemporary dreamer?

## Ideas for Writing

1. According to Lapham, so many people arrived from so many places all at once that "the volatility of the abruptly formed mass" produced a kind of happy chaos in California. Do some research into the recent history of immigration to the state, then indicate in an essay how Lapham's phrase could be both an explanation and a defense for what many contemporary observers see as the **unhappy** chaos of growth in today's California.
2. Lapham sees westward expansion as a facet of the American dream, but he also claims that the final stopping point, California, fosters its own version of

the dream. Drawing on his essay as well as other explanations of the dream, explain what makes the California dream unique. (Helpful hint: compare Fischer's "You See Gridlock, I See Heaven.")

---

# What the Railroads Will Bring Us
## HENRY GEORGE

*Henry George (1839–1897) was born in Philadelphia but settled in California after landing in San Francisco while working as a seaman. While there, he made his living as a printer, and he also wrote for newspapers. He completed the most influential of his handful of books,* Progress and Poverty, *in 1879. He believed that poverty could be remedied if the government eliminated all taxes but that on the unimproved value of land. It was an idea which made him famous in his day and which carries his reputation into the present, especially amongst economists. He moved to New York City in 1880. This selection, originally published in* Overland Monthly *in 1868, was intended to prompt thought about what it would mean that the country would soon be connected coast-to-coast by rail.*

◆

Upon the plains this season railroad building is progressing with a rapidity never before known. The two companies, in their struggle for the enormous bounty offered by the Government, are shortening the distance between the lines of rail at the rate of from seven to nine miles a day—almost as fast as the ox teams which furnished the primitive method of conveyance across the continent could travel. Possibly by the middle of next spring, and certainly, we are told, before mid-summer comes again, this "greatest work of the age" will be completed, and an unbroken track stretch from the Atlantic to the Pacific.

Though, as a piece of engineering, the building of this road may not deserve the superlative terms in which, with American proneness to exaggeration, it is frequently spoken of, yet, when the full effects of its completion are considered, it seems the "greatest work of the age," indeed. Even the Suez Canal, which will almost change the front of Europe and divert the course of the commerce of half the world, is, in this view, not to be compared with it. For this railroad will not merely open a new route across the continent; it will be the means of converting a wilderness into a populous empire in less time than many of the cathedrals and palaces of Europe were building, and in unlocking treasure vaults which will flood the world with the precious metals. The country west of the longitude of Omaha, all of which will be directly or indirectly affected by the construction of the railroad (for other roads must soon follow the first), is the largest and richest portion of the United States. Throughout the greater part of this vast domain gold and silver are scattered in inexhaustible profusion, and it contains besides, in limitless quantities, every valuable mineral known to man, and includes every variety of soil and climate.

The natural resources of this country are so great and varied, the inducements which it offers to capital and labor are so superior to those offered anywhere else, that when it is opened by railroads—placed, as it soon will be, within a few days' ride of New York, and two or three weeks' journey from Southampton and Bremen, immigration will flow into it like pent-up waters seeking their level, and States will be peopled and cities built with a rapidity never before known, even in our central West. In the consideration of the effects of this migratory movement[,] of the economical, social and political features of these great commonwealths shortly to be called into vigorous being, and of the influences which their growth will exert upon the rest of the Union and the rest of the world[,] . . . a boundless and most tempting field for speculation is opened up; but into it we cannot enter, as there is more than enough to occupy us in the narrower range suggested by the title of this article.

What is the railroad to do for us?—this railroad that we have looked for, hoped for, prayed for so long?

Much of the matter has been thought about and talked about . . . there are probably but few of us who really comprehend all it will do. We are so used to the California of the stage-coach, widely separated from the rest of the world, that we can hardly realize what the California of the railroad will be. . . .

The sharpest sense of Americans—the keen sense of gain, which certainly does not lose its keenness in our bracing air—is the first to realize what is coming with our railroad. All over the state, land is appreciating—fortunes are being made in a day by buying and parcelling out Spanish ranches; the Government surveyors and registrars are busy; speculators are grappling the public domain by the hundreds of thousands of acres; while for miles in every direction around San Francisco, ground is being laid off into homestead lots. The spirit of speculation, doubles, trebles, quadruples the past growth of the city in its calculations, and then discounts the result, confident that there still remains a margin. And it is not far wrong. The new era will be one of great material prosperity, if material prosperity means more people, more houses, more farms and more mines, more factories and ships. Calculations based upon the growth of San Francisco can hardly be wild. There are men now in their prime among us who will live to see this the second, perhaps the first city on the continent. This, which may sound like the sanguine utterance of California speculation, is simply a logical deduction from the past.

After the first impulse which settled California had subsided, there came a time of stagnation, if not of absolute decay. As the placers one after another were exhausted, the miners moved off; once populous districts were deserted, once flourishing mining towns fell into ruin, and it seemed to superficial observers as though the state had passed the acme of her prosperity. During this period quartz mining was being slowly developed, agriculture steadily increasing in importance, and manufactures gaining a foothold; but the progress of these industries was slow; they could not at once compensate for the exhaustion of the placer mines; and though San Francisco, drawing her support from the whole coast, continued to grow steadily if not rapidly, the aggregate population and wealth of the state diminished rather than increased. Through this period we have passed. Although the decay of portions of mining regions still continues, there has been going on for some time a steady, rapid development of the state at large—felt principally in the agricultural counties and the metropolis, but which is now beginning to make itself felt from one end of the state to the other. To produce this, several causes have combined, but prominent among them must be reckoned the new force to which we principally and primarily look for the development of the future—railroads. . . .

It is not only the metropolis that is hopeful. Sacramento, Stockton and Marysville feel the general impulse. Oakland is laying out, or at least surveying, docks which will cast those of Jersey City, if not of Liverpool, into the shade; Vallejo talks of her coming foreign commerce, and is preparing to load the grain of the Sacramento and Napa valleys into ships for all parts of the world; and San Diego is beginning to look forward to the time when she will have steam communication with St. Louis and New Orleans on the one hand, and China and Japan on the other, and be the second city on the coast. Renewed interest is being taken in mining—new branches of manufacture are being started. . . .

The new era into which our state . . . has already entered [is] without doubt an era of steady, rapid and substantial growth; of great addition to population and immense increase in the totals of the Assessor's lists. Yet we cannot hope to escape the great law of compensation which exacts some loss for every gain. And as there are but few of us who, could we retrace our lives, retaining the knowledge we have gained, would pass from childhood to youth, or from youth into manhood, with unmixed feelings, so we imagine that if the genius of California, whom we picture on the shield of our state, were really a sentient being, she would not look forward now entirely without regret.

The California of the new era will be greater, richer, more powerful than the California of the past; but will she be still the same California whom her adopted children, gathered from all climes, love better than their own motherlands; from which all who have lived within her bounds are proud to hail; to which all who have known her long to return? She will have more people; but among those people will there be so large a proportion of full, true men? She will have more wealth; but will it be so evenly distributed? She will have more luxury and refinement and culture; but will she have such general comfort, so little squalor and misery; so little of the grinding, hopeless poverty that chills and cramps the souls of men, and converts them into brutes?

Amid all our rejoicing and all our gratulation, let us see clearly whither we are tending. Increase in population and in wealth past a certain point means simply an approximation to the condition of older countries—the eastern states and Europe. Would the average Californian prefer to "take his chances" in New York or Massachusetts, or in California as it is and has been? Is England, with her population of twenty millions to an area not more than one-third of our state, and a wealth which per inhabitant is six or seven times that of California, a better country than California to live in? Probably, if one were born a duke or a factory lord, or to any place among the upper ten thousand; but if one were born among the lower millions—how then?

And so the California of the future—the California of the new era—will be a better country for some classes than the California of the present; and so too, it must be a worse country for others. Which of these classes will be the largest? Are there more mill owners or factory operatives in Lancastershire; more brownstone mansions, or tenement-rooms in New York?

With the tendency of human nature to set the highest value on that which it has not, we have clamored for immigration, for population, as though that were the one sole good. But if this be so, how is it that the most populous countries in the world are the most miserable, most corrupt, most stagnant and hopeless? How is it that in populous and wealthy England there is so much more misery, vice and social disease than in her poor and sparsely populated colonies? If a large population is not a curse as well as a blessing, how was it that the black-death which swept off one-third of the population of England produced such a rise in the standard of wages and the standard of comfort among the people?

We want great cities, large factories, and mines worked cheaply, in this California of ours! Would we esteem ourselves gainers if New York, ruled and robbed by thieves, loafers and brothel-keepers; nursing a race of savages fiercer and meaner than any who ever shrieked a war-whoop on the plains; could be set down on our bay tomorrow? Would we be gainers, if the cotton-mills of Massachusetts, with their thousands of little children who, official papers tell us, are being literally worked to death, could be transported to the banks of the American; or the file and pin factories of England, where young girls are treated worse than even slaves on southern plantations, be reared as by magic at Antioch? Or if among our mountains we could by wishing have the miners, men, women and children, who work the iron and coal mines of Belgium and France, where the condition of production is that the laborer shall have meat but once a week—would we wish them here?

Can we have one thing without the other? . . .

. . . [I]t is certain that the tendency of the new era—of the more dense population and more thorough development of the wealth of the state—will be to a reduction both of the rate of interest and the rate of wages, particularly the latter. This tendency may not, probably will not, be shown immediately; but it will be before long, and that powerfully, unless balanced and counteracted by other influences which we are not now considering, which do not yet appear, and which it is probable will not appear for some time yet.

The truth is, that the completion of the railroad and the consequent great increase of business and population, will not be a benefit to all of us, but only to a portion. As a general rule (liable of course to exceptions) those who *have*, it will make wealthier; for those who *have not*, it will make it more difficult to get. Those who have lands, mines, established businesses, special abilities of certain kinds, will become richer for it and find increased opportunities; those who have only their own labor will become poorer, and find it harder to get ahead—first, because it will take more capital to buy land or to get into business; and second, because as competition reduces the wages of labor, this capital will be harder for them to obtain.

What, for instance, does the rise in land mean? Several things, but certainly and prominently this: that it will be harder in [the] future for a poor man to get a farm or a homestead lot. In some sections of the state, land which twelve months ago could have been had for a dollar an acre, cannot now be had for less than fifteen dollars. In other words, the settler who last year might have had at once a farm of his own, must now either go to work on wages for someone else, pay rent or buy on time; in either case being compelled to give to the capitalist a large proportion of the earnings which, had he arrived a year ago, he might have had all for himself. And as proprietorship is thus rendered more difficult and less profitable to the poor, more are forced into the labor market to compete with each other, and cut down the rate of wages. . . .

And so in San Francisco the rise in building lots means that it will be harder for a poor man to get a house and lot for himself, and if he has none that he will have to use more of his earnings for rent; means a crowding of the poorer classes together; signifies courts, slums, tenement-houses, squalor and vice. . . .

To say that "Power is constantly stealing from the many to the few," is only to state in another form the law that wealth tends to concentration. In the new era into which the world has entered since the application of steam, this law is more potent than ever; in the new era into which California is entering, its operations will be more marked here than ever before. The locomotive is a great centralizer. It kills towns and builds up great cities, and in the same way kills little businesses and builds up great ones. We have had comparatively but few rich men; no very rich ones, in the meaning "very rich" has in these times. But the process is going on. The great city that is to be will have its Astors, Vanderbilts, Stewarts and Spragues, and he who looks a few years ahead may even now read their names as he passes along Montgomery, California or Front streets. With the protection which property gets in modern times—with stocks, bonds, burglar-proof safes and policemen; with the railroad and the telegraph—after a man gets a certain amount of money it is plain sailing, and he need take no risks. Astor said that to get his first thousand dollars was his greatest struggle; but when one gets a million, if he has ordinary prudence, how much he will have is only a question of life. Nor can we rely on the absence of laws of primogeniture and entail to dissipate these large fortunes so menacing to the general weal. Any large fortune will, of course, become dissipated in time, even in spite of laws of primogeniture and entail; but every aggregation of wealth implies and necessitates others, and so that the aggregations remain, it matters little in what particular hands. . . .

Nor is it worth while to shut our eyes to the effects of this concentration of wealth. One millionaire involves the existence of just so many proletarians. It is the great tree and the saplings over again. We need not look far from the palace to find the hovel. When people can charter special steamboats to take them to watering places, pay four thousand dollars for the summer rental of a cottage, build marble stables for their horses, and give dinner parties which cost by the thousand dollars a head, we may know that there are poor girls on the streets pondering between starvation and dishonor. When liveries appear, look out for bare-footed children. A few liveries are now to be seen on our streets; we think their appearance coincides in date with the establishment of the almshouse. They are few, plain and modest now; they will grow more numerous and gaudy— and then we will not wait long for the children—their corollaries.

But there is another side: we are to become a great, populous, wealthy community. And in such a community many good things are possible that are not possible in a community such as ours has been. There have been artists, scholars, and men of special knowledge and ability among us, who could and some of whom have since won distinction and wealth in older and larger cities, but who here could only make a living by digging sand, peddling vegetables or washing dishes in restaurants. It will not be so in the San Francisco of the future. We shall keep such men with us, and reward them, instead of driving them away. We shall have our noble charities, great museums, libraries and universities; a class of men who have leisure for thought and culture; magnificent theatres and opera houses; parks and pleasure gardens.

We shall develop a literature of our own, issue books which will be read wherever the English language is spoken, and maintain periodicals which will rank with those of the East and Europe. The *Bulletin*, *Times* and *Alta*, good as they are, must become, or must yield to, journals of the type of the New York *Herald* or the *Chicago Tribune*. The railroads which will carry the San Francisco newspapers over a wide extent of country the same day that they are issued, will place them on a par, or almost on a par in point of time, with journals printed in the interior, while their metropolitan circulation and business will enable them to publish more and later news than interior papers can.

The same law of concentration will work in other businesses in the same way. The railroads may benefit Sacramento and Stockton by making of them work-shops, but no one will stop there to buy goods when he can go to San Francisco, make his choice from larger stocks, and return the same day.

But again comes the question: will this California of the future ... possess still the charm which makes Californians prefer their state, even as it is, to places where all these things are to be found?

What constitutes the peculiar charm of California, which all who have lived here long enough feel? Not the climate alone. Heresy though it be to say so, there *are* climates as good; some that on the whole are better. Not merely that there is less social restraint, for there are parts of the Union—and parts from which tourists occasionally come to lecture us—where there is much less social restraint than in California. Not simply that the opportunities of making money have been better here; for the opportunities for making large fortunes have not been so good as in some other places, and there are many who have not made money here, who prefer this country to any other; many who after leaving us throw away certainty of profit to return and "take the chances" of California. It certainly is not in the growth of local attachment, for the Californian has even less local attachment than the average American, and will move about from one end of the state to the other with perfect indifference. It is not that we have the culture or the opportunities to gratify luxurious and cultivated tastes that older countries afford, and yet those who leave us on this account as a general thing come back again.

No: the potent charm of California, which all feel but few analyze, has been more in the character, habits and modes of thought of her people—called forth by the peculiar conditions of the young State—than in anything else. In California there has been a certain cosmopolitanism, a certain freedom and breadth of common thought and feeling, natural to a community made up from so many different sources, to which every man and woman had been transplanted—all travelers to some extent, and with native angularities of prejudice and habit more or less worn off. Then there has been a feeling of personal independence and equality, a general hopefulness and self-reliance, and a certain large-heartedness and open-handedness which were born of the comparative evenness with which property was distributed, the high standard of wages and of comfort, and the latent feeling of everyone that he might "make a strike," and certainly could not be kept down long. . . .

In a country where all had started from the same level . . . social lines could not be sharply drawn, nor a reverse dispirit. There was something in the great possibilities of the country; in the feeling that it was one of immense latent wealth; which furnished a background of which a better filled and more thoroughly developed country is destitute, and which contributed not a little to the active, generous, independent social tone.

The characteristics of the principal business—mining—gave a color to all California thought and feeling. It fostered a reckless, generous, independent spirit, with a strong disposition to "take chances" and "trust to luck." Than the placer mining, no more independent business could be conceived. The miner working for himself, owned no master; worked when and only when he pleased; took out his earnings each day in the shining particles which depended for their value on no fluctuations of the market, but would pass current and supply all wants the world over. When his claim gave out, or for any reason he desired to move on, he had but to shoulder his pick and move on. Mining of this kind developed its virtues as well as its vices. If it could have been united with ownership of land and the comforts and restraints of home, it would have given us a class of citizens of the utmost value to a republican state. But the "honest miner" of the placers has passed away in California. The Chinaman, the mill-owner and his laborers, the mine superintendent and his gang, are his successors.

This crowding of people into immense cities, this aggregation of wealth into large lumps, this marshalling of men into big gangs under the control of the great "captains of industry," does not tend to foster personal independence—the basis of all virtues—nor will it tend to preserve the characteristics which particularly have made Californians proud of their state.

However, we shall have some real social gains, with some that are only apparent. We shall have more of home influences, a deeper religious sentiment, less of the unrest that is bred of an adventurous and reckless life. We shall have fewer shooting and stabbing affrays, but we will have probably something worse, from which, thank God, we have hitherto been exempt—the low, brutal, cowardly rowdyism of the great eastern cities. We shall hear less of highway robberies in the mountains, but more, perhaps, of pickpockets, burglars and sneak thieves.

That we can look forward to any political improvement is, to say the least, doubtful. There is nothing in the changes which are coming that of itself promises that. There will be a more permanent population, more who will look on California as their home; but we would not aver that there will be a larger proportion of the population who will take an intelligent interest in public affairs. In San Francisco the political future is full of danger. As surely as San Francisco is destined to become as large as New York, as certain is it that her political condition is destined to become as bad as that of New York, unless her citizens are aroused in time to the necessity of preventive or rather palliative measures. And in the growth of large corporations and other special interests is an element of great danger. Of these great corporations and interests we shall have many. Look, for instance, at the Central Pacific Railroad Company, as it will be, with a line running to Salt Lake, controlling more capital and employing more men than any of the great eastern railroads who manage legislatures as they manage their workshops, and name governors, senators and judges almost as they name their own engineers and clerks! Can we rely upon sufficient intelligence, independence and virtue among the many to resist the political effects of the concentration of great wealth in the hands of a few? . . .

With our gains and our losses will come new duties and new responsibilities. Connected more closely with the rest of the nation, we will feel more quickly and keenly all that affects it. We will have to deal, in time, with all the social problems that are forcing themselves on older communities (like the riddles of a Sphinx, which not to answer is death), with one of them, the labor question, rendered peculiarly complex by our proximity to Asia. Public spirit, public virtue, the high resolve of men and women who are capable of feeling "enthusiasm of humanity," will be needed in the future more than ever. . . .

Let us not imagine ourselves in a fool's paradise, where the golden apples will drop into our mouths; let us not think that after the stormy seas and head gales of all the ages, *our* ship has at last struck the trade winds of time. The future of our State, of our nation, of our race, looks fair and bright; perhaps the future looked so to the philosophers who once sat in the porches of Athens—to the unremembered men who raised the cities whose ruins lie south of us. Our modern civilization strikes broad and deep and looks high. So did the tower which men once built almost unto heaven.

## Questions for Discussion

1. George talks about the benefits of the railroad, but also the negatives. Make a list of the plusses and minuses as developed in the selection, then indicate whether you think he finally comes down on one side or the other.

2. When George talks about the "peculiar charm of California," he begins by listing what it is not before going on to indicate what it is. What are the elements on either side, and to what does he ascribe the charm in the end?
3. According to George, people in California live in a spirit of true sharing, partly because, at his time, the state was made up almost entirely of immigrants. (Like many of his time, he is blind to the Native American population.) Does he effectively convey his optimism about the spirit of the true Californian? How does he justify his pessimism about the future influx of immigrants?

## Ideas for Writing

1. Does it stand to reason that with an increase in population, labor gets poorer but capital gets richer? As a test case, do some research about wages in the

### California's Population: Growth Since Statehood

| Year | Population |
| --- | --- |
| 1850 | 92,597 |
| 1860 | 379,994 |
| 1870 | 560,247 |
| 1880 | 864,694 |
| 1890 | 1,213,398 |
| 1900 | 1,485,053 |
| 1910 | 2,377,549 |
| 1920 | 3,426,861 |
| 1930 | 5,677,251 |
| 1940 | 6,907,387 |
| 1950 | 10,586,223 |
| 1960 | 15,717,204 |
| 1970 | 19,971,069 |
| 1980 | 23,667,902 |
| 1990 | 31,400,000 |
| 2003 | 35,591,000 |
| Projected 2020 | 45,821,900 |

*Source:* U.S. Census Bureau, State Department of Finance.

profession you plan to enter, then write an essay explaining your position on George's claim.

2. George claims that the state will gain the civilizing influence of culture once it is connected to the larger world via the railroad. If that was true in his time, it must be doubly true now that airline travel has connected all parts of the world together. Write an essay that talks about the cosmopolitan influences in the California of today. Explain whether they truly improve life in the state, and how.

# You See Gridlock, I See Heaven
## DOUGLAS FISCHER

*Douglas Fischer is a staff writer for the daily* Oakland Tribune, *with primary responsibility for writing about environmental issues. His series of investigative articles, "A Body's Burden: Our Chemical Legacy," which appeared in 2005, brought to public attention the problem of chemical absorption by the body through a study of an average family's toxic exposure.*

◆

The dream started to crumble in 1964. By '76 it was mostly gone. And California today is the better for it in ways no one foresaw 30 years ago.

California built itself in the '50s and '60s. At one point the state had half of NASA's prime contracts, a net flow of nearly 1,000 new residents per day, a free university system and all the water Southern California needed.

It was a stunning run that established California as the prototypical "New West" and seemed limitless at its height and scope. But it came at a price.

So what if a few of the world's foremost salmon runs disappeared behind the concrete dams that went up in that era? The farmland that water system irrigates now accounts for one-eighth of total U.S. agriculture income.

And California's welfare and education systems, once the envy of the nation? Taxpayers eventually revolted as new arrivals took advantage of the safety net. Today [2006] California sits in the bottom half in the nation in education spending per pupil.

Historians disagree on what marked the end of that so-called golden era—when this paradise that was California ceased to be.

Some say the cracks appeared as early as 1962, when California passed New York as the nation's most populous state and newspapers and civic leaders began to wonder whether such growth might soon be an inconvenience. Others say the edifice came down in 1978, when Proposition 13 froze property taxes at 1975's level and rewrote state spending policy.

It's tempting to say the state remains moribund with this sense of malaise. Sky-high housing costs are pricing the state's 30-somethings right out of the market. Political squabbles have Sacramento gridlocked. More than 650 people a day moved out of state last year [2005].

But while the nation's attention remains riveted on California's collapse, an equally fervent groundswell has been moving unnoticed for years. And it is that wave of new immigrants—mostly foreign born, considerably browner than the previous wave, but equally desirous of cashing in on California's dream—that makes this state such a vibrant place today.

"We are a magnet for people all over the world, who just can't wait to get here," said Jim Quay, executive director of California Council for the Humanities. "If there's a tarnish on California's golden dream, it sure hasn't been communicated to the rest of the world."

The era was also one of social unrest, riots, economic downturns, which upended the state's sense of order and rewrote the nation's priorities. Norman Mailer wrote that this was really the bubbling over of a full-scale struggle that had been simmering unnoticed for 20 years: "It was whether the country would go mad or not." California is where the lid blew off.

Take the Free Speech Movement at the University of California, Berkeley. The 1964 protests alienated a tax base that didn't understand why they had to pay to educate a bunch of ill-mannered ingrates. Ronald Reagan swept into the governor's mansion in part on the promise to "fix the university." State support for its crown jewel was never the same.

But the riots launched a student movement that eventually shook the nation in the late 1960s and revolutionized higher education in the country. And it came, organizer Mario Savio said, because of the political character of the Bay Area.

"This is one of the few places left in the United States where a personal history of involvement in radical politics is not a form of social leprosy," he wrote in "West of the West."

The Vietnam War protests shook the nation to its soul, and the military-industrial complex—the economic engine for Southern California and Silicon Valley—never again had the same prestige and unquestioning shine.

Education spending tumbled from fifth in the nation in 1965 to 41st at its nadir in 1995; highway congestion doubled and doubled again.

More than 239,000 Californians left the state last year, according to the U.S. Census. Yet 232,700 foreigners arrived hoping to call California home.

"Rightly or wrongly, California is still called 'Gold Mountain' in China," said Him Mark Lai, a board member of the Chinese Historical Society of America. "You still have that conception that it is easier to make a living."

But if your beloved state once seemed just right with 11 million people calling it home, it surely is insufferable with 35 million. Ham Forkner is one such soul, and he's fed up.

Forkner grew up in Berkeley and loved it. He graduated from Cal in '40 and still comes back every year for the reunions. But he'll never live here. "California's changed a hell of a lot. I can't stand it anymore," he said from his home in western Montana. "But it was a beautiful place to grow up."

Check just about any barometer against past decades, and Forkner has a point: Life today is more hemmed in, congested, harried.

Want to take the mountaineer's route up Mt. Whitney, California's highest point? Better be among the first 15 that morning to request a trail permit.

Figure a Sunday drive down the coast would be nice? Pack a lunch. Paul Vieregge, one of the founders of the Monterey Jazz Festival, remembers when traffic was so thin on Route 1 through Big Sur he'd sit on the porch of the old d'Angulo ranch house with his friends and bet against the direction of the next car. Sometimes he'd wait hours before collecting.

Today, that stretch of highway sees 800 cars an hour on an average evening.

But for every story like Vieregge's, others have tales of change for the better.

Lai recalls that San Francisco's Chinatown in the early '60s was in danger of quietly disappearing. Government quotas keep a tight lid on the number of Chinese legally entering the United States, and Chinatown was slowly stagnating, he said.

Then Congress in 1965 loosened the quotas. Immigrants flocked to the States, with San Francisco as a top destination. "Chinatown from that point on becomes a lot more diverse," Lai said, noting that post-'65 immigrants tended to be more educated and arrived with business backgrounds or from urban hubs like Hong Kong. "It's really at that point that you start to have other than Cantonese food" in Chinatown restaurants.

So what happened? Like all myths, the notion that California was a paradise so many years ago is a blend of truth and fuzzy recollection. Likewise, the sense that California has been on the skids ever since mixes hard-edged reality and utter fiction.

Where the good times were depends, historians say, on the color of your skin. The first immigrant wave, spanning from World War II to the mid-1970s, drew people from throughout the United States—Kansas, Ohio, Arkansas. The second wave, equally as potent, drew chiefly foreigners and continues today.

"Those two demographics look remarkably the same, except in the second half the people are darker," said Richard Walker, a geography professor at UC Berkeley and head of the California Studies Center.

But skin color alone did not mark the times. Walker notes that the second wave peaked during a meaner era: Taxpayers were revolting, social services were being trimmed and California schools took a dive. There was a recession, a lot of homelessness and residents started getting a little nervous.

In the early 1990s California absorbed nearly one third of all immigrants arriving in the United States. Not coincidentally, voters in 1994 overwhelmingly passed Proposition 187 to ban some of their children from public schools.

But that era, too, passed. The people were here to stay; they started building California. Politicians found it hard to be anti-immigrant when much of the electorate was foreign born. And the children were already in the schools. "It's a fait accompli," Walker said. The point is, California has always been growing like crazy. It's always been a boom state during boom times. It has always drawn in people like a vacuum cleaner.

"It's just that where you put the nozzle of the vacuum cleaner has changed."

And that will make for a very different California in a few decades, said Hans Johnson, a demographer for the Public Policy Institute of California. Five years from now, according to population projections, Hispanics will surpass whites and become the largest ethnic group in the state.

And it's not just from immigration.

Already Hispanics account for more than half the births in the state. Whites, meanwhile, have dropped from 70 percent of all births in 1970 to about 30 percent now. And California's whites on the whole are an older, grayer crowd. The median age for white females, according to 2000 census data, is 41 years old. The median age for female Hispanics, on the other hand, is 25.

"The single largest group of children in California are not whites but Hispanics," Johnson said. "By 2040, (Hispanics) will almost constitute a new majority."

But surely these crowds are arriving—or being born into—a California considerably degraded since its heyday in the '50s. Again, historians say, that's a matter of perspective.

Paul and Penny Vieregge have watched as Californians discovered Big Sur. They remember when the phone line stopped at Pardington and the Nepenthe restaurant hosted the big end-of-season closing party before the area shut down for winter. Is that spirit gone?

"Yes. Completely," Penny Vieregge said without pause. "What we have now are third, fourth, fifth home owners. Gated communities. Our volunteer base is just about belly up."

Sylvia McLaughlin recalls the days in the early 1950s when she and her husband would drive down the Peninsula to look at all the fruit trees in blossom. Needless to say, those are long gone. Today, farmland along the Interstate 80 corridor between the Bay Area and Sacramento and prime Delta bottom land near Tracy are rapidly disappearing beneath housing tracts.

This growth has McLaughlin, who co-founded Save The Bay in the 1960s, wondering what's next. "We've fought for the Marin Headlands. We've fought for all the ridge lines. You just try to save the outstanding, wonderful natural areas that we're endowed with here."

In that way, the party isn't over. California has the world's sixth largest economy, producing $1.5 trillion in goods and services annually. Home sales may have slowed recently, but people still will pay dearly to live here: The median price for a single-family home in the Bay Area—$625,000—is still almost 17 percent higher than a year ago.

Stephen Levy, director of the Palo Alto-based Center for Continuing Study of the California Economy, believes that California remains a powerhouse.

"We still have tremendous economic opportunities and a young and vibrant population," he said. "The difference from 50 years ago is we are now ambivalent about growth. There is no consensus."

And that ambivalence has led to paralysis—something unknown a generation ago, as Gov. Edmund "Pat" Brown was ushering his water project and freeway system past voters.

Five years ago, when a reporter walked into Levy's office confusing this ambivalence with a sense of stagnation, Levy grew visibly frustrated. Today he still believes the state has the industries and opportunities found here a generation ago.

"The question is whether we still have the will to have world-class education, world-class infrastructure and world-class places to live and work," he said.

After all, California still leads the nation in patents, foreign trade, venture capital, Levy said.

Hollywood is still Hollywood. It drives the nation's culture, spilling over into music, toys, architecture. California's defense and aerospace companies have less clout, but Silicon Valley still drives the computer industry.

"And despite a few bumps along the road, we still have held onto our tolerance and attitudes," Levy said.

He knows. He grew up in 1950s Los Angeles. His mother ran an apparel factory, and the evolution of his mom's floor workers was the California story writ small.

In the '50s they were white and black. By the '60s they were black and Latino. By the '70s they were Latino and Asian. "But it was always multicultural and fascinating. It all worked."

The point, he added, hitting the table for emphasis, is that "everyone here was new—whether 'new' was New York or Mexico or the Philippines.

"And that made the difference."

## Questions for Discussion

1. Why is there so much pessimism about the state of the Golden State these days? Make a log of the examples Fischer gives to suggest that the dream is dead.
2. Fischer makes the case that there is just as much optimism about California now as there ever has been, but he says that it occurs in different people now than it did before. Who are the current California dreamers, according to the article, and what historical markers show the birth of their dream?
3. What are Fischer's predictions about the future of the state, and how does he support his claims?

## Ideas for Writing

1. Fischer cites Stephen Levy to suggest that the dream retains its hopes despite change. If you live in California, interview some people who are new-comers to the state. Address these questions in an essay based on their experience: What hopes did they bring? Have those dreams been fulfilled? Does their experience support or refute Fischer's characterization of the dream? If you live elsewhere, interview some newcomers to your state. Do they have a dream? If so, evaluate its resemblance to the California dream.

2. Being negative about the results of growth is commonplace, especially when growth threatens people's familiar way of doing things. Find a community in which growth is perceived as a negative. Talk to some people firsthand to find out what form these pessimistic views may take. In an essay, explain any similarities with the examples Fischer gives, then indicate whether there is a common cause for these points of view.

---

# Graduation Marks Triumph for Homeless Woman

## CHRIS MORAN

*Chris Moran is a staff writer for the* San Diego Union-Tribune, *a daily newspaper in San Deigo, California. He has covered many items of local and national importance, focusing on politics and social issues. In 1999, he won an Education Writers Association award for his feature story, "A Life's Lesson." He has also been honored by the San Diego Press Club for his coverage of education issues.*

---◆---

Chula Vista—By her own description, Debbie Berry was "bored and fat," sitting on an overstuffed love seat in front of the television that day in 2000 when she thumbed through the course schedule. It was no special invitation. Southwestern College mails out 100,000 of these three times a year.

But only to those with fixed addresses. Berry didn't get mail where she had lived the year before—a nylon camping tent in a dried river bottom behind Smart & Final on Main Street.

The course schedule arrived at an 800-square-foot mobile home she shared with her boyfriend, Billy Stewart, four cats, a macaw, an African gray parrot and a 125-pound Rottweiler. She was still unemployed, but welfare checks allowed her to cover the monthly rent for her space in the mobile home park off Broadway in northern Chula Vista.

Berry remembered that she oohed and aahed as she flipped through the offerings until Stewart said to her, "Why don't you just go?"

So she did.

She commuted across town on the bus. She got financial aid to cover tuition and most of her books. During her second year, she took a final exam while suffering from what turned out to be a ruptured hernia, and she was in surgery within hours of finishing the test.

Friday, she was to march in Southwestern College's graduation ceremony to receive her associate's degree in anthropology. Debbie Elizabeth Berry is one of more than 1,300 new degree recipients.

She has a sense of humor about her story, though it's difficult to tell where she draws the line between bad luck and taking responsibility for a tough life.

It's bad luck that when she and Stewart bought a camper as a first step out of the river bottom and parked it on the street, it was totaled by an out-of-control car. But before she was homeless, she had a job and an apartment, a mom who would have taken her in and a boyfriend to help pay rent.

First she lost her kids in court. Then she lost her father. Then she lost her will to keep working.

"It was life. It wasn't chosen, but it happened," she said.

She did choose to enroll in two of the courses from the Southwestern schedule. For four years, she built on that foundation, brick by academic brick.

There's no defensive laughter or resignation in her voice, just unabashed glee when she says, "I have a degree."

One of Berry's most vivid memories of homelessness was the police helicopter that hovered periodically above the camp. Often, she surmised it was taking some sort of informal aerial census.

But one night during the last El Niño winter, the police used the helicopter to broadcast a warning: get out. Floodgates were going to open and her camp would soon be inundated. So she had to flee even a squatters' camp.

She remembers the people she lost, too. A friend died in her arms on the street. Another camp resident died when he was transferring fuel to a propane tank and it blew up in his face.

She'd never envisioned this sort of desperation as a child in Scottsdale, Ariz.

"Being from an upper-middle-class neighborhood, growing up you wonder how people get themselves in that sort of position," Berry said.

For her, it was emotional collapse. First, she lost a bitter custody battle for her two daughters in a case that included allegations of child abuse, heavy drinking and appalling profanity. Then her father died.

"I literally gave up on everything," Berry said.

She moved out of the motel she was managing. For a time, she lived in an apartment, but without a job she couldn't make the rent. So out she went.

Why didn't she go back to her mom's house in Arizona?

"Pride," Berry said. She'd rather live on the streets than go back to Arizona and admit that her California dream had turned sour. To this day, she hasn't told her mother her story. Berry said her mom would probably learn about her saga this week when she arrives to attend the graduation and perhaps reads this newspaper article.

Homelessness subjected Berry to the whims of weather, the indignity of having no restroom and long stretches without a shower, but it also taught her some things.

There was a fraternity of the dispossessed. One lady took her under her wing, gave her tips on how to stay safe as a woman on the street. Another friend told her and Stewart about putting a pallet under the tent to keep dry at night. The group had communal meals, generally a stew with whatever the group had scavenged during the day: cans of soup, vegetables, meat discarded by the Smart & Final.

Berry would cook the mishmash in a pot over an open fire. She never had any trouble with the guys, and Stewart was there to protect her.

Berry still cooks for the guys now and then. They'll come by the mobile home once or twice a week, where Berry cooks on a gas range. She and Stewart have kept a few certificates their friends received for completing alcohol and drug abuse rehabilitation classes. They're tucked into grooves in the wood panel walls.

The love seat she was sitting on the day the course schedule landed on her lap is furniture she and Stewart found on a front lawn, left for discard. They carted it home in a wheelbarrow.

"We're still not completely out of the homeless situation yet," Berry laughed.

"We still look for good bargains."

Berry won't be sticking around San Diego after graduation. She's going to live with her mom in Arizona. But it's Mom, not Berry, who needs help. She has been weakened by cancer, and her second husband died late last year.

Berry is not sure what's going to become of her and Stewart, though she suspects he will follow her to Arizona.

She plans to continue her education. She hopes someday to work as an archaeologist and sift through the ruins of ancient Indian civilizations in Arizona.

Being homeless taught her things she couldn't learn in the classroom. She said that in a catastrophe, such as an earthquake, what she's learned will serve her well.

"I know I could be on the streets and survive," Berry said. "Not a lot of people can say that."

## Questions for Discussion

1. Journalists are supposed to be objective in their reporting. However, in this piece, Moran gives hints that he is happy for Debbie Barry and proud of her success. Where do you find this coming through in the article? Do you think it compromises the integrity of the piece?

2. The article mentions the California dream once, as something Barry stubbornly clung to. What elements of the traditional dream did she achieve in the end? Do they match the dream in the way you understand it or as it's defined by the other writers in this chapter?

3. What can you determine about Debbie Barry's character from the evidence you glean in this reading? What do you think is not said, but implied, in the details Moran gives about her, either positive or negative?

## Ideas for Writing

1. Education is an important part of the California dream for a lot of people, but education funding in the state has been in jeopardy for the past several years. Do some research into fees at community colleges, then write an essay in which you compare the current situation with that in other states and also with what has happened in California over the past decade or so. (Helpful hint: compare William E. Piland "College in California: Options Reduced?" in Chapter 3.)

2. It's hard to imagine that misfortune could take a person from a middle-class life to living in a squatters' camp, but according to this article, it happened to Debbie Barry. Do some research into homelessness in your community. For

example, you could talk to people in agencies devoted to aiding the home-less, or search your local newspaper for articles similar to Moran's. Then, write an essay in which you evaluate the causes of the problem and discuss what is being done to help the homeless in your community.

---

# My Place in California
## DJ WALDIE

*Donald Waldie lives in Lakewood, a suburb of Los Angeles, in the house which his parents bought before he was born. He walks to work at the Lakewood City Hall, where he serves as the city's public information officer. He has turned what might otherwise be seen as a narrow life into one given to contemplating the mysteries of suburban life and expounding, though subtly, the argument that there is more to the suburbs than they are often given credit for. His books include* Holy Land: A Suburban Memoir *(1996),* Real City: Downtown Los Angeles Inside/Out *(with Marissa Roth, 2001), and* Where Are We Now: Notes from Los Angeles *(2004), from which this selection is taken. His articles appear regularly in the* Los Angeles Times, LA Weekly, *and* Los Angeles Magazine.

---◆---

Where I live is where most Californians live—in a tract house on a block of more tract houses in a neighborhood hardly distinguishable from the next and all of them extending as far as the street grid allows. My exact place on the grid is at the extreme southeast corner of Los Angeles County, but that's mostly by acci-dent. While I reside in Lakewood, I live in suburbia, where my home might as well be almost anywhere in the state.

I've lived here my whole life, in the 957-square-foot house my parents bought in 1946 when the idea of suburbia was brand new, and no one knew what would happen when tens of thousands of working-class husbands and wives—young and so inexperienced—were thrown together without any instruction manual and expected to make a fit place to live. What happened after was the usual redemptive mix of joy and tragedy.

At least their suburbia wasn't an oil company camp in Oklahoma, a walk-up tenement in a crabbed Midwestern town or a shack at the end of a dirt road somewhere in the border South.

There are Californians who don't regard their tract house as a place of pilgrimage, but my parents and their friends in Lakewood did. They weren't ironists. They were grateful for the comforts of their not-quite-middle-class life. For those who came to Lakewood, the aspiration wasn't for more, but only for enough.

It's slightly more than fifty years since an idling road grader waited for the last harvesters to begin the building of Lakewood, the start of a very long line of machines that eventually scraped the rest of Los Angeles County into suburbia. Despite everything that was ignored or squandered in its making, I believe a kind of dignity was gained. More men than just my father have said to me that living here gave them a life made whole and habits that did not make them feel ashamed. They knew what they found and lost.

Mostly, they found enough space to reinvent themselves, and later, some knew that the work had gone badly. Some of them, the men particularly, gave up what little adolescence they retained after the Depression and the second world war. That loss made them seem remote to their sons and daughters.

Urban planners tell me that my neighborhood was supposed to have been bulldozed away years ago to make room for a better paradise of the ordinary, and yet these little houses on little lots stubbornly resist, loyal to an idea of how a working-class neighborhood should be made. It's an incomplete idea, but it's still enough to bring out four hundred park sports coaches in the fall and six hundred to clean up the weedy yards of the frail and disabled on Volunteer Day in April and over two thousand to sprawl on lawn chairs and blankets to listen to summer concerts in the park. I don't live in a tear-down neighborhood, but one that makes some effort to build itself up.

Suburbia isn't all of a piece, of course, and there are plenty of toxic places to live in the gated enclaves and McMansion wastelands of Los Angeles. Places like that have too much—isolation in one and mere square footage in the other—but, paradoxically, not enough. Specifically, they don't have enough of the play between life in public and life in private that I see choreographed by the design of Lakewood. There's an education in narrow streets when they are bordered by sidewalks and a shallow setback of twenty feet of lawn in front of unassuming houses set close enough together that their density is about seven units per acre.

With neighbors just fifteen feet apart, we're easily in each other's lives in Lakewood. You don't have to love all of the possibilities for civility handed to us roughly by the close circumstances of working-class suburbia, but you have to love enough of them, or you live, as some do, numbly or in a state of permanent, mild fury.

I once thought my suburban education was an extended lesson in how to get along with other people. Now, I think the lesson isn't neighborliness; it's humility. Growing up in Lakewood; the only sign of a man's success I can remember was the frequency with which a new car appeared in a neighbor's driveway. Even today, it's hard to claim status in Lakewood through personal gain (in our peculiar American way) because this is a suburb where life is still pretty much the same for everybody, no matter what you think you're worth.

Lakewood's modesty keeps me here. When I stand at the head of my block and look north, I see a pattern of sidewalk, driveway and lawn, set between parallel low walls of house fronts that aspires to be no more than harmless. We are living in a time of great harm now, and I wish that I had acquired all the graces my neighborhood gives.

Loyalty is the last habit that anyone would impute to those of us who live here; we're supposed to be so dissatisfied. But I'm not unusual in living in Lakewood for all the years I have. Nearly twenty-seven percent of the city's residents have lived here thirty years or more. Perhaps, like me, they've found a place that permits restless people to be still. The primal mythmakers of Los Angeles are its real estate agents, and one of them told me that Lakewood attracted aspirant homebuyers because "it's in the heart of the metroplex." Or, maybe, it's just in the heart. I live here because Lakewood is adequate to the demands of my desire, although I know there's a price to pay.

A Puritan strain in American culture is repelled by desires like mine, and has been since a brilliant young photographer named William A. Garnett, working for the Lakewood Park corporation, took a series of aerial photographs in 1950 that look down on the vulnerable wood frames of houses the company was putting up at the rate of five hundred a week. Even after fifty years, those beautiful and terrible photographs are used to indict suburbia. Except you can't see the intersection of character and place from an altitude of five hundred feet, and Garnett never came back to experience everyday life on the ground.

The everyday isn't perfect. It confines some and leads some astray into contempt or nostalgia, but it saves others. I live where I live in California because here the weight of my everyday life is a burden I want to carry.

## Questions for Discussion

1. What tone does Waldie set with his first line? What evidence do you find that he continues in this voice throughout the essay? What does this point of view contribute to the essay?
2. Waldie talks about his parents coming to California with hopes not of "more, but only for enough." In what ways, according to the piece, is Lakewood suited to that kind of dream? Does this seem at odds with the California dream as you understand it?
3. Waldie suggests that the choices Lakewood offers are limited, yet he claims to be happy staying there. Explain the paradox that this creates, and indicate what keeps him from giving in to the "state of permanent, mild fury" which he says can affect people in a place like this.

## Ideas for Writing

1. This essay talks about a neighborhood in greater Los Angeles, but Waldie says that the place he describes could be almost anywhere in California. Maybe, Lakewood could be anywhere in the US. Think about how Lakewood is described. Does it resemble the suburbs you know? Do some research into the critiques of American suburban life, then write an essay in which you evaluate suburban values and respond to these critiques.
2. More than once, Waldie uses the word "grid" to describe Lakewood. His book *Holy Land* discusses grids at length, pointing out that, among other things, concentration camps and jails are arranged in grid-like format. Evaluate the architecture of a place you know, and explain in an essay whether it is structured, like these places, to enforce conformity on its users. Then, apply the argument to your neighborhood. Does it seem to be designed to hem you in, or to offer you a sense of freedom?

---

# Statement to the House
# Un-American Activities Committee
# (April 1951)
## ROBERT LEES

*Robert Lees (1912–2004) was a Hollywood screenwriter, famous for writing comedy, including several Abbott and Costello films. Born in San Francisco, California, Lees was well-regarded in the 1940s and*

*1950s, but his career was virtually destroyed when he was put on the Hollywood blacklist by the movie studio bosses during the McCarthy Era for alleged Communist activities. As a result of his blacklisting, he had associates submit manuscripts to the studios under the pseudonym "J. E. Selby."*

————————— ✦ —————————

I believe no man who has made writing his profession can completely disassociate himself from people. He writes about them—he writes for them. They are both his inspiration and his audience. Their political freedom guarantees the necessary tools of his trade—freedom of thought and expression. I emphasize this relationship because it explains why I believe a writer must also function as a citizen.

In my career as a writer I have worked in the motion picture industry for the past seventeen years, starting when I was old enough to vote. Before that I had attended grammar and high school in San Francisco where I was born. My parents were also native San Franciscans. In the early thirties, I moved with them to Los Angeles. The depression ended my college career at U.C.L.A. before I could complete my freshman year. After a short experience in films as an extra and bit player, I started as a screen writer at Metro-Goldwyn-Mayer. My name has been associated with over fifty short subjects for that company, mostly Robert Benchley and Pete Smith comedies. Two of these won Academy Awards.

Since then I have received writing credit on some fifteen feature films, starring such comedians as Claudette Colbert and Fred MacMurray, Olsen and Johnson, Abbott and Costello. I certainly don't think I have been summoned to Washington because of these comedies. I believe I am here because in those seventeen years that I have worked as a writer I have functioned as a citizen.

I firmly supported the election of Franklin Delano Roosevelt. I joined with other writers and artists in actively campaigning for him. Being concerned with the rise of fascism in Italy, Spain and Germany, I and others in Hollywood protested these dictatorships. During the war I worked to better our relations with our Allies. For these same reasons I did several scripts for War Bond Shorts. I went to Washington and helped prepare a technical film, "Substitution and Conversion," which was requested by General Sommervell. The film not only played in theatres, but in shops and warplants. For these pictures I was given a commendation by the War Department and the War Activities Committee.

Since that time, since the death of President Roosevelt, I have felt a growing concern, along with many others, that our subsequent foreign policy has not been successful in achieving the peace the world fought so hard to obtain, I have been concerned with the Administration's "get tough" program on one hand and the fears of my two young children who tell me about the Atom-Bomb drills they have been practicing in school. I am concerned with the loyalty oaths, the thought control, and the endless investigations which have come about because today we must believe that those who were our allies in the last war are now our enemies, and that those who were our enemies are now our friends.

Because of my concern, and because I am a writer who has functioned as a citizen, this Committee demands that I either conform to their dictates or be forced into silence.

It is my beliefs that cause me to be summoned here. It is because of the people I may know who have shared these beliefs, people whom the Committee wishes me to expose as subversive by the Committee's standards, that I have been summoned here. I am asked to purge my friends and my conscience under threat of having my seventeen years of work and devotion to my craft end in blacklist.

When I first decided to make writing my career, I did so because of what I felt about people. I have learned more about people and about writers and the tradition of writing since then. I know that I cannot write that war is preferable to peace, or that bigotry or conformity are virtues, or that one race or one chosen group are superior to any other and can dictate how others should live, or how others should think. I cannot, because no man of integrity can successfully write what he doesn't believe. And no writer, who is a true American, can ever force himself to betray his citizenship and his friends, or write the kind of material that will be forced upon the American people if this Committee has its way.

---

# Blacklist: A Different Look at the 1947 HUAC Hearings

## MICHAEL MILLS

*Michael Mills is the author of several prominent film-related web-sites, most notably* The Palace *(www.moderntimes.com/palace). He is committed to understanding the relationship between movies and history. He is also a photographer and a lover of jazz music.*

———————————— ✦ ————————————

According to the experts, the start of the cold war with the Soviet Union began in July 1947 when Stalin refused to accept the Marshall Plan for the Soviet Union. Although Soviet-American tensions had been mounting ever since the Bolshevik Revolution, they were briefly relaxed during the alliance to defeat Nazi Germany. By the spring of 1947 the euphoria created by the allied victories was waning. Meanwhile the Soviet Union continued its free and unabated domination of a tattered Europe. Marxist principles appeared to be gaining a foothold in much of the world. It appeared to some Americans that the terrible sacrifices by so many during the war years had been in vain.

The menace of German agents and fifth columnists had given way to Communist spies and "fellow travelers" more menacing than their predecessors, because they spoke without accents and looked much like the rest of us! The widespread and popular notion, many concluded, was that American Communists were conducting atomic espionage for the Soviet Union. It was in this capricious environment, that the conviction of Alger Hiss (1948), the rise and fall of Senator Joseph R. McCarthy (1950–1954), and the executions of Julius and Ethel Rosenberg would open the door to one of the most disquieting periods in American history.

In 1946, for the first time since the Hoover administration, the Republican Party had won control of Congress. Political events in Europe and the rest of the world bewildered most Americans. Early polls indicated official U.S. foreign policy at odds with that of the average citizen. As a result, President Truman came to be regarded by many as being soft towards Communism, especially "domestic" Communism. Because of the newly empowered Republican majority and to combat these increasing uncertainties, Truman put into effect the first of many of the so-called "anti-Communist loyalty acts." However, rather than shoring up a perceived weakness within his administration, these executive mandates lent credence to Truman's detractors, and fueled his own self-doubts.

A revitalized HUAC (inactive during the war years) now under the leadership of the contemptuous J. Parnell Thomas, (R-New

Jersey—who would later himself be jailed for accepting kickbacks) launched multiple investigations into Communist infiltration of organized labor, the Federal government, and most audaciously— Hollywood. The assault on the film industry was in many ways a predictable aftermath of the recent release of films of predominantly liberal sentiment. The apolitical fledging American style film noir which took a disparaging view of life under any system of government was cresting. And there was, it must be said, at least a modicum of factual substance to the committee's charges. A number of Hollywood directors, screenwriters, and actors had joined the Communist Party or contributed funds to its activities during the Depression of the 1930s. It was to these especially strident participants that HUAC was most mindful.

In September 1947, Thomas's committee subpoenaed 41 witness, nineteen of whom declared their intention to be "unfriendly" (ie, to refuse to answer questions about their political affiliations). Of the nineteen, eleven were directly questioned about their membership in the Communist Party. German émigré playwright Bertolt Brecht left the country the day after his appearance, leaving just 10—the infamous Hollywood Ten.

To counter what they claimed were reckless attacks by HUAC, a group of Hollywood liberals led by actor Humphrey Bogart, his wife Lauren Bacall, John Huston, William Wyler, Gene Kelly and others, established the "Committee for the First Amendment" (CFA). The CFA traveled to Washington to lend its support as the eleven unfriendly witnesses began their testimony. However, as the eleven began to respond to their inquisitors with as much disdain, and often with histrionics far more brusque than their accusers, the embarrassed First Amendmenters began to unravel. Director Edward Dmytryk, one of the Ten, said later, "I was so happy with the support of the CFA and others, but when (screenwriter) John Howard Lawson began haranguing the committee members, I died. We lost it right then and there!" Humphrey Bogart wrote a piece for the March 1948 issue of *Photoplay* magazine entitled "I'm No Communist," in which he admitted being "duped." His trip to Washington, he said, had been "ill-advised." John Garfield wrote a similar article called "I'm a Sucker for a Left Hook." Edward G. Robinson lamented "the Reds made a sucker out of me."

The Truman administration was by now largely responsible for much of the anxiety and anti-Communist fervor surrounding the post-war period. As the elections of 1948 approached, the

White House grew more and more unreasonable in imposing the loyalty oaths now being administered to all Federal employees. In a speech at a Democratic fund raiser, Truman vowed that all Communists and Communist sympathizers would be, without deliberation, removed from the government! The President now emerged more and more inclined to apply any tactics necessary to ease the discerned tensions. He played right into the hands of the tyrannical red-baiters.

It was at the later HUAC hearings of March 1951 led by John S. Wood (D-Georgia), and the 1952 Internal Security subcommittee headed by Senator Pat McCarran, that the "naming-of-names" became the watch words. By 1951, Joseph R. McCarthy was in full blossom. The entire country, Congress, and the Truman administration share equally in what was to come. It was from these latter hearings in Washington and in Hollywood that the infamous blacklist evolved. By that time, and as a direct result of these more recent hearings, more than 324 people had been fired by the studios and were no longer permitted to work in the Motion Picture Industry.

## Questions for Discussion

1. Lees makes much of the distinction between his roles as "writer" and "citizen." What is the crucial difference, according to his statement? Is it a difference that you see as compelling in his defense of himself?
2. What is Lees' strategy in reciting the details of his early life in his statement?
3. How does Lees' tone change as the essay makes its concluding points? Talk about both the style and the content in the last several paragraphs, contrasting them with what came earlier.

## Ideas for Writing

1. Do some further research on the Hollywood Ten or the Hollywood Blacklist. Write an essay on the long-term effects of the investigations of the House Un-American Activities Committee on people involved in the film business.
2. Find out more about the Committee for the First Amendment (CFA) and its later disaffection and disillusionment (as Mills claims) with its cause. Then write a statement which you might read if you were called to testify in front of the House Un-American Activities Committee. What support would you offer in defense of those being investigated?

# The Third California
## JOEL KOTKIN AND WILLIAM FREY

*Joel Kotkin is an expert on economic, political, and social trends. He has written several books, the newest of which is* The City: A Global History *(Modern Library).* The New Geography *(Random House, 2000) was a bestseller describing how digital technology changed the US. Kotkin serves as an Irvine Senior Fellow at the New America Foundation, which is dedicated to bringing new ideas to the forefront of public discourse.*

*William Frey, PhD, is a demographer and sociologist specializing in US demographics. His academic affiliations include being a Visiting Fellow at the Brookings Institution Center on Urban and Metropolitan Policy in Washington, DC, and faculty appointments at the University of Michigan Population Studies Center and as Senior Fellow at the Milken Institute in Santa Monica, CA.*

---- ◆ ----

*Away from the coast, the goals of building a life and raising a family are still possible.*

The last great frontier for upward mobility in California extends from the far eastern suburbs of greater Los Angeles to the Sierra foothills in Northern California. It is there that the "California dream"—a place to create a new life and raise a family—is still possible. Call it the "Third California."

That may come as a surprise. Some coastal residents regard inland California as a failed geography of rising poverty, crummy jobs and unremitting ugliness. But in recent years, more and more higher-end and professional jobs have begun moving east, and with them a new emphasis on improving the quality of life in such cities as Bakersfield, Modesto, Ontario and Riverside.

The "First California" (the older, settled area around San Francisco Bay) and the "Second California" (the later-developed urbanized region along the Southern California coast) have run out of room to grow. These Californias, as those of us who live here know, are congested and expensive—and may be increasingly hemmed in economically as well. The pace of new job creation is measured, at best, with the exception of San Diego and Orange counties.

By contrast, the Third California is growing four times faster than the rest of state and now represents about 30% of the state's total population, or about 9 million people, according to 2000 census data. By 2050, more than 21 million people, or 38% of the state's population, will live in inland California, according to census projections. Virtually all the areas of fast-paced economic growth in the state—Bakersfield, Riverside and Stockton—are located there.

Coastal Californians migrating inland do so for many of the same reasons that earlier generations of Americans left the Midwest, Northeast and South. The cost of housing is by far the biggest factor driving the migration. Today [2006], only 11% of the households in San Francisco and Orange counties, and 17% in heavily minority L.A. County, can afford a median-priced house. By contrast, affordability rates, though down from earlier this decade, are closer to 30% in most inland regions.

For many, this means the future lies east, and families are prominent in this movement. The under-35 population in the inland region has increased dramatically, and from 2000 to 2004, the number of children younger than 15 rose faster in inland areas than along coastal California, according to 2004 census data.

The "eastward surge" is also multiethnic. Latinos, who make up an ever-increasing share of California's new families, account for about half of Third California's growth since 2000.

Still, most assessments of Third California are not flattering. According to Stephanie Pincetl, a UCLA professor, the Central Valley is, at best, a product of "malign neglect" as it has shifted from an agricultural cornucopia to "an almost unbroken chain of smog-choked cities and suburbs."

The appraisals of environmentalists and academics who live in the Inland Empire are rarely more charitable. The challenges in Third California are many. Much of the job growth has been heavily dependent on population movement, which has sparked a boom in construction and lower-paying retail jobs. A sharp decline in housing construction, or even a mild slowdown in migration patterns, would leave much of the region vulnerable to a downturn.

More serious, many inland areas, with the exception of Sacramento and the western reaches of the Inland Empire, are home to a large, highly uneducated population, including many people who have recently arrived from Mexico and Central America. In Fresno and the rural reaches of the Central Valley, per-capita incomes are among the lowest in the state, and unemployment rates among the highest in the country.

Yet the 2000 census revealed that in Sacramento and the Inland Empire, the number of educated people was on the rise. Most intriguing, these areas experienced a nearly 40% growth in residents with graduate degrees, a rate of increase larger than along the southern coast and close to Bay Area levels.

The apparent movement of professionals into parts of inland California may signal a longer-term shift in the region's ability to compete in high-skilled industries. The signs since 2000 are particularly encouraging, as migration and economic flows from the coastal regions have strengthened.

The higher-end jobs moving east are in warehousing, manufacturing and construction, according to a 2005 report by the Bureau of Labor Statistics. As a whole, California has lost about 260,000 industrial jobs since 2000, but the number of those jobs has actually risen around Bakersfield, Fresno, Riverside-San Bernardino and Sacramento.

More significant is the shift in white-collar professions. Since 2002, San Francisco has lost 5.2% of its high-end jobs. Most areas in Third California, by contrast, have enjoyed gains, with Bakersfield, the Inland Empire and Stockton all adding such jobs at double-digit rates, according to the BLS.

There are other signs that more skilled people are headed inland. One is increased construction of higher-end housing in Bakersfield, Chino and Sacramento. The wealthier newcomers are becoming a force for other improvements—revived downtowns, better schools, more parks and open space.

"There's a fundamental shift in the market today," said Inland Empire economist John Husing. "We're seeing a mass migration of highly skilled people to this region. Go to any area now and it's exploding, bringing professionals."

If Husing's observation proves accurate, it is good news for all California. Facing growing competition from such lower-cost states as Arizona, Nevada and Texas for young families, upwardly mobile professionals and higher-end jobs, the Golden State needs an outlet for the aspirations of its people, and the Third California may be the place.

## Questions for Discussion

1. For the people who move there, the "Third California" is a place to pursue the dream, but others denigrate it. Contrast the good and the bad points of the third California using material you glean from this article.

2. The third California, according to Kotkin and Frey, gives people a chance at a middle-class life which might not be available to them in the more traditional, but now quite expensive, places to live. What elements of the dream do the writers name, and how do these support descriptions of the dream you see elsewhere in this chapter?

3. Kotkin and Frey call the third California "the last great frontier for upward mobility," using language which suggests hope for the future. Where else do they discuss what will become of the third California, and what tone do they use?

## Ideas for Writing

1. Research a city like Bakersfield, Fresno, or San Bernardino, California, online. What is it doing to attract new residents? Can you find evidence that there are long-time residents who resent the fact that newcomers are changing the way of life? Write an essay in which you explain and contrast the two points of view.

2. Choose a neighborhood in a California city you'd like to live in, and find out how much it costs to buy a place there. Write an essay in which you explain how you could afford to live there, or why you could not. Talk about the ways in which California's affordability or lack of it has an impact on people's ability to live their California dream.

## Thinking and Writing about Chapter 1

### Connecting the Essays

1. Kevin Starr says that from the first, California "was caught in a paradox of reverent awe and exploitative use." Could it be that the displacement to the third California which Kotkin and Frey write about is just another example of this exploitation? Contrast the problem as Starr explains it with the demands made by the migrants Kotkin and Frey describe.

2. Compare the enthusiasm about California cited by Douglas Fischer with the hopeful tone of Lewis Lapham or the more somber one of Waldie. Is any one of them wholly right about California and the dream as you know it, or is the truth found in taking bits and pieces from each?

3. Both Moran's article and the statement by Robert Lees (as well as its contexts) concern themselves with dreams displaced. Compare and contrast the reasons for this displacement, and explain why it might be said that the California dream is sometimes not something that the individual can control, no matter how hard he or she tries.

4. When DJ Waldie suggests that life in Lakewood, California is hardly dream-like, he speaks as someone who has always lived there. This pessimism seems

to be shared by those who examine life in the "third California," according to Kotkin and Frey. However, they also explain that things are improving there as more people move in. Explain which opinion reflects your viewpoint on life in the suburbs. Consider whether there might be some essential connection between one's viewpoint and how long—or whether—he or she has lived in California, or in a suburb in another state.

5. Henry George verges on panic when he talks about the number of new people coming to California. Do you sense something of the same tone in more recent writing about the state? Compare Douglas Fischer's or Kevin Starr's selection for evidence as you write.

## Extending the Theme

1. Popular culture has an important part in disseminating the California dream around the world. Discuss several movies and/or songs which describe the dream. Are they all positive, or can you also find some anti-dream messages in them? Write a piece in which you speculate on the social function of these artifacts of popular culture as they portray the dream.

2. What is the official version of itself which the state of California offers to the world? Go online and check out www.ca.gov. Do the messages in word and text complement each other? Do they reinforce the dream? How do you think the message is interpreted by people who have never experienced California for themselves? Write an analysis of the state's website as it relates to these topics.

3. Do people born in California have a different notion of the dream, and the place itself, than do newcomers? Talk to some long-time residents and to some people who have arrived more recently, and write an essay which contrasts their attitudes, hopes, and fears as they pertain to California.

4. Do you think that the California dream changes over time, or is it an endless reinvention of the same theme? Explain your response by writing an essay which makes reference to some accounts of the dream with which you are familiar.

5. Take up one of the issues that threaten the state—growing population, urban breakdown, the destruction of the environment, etc. Do some further research to find out what experts are saying might happen if current trends continue, then write about whether you see the future as bright or bleak, and why.

# Arrivals, Departures, and Culture Clashes

*Crash*—the title of the film which won an Academy Award in 2006—is almost the only word needed to summarize many people's California experience. The state's many groups co-exist, peacefully for the most part, but occasionally they find themselves in conflict, smashing into each other on the way to achieving their California dreams.

It's a challenge that every resident needs to come to terms with, because though the numbers ebb and flow, California is gradually increasing in population. And along with numbers comes diversity, as modern air travel makes it possible for people from every spot on the globe to live in the state, establishing communities or blending into the larger culture.

This infusion of new people brings with it both variety and tension—within people themselves as they struggle with the changes which come from being somewhere unfamiliar, amongst groups as they tussle for space in a place which is becoming ever more crowded, and within and between groups as they compete for resources while in many cases attempting to maintain the identity which formed them in whatever place they originated from.

For some people, the definition of self as they live it in California involves replicating their home culture as closely as possible. This is reflected in their dress, their food, and their family life. For others, it means throwing off the past and creating a new self, one whose core value might be rooted in the idea that endless reinvention is possible. For these folks, California is more than a physical place—it's a mental landscape which unfolds in endless sets of possibilities.

Even the word "Californian" is not uncomplicated to define. On the one hand is the idea that Californians are a distinct breed of American, formed of different stuff than people in other parts of the country. On the other is the notion that there is no one way to define the term at all, because to be from California signifies having the freedom to be different in a million and one ways. The essays in this chapter reflect the impossibility of fixing the definition of a "Californian" in any simple way.

The writers in this chapter don't necessarily concern themselves with immigration's positive or negative consequences for the state in terms of economics, politics, or resources. All of those topics are covered elsewhere in this book. Rather, these essays focus on the *experiences* of people who live in the state, whether they be immigrants or lifelong residents. Each speaker in the chapter tries to sort out the question of identity and how individual choices merge or clash with others' cultural practices. Often, these dictates have been brought from the home country by parents, and the struggle becomes inter-generational, as the young adopt new ways to the chagrin of their parents.

The first selection lays the groundwork for what follows. Carey McWilliams, speaking from the middle of the past century, outlines the rapid pace at which the population of California was changing in his time. Despite some lulls since, the state is now growing at an even greater rate. You will likely hear in McWilliams a forerunner of today's panic over the influx of people to the state and the changes which that brings.

Speaking much closer to the present, David Rieff talks about the state's largest city, Los Angeles, describing it as if it had been colonized by foreign invaders, which is exactly how many people view immigrants and immigration in California. In a similar thematic vein, Mike Davis takes a critical viewpoint on the strategies which privileged people use to create borders to contain or exclude those viewed as alien. He argues that there is a "third border" which serves to demarcate territory deemed inappropriate for Latino occupation, a problem which is not confined to California.

Machico Yasuda, Alizah Salario, and Donna Mungen take on the question of how to understand the cultural outsider, in each case discussing young people. Yasuda focuses on the ways in which children may resist the attempts of their parents to help them retain their home culture.

Salario and Mungen discuss youth who have chosen to act in a way of which the culture disapproves. Each of these writers attempts to decipher the choices made by certain Californians, not assuming automatically that the actions of these young people are dismissible as simply evil. What unites these two pieces is their similar focus on youth violence as an expression of identity.

lê thi diem thúy talks about family dynamics, portraying a refugee family while explaining their values and confusion about how things are done in their new land. As she describes where they live, she evokes the same spirit as does Ishmael Reed, who asks for a new look at what to many might be an easily stereotyped place, his neighborhood in Oakland. Each gives a new way to view an economically disadvantaged community.

As you read, think about your own experience as either a native or newcomer to, or observer of, California. If you live in the state, what issues face you as you try to mediate between your desires to live life as you wish and the values of your home culture, especially if those conflict with the mainstream culture? If you are outside of California, what is your understanding of the state's multiple cultures, and how might you see yourself fitting into these complicated dynamics if you were to end up relocating there?

---

# Population Whirligig
## CAREY MCWILLIAMS

*Carey McWilliams (1905–1980) completed his undergraduate and law degrees at USC and then practiced law in LA for a decade. The economic upheaval of the Depression inspired him to examine the social conditions of California's migrant farm workers, which he detailed in* Factories in the Field *(1939). In 1939, he took a job as the head of the California Division of Immigration and Housing, a post he held for four years. This position allowed him to focus government attention on the evils of Japanese internment during World War II, though the hearings he forced were ultimately unsuccessful in fostering change. In the 1950s, no longer working for the government, he spoke out against McCarthy's anti-Communist campaign. He served on the editorial staff of* The Nation *for many years.*

———————— ✦ ————————

The states of the Ohio and upper Mississippi Valley have always been characterized by a high degree of homogeneity which has reflected, as Dr. Dan Elbert Clark has written, "a general similarity of physical environment and common purposes and needs," and, also, a similar pattern of settlement through the gradual extension of the frontier. Similar observations might be made of both the South and the West; but no such homogeneity has ever existed in California. For California has always occupied, in relation to the other regions, much the same relation that America has occupied toward Europe: it is the great catch-all, the vortex at the continent's end into which elements of America's diverse population have been drawn, whirled around, mixed up, and resorted. Basically, the explanation for California's diversity is to be found in three factors: the reasons which have prompted people to move to California; the diversity of resources in California; and its geographical position.

Since California was essentially a mining *and* agricultural frontier, it naturally attracted a different type of migration than that which was drawn to the usual frontier settlement. Mining frontiers always attract a great diversity of types. From 1848 to the present time [1940s], people have been attracted to California for a variety of reasons and the diversity of motivations has been reflected in the variety of types. Through the years, thousands of people have come to California primarily because they found the climate attractive; because California was a pleasant place in which to retire; and for a variety of non-economic motivations. The discovery of gold made California world-famous, and curiosity alone, has drawn thousands of migrants westward. Capitalizing on the gold rush legend, California has consistently sought to attract new residents through aggressive promotion campaigns often financed by grants of public funds. The non-economic attractions of California have not been limited to any one class, or type, or group, but have had the widest possible appeal. For better or worse, the legend of California as a "Land of Promise" is now too firmly rooted in the consciousness of the nation to be offset by "warnings," hostile legislation, or other measures aimed at diverting the flow of migration.

The reasons which have prompted people to migrate to California have also been closely related to the diversity of opportunities in California which in turn reflects the great geographical diversity of California as a state. The geographical diversity of California is so great as to make of it an anomaly even among states which also show a great range of environmental conditions. In this sense, California is beyond any doubt a special case. In the variation of climatic conditions; in the diversity of its soils; and in contrasting topography, California shows a truly astonishing diversity. "In no similar area in North America," writes

Dr. R. T. Young, "are there such great extremes of climate or more marked differences in the corresponding life. . . . Even the *flora and fauna* of California are peculiar to themselves." There is, however, a special feature about the geographical diversity of California. "The conspicuous fact about California's environment," writes Dr. John Walton Caughey, "appears to be its versatility." California's environment is certainly one of the most versatile, the most plastic and adaptable, to be found anywhere in the world. The diversity of California's agriculture is almost matched by the diversity of its mineral production. Economic geographers have consistently emphasized that California is one of the most perfectly balanced, most nearly self-sufficient regions in the nation. It has been able to offer, therefore, a wide range of opportunities in almost every significant field of economic activity.

The geographic location of California has also been of prime importance in attracting a most diverse migration. It has been to Asia what New York has been to Europe: the first landing place for east-bound migrants from across the Pacific. It has also been the terminus of the westward movement. Chinese, Japanese, Filipinos, and Russians have come to California from the East. By reason of its position, it has also drawn migrants from Mexico, Central and South America. From many points of view, therefore, California has occupied a unique geographic position which has enabled it to attract migrants from all corners of the world. The completion of the Panama Canal, for example, greatly shortened the distance, measured in time, between California and Europe. The expansion of population in Europe has long blinded people to the central position which California occupies on the global maps. In the last century, California has steadily moved toward a more central position in world affairs. In 1848 it was one of the most remote areas of the world, the last frontier of America, in a world in which the United States still occupied a subordinate position to Europe. Today, the United States is the world's first power; and California, no longer a frontier, occupies a more central position, in terms of our global interest, than the older settlements on the eastern seaboard. The movement to locate the headquarters of the United Nations in San Francisco was a symbolic recognition of the fact that California, in geophysical terms, today occupies a central position in world affairs.

The marks of migration can be seen, not only in the diversity of California's population, but in the curious manner in which the migrants have been re-grouped within the state. "Migration," wrote Dr. Robert E. Park, "has had a marked effect upon the social structure of California society . . . where a large part of the population, which comes from *diverse and distant* places, lives in more or less *closed communities*, in intimate economic dependence, but in more or less complete cultural independence of the world about them" (italics mine). Just as the aged have their "retirement colonies" in California, so one can find colonies of Portuguese dairy farmers, Armenian raisin-growers, Yugoslav fishing colonies, Japanese produce-farmers, as well as a miscellany of Chinatowns, Mexican "jim-towns," and Russian Molokan settlements. Even the rich have their colonies. Pasadena, for example, is the home of families whose wealth is based on inheritance; the rich European refugees are clustered along the Riviera; and the nouveau riche are to be found in Beverly Hills and Bel-Air. For the disposition of racial and ethnic minorities to settle in colonies finds its counterpart in the disposition of social classes to segregate themselves. Dr. Park's characterization of Southern California as "a congeries of culturally insulated communities" can be applied, with some modifications, to the entire state.

If California's population represented a thorough cross-section of the American people, its diversity might have less significance for the differences would tend to cancel out. But the population of the state really represents a selection, rather than a cross-section, of the national population, and a selection of this sort tends *to heighten*, to emphasize, the diverse traits and characteristics of the populations from which the migrants have been drawn. Throughout this chapter, I have had occasion, again and again, to stress the point that national population trends are heightened in California; that they appear in a more extreme form here than elsewhere. This tendency reflects the fact that the population of California has been selected, rather than drawn at random, from every state, every class, every race, every ethnic element in the American population. Immigration to America has, also, been selective; but a selection from an already selected population brings into sharp focus the more striking traits and characteristics of the base population. It is for this reason that one can say that the Californians are more like the Americans than the Americans themselves. Lord Bryce, who saw California clearly and saw it whole, observed that the Californians were "impatient . . . for the slow approach of the millennium" and were always "ready to try instant, even if perilous, remedies for a present evil."

But there is still another dimension to the impact of migration in California which must be explored even if it cannot be exactly defined. If one can imagine a situation in which a *selection* of the American people had been drawn to a region the environment of which was more like that of the rest of the country than California's, the social and cultural consequences would be entirely different from what they have been in California. For California *is different*, and the totality of its differences has been brought to bear upon its selected population. If all of the migrants to California had come from a single place of origin, or if they all had a common cultural background, *and* if the physical environment into which they moved, had not been strongly different from the environment which they left, more of the customs and traditions of the area of origin would have been transplanted in California. But, as Marion Clawson has said, "the very diversity of California's migration, *as well as* the fact that the physical environment in the state differs from that in the areas of origin, has led to some abandonment of the old forms and traditions and to the evolution of certain new ones."

Migration naturally tends to weaken the well-established family ties, social customs, and the traditions of migrants; but, in California, this tendency has been given a special emphasis by reason of the novelty of the environment. In surveying the culture of California, one will find in every field—in mining, agriculture, industry, technology, gardening, architecture—that the novelty of the environment and its compulsive quality have *forced* an abandonment of the imported cultural pattern in many important respects. "So great a departure from the climate of the Midwest and East," reads an early report of the Commission of Agriculture, "subjected the culture of the soil to novel conditions, unsettling old traditions, and defying some of the most tenaciously held lessons of experiences in the older parts of the country." From a statement of this sort, one turns to a recently published work, *Pacific Coast Gardening*, by Norvell Gillespie, and is there informed that both the technique and timing of gardening on the Pacific Coast are quite unique and that success depends on a know-how which cannot be imported but must be discovered here, by a painful trial-and-error process.

The culture of California has two striking characteristics: the willingness of the people to abandon the old ways, *and* the willingness with which people will try new forms and modes, and the inventiveness which they show in devising such modes and forms. These inter-related dynamics are at work in every phase of the culture of the state; in its politics no less than in its agriculture. Migration accounts for the weakening of old ties but it is the challenge of a novel and highly versatile environment which explains the inventiveness, the quickness with which something new is devised. This latter statement, however, requires some refinement. The inventiveness of the people can be measured by the degree to which the new environment differs from the old. Kansas differed from Illinois as Illinois differed from Pennsylvania, but the degree of these differences is slight when measured against the degree by which California differs from all of these states. In discussing the diffusion of cultures, Arnold Toynbee has suggested that: The greater the difficulty of the environment, the greater the stimulus to inventiveness; and the related generalization that new ground provides a greater stimulus to activity than old ground. California was both new and difficult. Its difficulties consisted not in a meagerness of resources but in the fact that its resources could be unlocked only by untried, freshly devised methods. In these dynamics is to be found the basis for the belief, dating from the first American impressions of California, that this state held, as William James phrased it, the promise of "the new society at last, proportionate to nature."[1]

## Questions for Discussion

1. What are McWilliams' reasons for choosing the image of the "whirligig" to describe California's population? Why is it an appropriate image to describe the people in the state, even today?

2. McWilliams claims that California is a "special case" in the way it attracts immigrants, compared to the rest of the US. What are its appeals, according to the piece?

3. McWilliams says that California's population groups itself into colonies that remain closed to the world around them. But near the end of the selection, he seems to challenge this claim by saying that California weakens ties and traditions and forces people to abandon old ways and invent new ones. Which do you think is the more accurate statement, and how do you explain the seeming contradiction in his argument?

## Ideas for Writing

1. Do some research on recent immigration to California. Are people still coming for the same reasons they were when McWilliams wrote in the mid-20th

---

[1]For an interesting account of the relationship between mobility and crime see; Final Report on the Special Crime Study, Commission on Social and Economic Causes of Crime and Delinquency, Sacramento, June 20, 1949.

century? You might use hard data to make your case, or you might bounce some of McWilliams' reasons off a couple of immigrants you interview, if you live in California. Do they agree that the state presents the same opportunities now as it did approximately sixty years ago, when McWilliams wrote?

2. McWilliams describes California as no longer being a "frontier," but rather as having a "central position" in the world. Do some research on the industry, economy, population, politics, and/or other facets of life in the state now, and write an essay in which you argue either that California should be seen as the center of the world, or that it occupies a place on its margins.

---

# Excerpt from *Los Angeles, Capital of the Third World*

## DAVID RIEFF

*David Rieff was born in Boston in 1952, educated at Princeton, and then took a post as an editor at a New York publishing firm. Just before he turned forty, he left that job to write about topics ranging from immigration in LA (the selection here comes from his 1991 book,* Los Angeles: Capital of the Third World*) to, more recently, global military campaigns, particularly those in Bosnia, Afghanistan, and Iraq. Aside from publishing half a dozen books, Rieff has written for most major US newspapers as well as magazines like* Harper's Magazine *and* The New Republic. *His mother was famed activist and intellectual Susan Sontag.*

---

◆

---

[H]undreds of thousands continue to come north along this stretch [Interstate 5] each year. In 1990, the INS stations in the area between San Diego and the Oceanside checkpoint caught half a million illegal immigrants. Homeowners in northern San Diego Country, which had been increasingly selling itself in Southern California as the ideal place to live for those who wanted to find affordable housing far enough from L.A.'s burgeoning crime and traffic problems but close enough to commute to the city to work, now found that their fine homes were in the middle of another thoroughfare, the entry route for illegal aliens. They might be taking a morning jog through one of the county's parks or idyllic canyon roads only to stumble on an encampment of migrants. On the main streets of small rich towns like Costa Mesa and Mission Viejo, one now saw clusters of Mexican men. Whether they were looking for work, or a ride north, or were simply unsure of what to do next, was unclear. What was clear is that they were everywhere.

Surprise, surprise, the United States turned out to border on the Third World after all. It was not just an abstraction, or a black hole, or the place you drove down to from Los Angeles for some cheap and dirty fun or some good fishing. It had its own dreams and they were pressing steadily closer. To many people in Southern California, it appeared harder and harder to know just where Mexico now ended and the United States began, harder to confute those exuberant Third World-loving activists who were describing L.A. to anyone who would listen not as the most quintessentially American of cities, but rather as the capital of a new country that they had taken to calling Mexamerica. "Los Angeles," wrote Lester Langley, in his book *Mexamerica: Two Countries, One Future*, "is for the American Southwest and Mexico's northern third what Mexico City is to the southern and central regions of Mexico proper."

"Mexico proper"! It was language to make a Chicano militant pinch himself with gleeful wonder. Under the circumstances, was it any surprise that even more sober Mexican-American politicians in Los Angeles increasingly were couching what were at root entirely conventional ambitions in the giddy rhetoric of return and reconquest? "The legacy of Los Angeles left by its founding fathers and mothers, Spanish, Indian and Mexican," State Senator Art Torres declared, "is now being reclaimed by a new generation of leaders. . . . Our modern metropolis is returning to the enduring Pueblo de Los Angeles of years past." The fact that Torres's rosy evocation of eighteenth-century L.A. was not much closer to historical accuracy, let alone applicable to the contemporary city, than Helen Hunt Jackson's portrait of a colonial arcadia in *Ramona* had been was beside the point. What mattered was that, from the Mexican-American point of view, the tables were finally turning.

Many Chicanos, not only militants or politicians who naturally viewed the new immigration as demographic good news for their own chances at higher office, reveled in being able to respond to Anglo complaints concerning Hispanics who refused to learn English or more generalized fears of a Mexican "takeover" of L.A. with exultant gibes of their own. It was an understandable reaction. There are a great number of Chicanos throughout greater L.A., after all, who, if their roots in the region do not go back to the days of the Pueblo, do reach back five or six generations. Ignored for so long, they could be forgiven for wanting to get a little of their own back. As for the militants, many of them had taken to denying that Los Angeles was in any legitimate sense a part of the United States at all. Conjuring up the mythic Aztec homeland of Aztlán, they described themselves not simply as a disadvantaged group within the American polity but rather as a colonized people, whose land had been usurped when Mexico was forced to cede the Southwest to the United States in the treaty of Guadalupe Hidalgo in 1847.

"In the spirit of a new people," began the preamble to the *Plan de Santa Barbara*, the quintessential statement of late-sixties Chicano militancy, "that is conscious not only of its proud historical heritage, but also of the brutal 'Gringo' invasion of our territories, we, the Chicano inhabitants and civilizers of the northern land of Aztlán, from whence came our forefathers, reclaiming the land of their birth and consecrating the determination of our people of the sun, declare that the call of our blood is our power, our responsibility and our inevitable destiny." Most of this bluster, of course, no more defining of the Chicano community (unsurprisingly, many of the *Plan*'s principal drafters went on to careers in mainstream politics, journalism, and the arts) than the Port Huron statement of the radical Students for a Democratic Society in the same era defined an American polity that went on to elect Nixon, Carter, Reagan, and Bush. But however inflated Chicano rhetoric could be at times, the nature of Mexican-American identity was unquestionably anomalous. Mexican-Americans were not exactly an ethnic group, not exactly a race or people (for all the talk about *La Raza*, the race, the difference between a light-skinned Mexican from the northern state of Chihuahua and a copper-skinned Indian from Michoacán was as great as between a Swede and a Sicilian), not exactly an immigrant group, and yet at the same time were all those things.

In coming to America, and, more particularly, to Southern California, which less than a hundred and fifty years before had been Mexican, they were both immigrating—it was pure rhetoric to assert that a peasant from the Altos de Jalisco had any organic relation to Alta California; that peasant barely had any real sense of the lowlands of his own state—and returning. In other words, the movement had as much of the experience of an American from, say, New York moving to California as it did of a Korean coming from Seoul or Pusan. Koreanness, after all, had not been a latent possibility in the Southland since its early settlement; but Mexicanness had. And if the United States was a country perpetually up for grabs, the new arrivals from Spanish America were making their claim not only on the basis of a vision of the future but on a memory of the past, and they arrived with, psychologically at least, deeds and titles in their pockets.

The prospect was one that some Anglos at least had been conscious of for a long time. As far back as 1946, when the glorious suburban dreams of postwar Los Angeles were still in their infancy, Carey McWilliams could assert with steely prescience that the Mexican influence in Southern California, far from having been successfully exorcised, was just about as abiding and irreducible a characteristic of the region as its desert topography. "In view of the size of this Mexican colony," McWilliams concluded, at a moment when there were only 300,000 people of Mexican origin in greater L.A., that is, one-tenth the present figure, "and its proximity to the Mexican border, it is not unlikely that, in the future, some fusion of the two cultures will occur." Now, forty-five years later, Chicano militants and Valley housewives seemed united in intuiting that this fusion was at last taking place, with, if anything, its Mexican component gaining the upper hand on the simple grounds of fecundity, or what Carlos Fuentes once playfully referred to as "the chromosomatic imperialism" of the new Hispanic immigrants.

And given this demographic outlook, what other destiny was really possible for Los Angeles? In 1990, most projections pegged the Hispanic population of the United States, then thought to stand at about seventeen million people, as doubling to thirty-six million by the year 2010. This could mean, among other things, that Hispanics would outnumber blacks. In California as a whole and Southern California in particular the change would be even more dramatic. Hispanics made up 14 percent of the region's population in 1970 but would constitute 40 percent by the year 2000. In the same period, the white population was expected to decline from 75 to 40 percent of the whole. Add the likelihood that the old would be disproportionately Anglo and the young disproportionately Hispanic, and you began to see why this new immigration was so unsettling to so many people.

But more important even than the raw statistics themselves was the perception among many Angelenos that neither the new Mexican and Central American immigrants nor, increasingly, the children of the Southland's Chicano population were interested in assimilating, at least according to those myths and norms ingrained in the American imagination since the great European immigration of 1990. Everywhere in Anglo L.A., one heard jaundiced assertions about the new immigrants refusing to speak English, or become Americans. If immigration was a journey, then Hispanics, it seemed, were refusing to make the trip even as, in reality, they were crossing the frontier in ever-increasing numbers.

To many Anglos, particularly those whose ancestors had themselves made the immigrant passage, this seemed like a betrayal. The Hispanics, I was told repeatedly, in tones of wonder and incomprehension as often as of bitterness, did not love America. European immigrants had never expected the larger society to acknowledge the national holidays of Poland, Italy, or Ireland. Their festivals recalled notables of their ethnic groups who had made a contribution to America—Columbus Day for Italians, and, for the various other groups, days honoring Revolutionary War-era generals, von Steuben for the Germans, Lafayette for the French, and so on. But for Mexicans, whose ancestors had *fought* the United States, such a strategy was obviously unworkable. Indeed, scarcely a month went by without calls from the Mexican-American community in California for statues to General Kearny or Stockton or Frémont, those paladins of the Anglo victory in nineteenth-century California, to be removed from the public squares in which they had for so long occupied pride of place.

The real parallel was to the American Indians. After all, it was clear even to the most patriotic Americans that a descendant of the Cheyenne or the Sioux who had fought the U.S. Cavalry across the plains of the West had little reason to take any pleasure in American history. But the Indians had been largely exterminated—even the names of the great tribes of Southern California, the Diegueno, the Gabrieleno, and the Chumash, being unknown to most Angelenos—and the new Hispanic immigration was the first time an immigrant group could manifest a bitterness similar to that felt by both Native Americans and, of course, blacks. Even the Asians, no matter how badly their ancestors were treated in California, could not muster the same kind of rancor. Unlike the Hispanics, they were doing well economically, and money is a wonderful bandage for history's wounds. Moreover, the commercial aspirations of Asian-Americans made it impossible for them to criticize a capitalist system that was serving them well. "I'm a professional businessman, not a professional Pakistani," was the way a character in *My Beautiful Laundrette*, Stephen Frears's film about the new multiracial London, tells off a black squatter who has appealed to him on the grounds of racial solidarity, and it was a story that might just as well have been told about Los Angeles.

Predictably, liberal Anglos pointed reassuringly to statistics demonstrating that the new Hispanic arrivals were learning English just as earlier immigrant groups had done. But though that was certainly true to some extent, and, moreover, though the militants tended to drown them out, L.A. was full of Chicanos who considered themselves white (as they were; a northern Mexican is often lighter-skinned than a Southern Italian), and fuller still of people who wanted nothing better than to assimilate in the old-fashioned way, and as quickly as possible, it was not the whole story. To begin with, the Spanish language simply had another standing than Italian had had in New York in 1900, or, for that matter, Korean had in Los Angeles in 1900, no matter how many signs in Hankul one saw on Olympic Boulevard. The proximity to the Mexican border, and, by extension, to all of Spanish America, changed everything.

There was also the constant traffic across the border. To be sure, many of the Italians, Slavs, Irish, and Jews who immigrated to America eventually returned home for good—as many as 10 percent by some estimates—while even among those who accepted the bounty of Ellis Island there were a good number who made at least a trip or two to the old country at some time in their lives. But they were scarcely in a position to go back for Christmas or Easter, as many Hispanic immigrants who were in L.A. legally were wont to do, much less work for a while in L.A., then go home, then return, then go home again, as so many illegals did, turning the border into a sort of risk-laden turnstile. When the U.S. Congress in 1986 passed a revised immigration law that offered amnesty to hundreds of thousands of illegal aliens, one of the measure's first effects was, the following Christmas, to hopelessly snarl traffic at all the major border crossings into Mexico as people traveled south to see their relatives.

Mexico was so close. With the exception of Canada and the Caribbean, immigrants to America had never come from so nearby before. It was not just a matter of a Hispanic immigrant in L.A. being able to live an entire existence, albeit an economically deprived one, in Spanish. That, after all, was true in Koreatown as well. But not only was L.A. close to Mexico but it had never succeeded in ridding itself of its Hispanic nature in the first place. The centrality of the Mexican shadow world was confirmed as much by what was missing from the image L.A. presented to the world as by what was present in it. Los Angeles is a city of discrete communities, many of which had campaigned energetically to have their identities acknowledged on freeway signs and markers along the major surface streets. At last count, there were more than four hundred of these signs strewn across L.A. They inform passing motorists that they have just crossed into or out of Downtown, Carthay Circle, Echo Park, Miracle Mile, or Larchmont.

These are imaginative jurisdictions, of course, neighborhoods rather than independent towns, but like actors hungry for screen credit the acquisition of one of these signs was an important measure of success. It is a distinction by no means restricted to residential areas and a few older commercial zones like the Miracle Mile. Immigrant communities are designated as well, and you don't need to read the shop signs in Los Angeles to know when you are in Little Tokyo, Koreatown, or Chinatown. But you can drive from City of Industry in the east to the Pacific Ocean in the west in L.A. and never encounter a sign, for all the loose, jumpy talk about diversity, that announces that you have crossed into Chicanotown, Little El Salvador, or Jaliscoville. It is as if that is information at once both too unmanageable and too obvious to fit suitably on a rectangular piece of metal, stenciled alongside the shield of the city of Los Angeles.

But if no text at least a subtext, as the Method actors say. In L.A. even the most anodyne sight can awaken, to anyone sensitive to what lies beneath the city's triumphalist surface, the ghosts of Mexican Southern California. I heard people with no conceivable interest in Mexico remark absently over lunch that today was Cinco de Mayo, or even some other, far more obscure, Mexican national holiday or Hispanic Catholic festival. Then there was the cruder though almost never remarked-upon fact that something like half of L.A.'s streets have Spanish names, sometimes even Spanish versions of names, like Santa Monica or Santa Barbara, that have perfectly serviceable English equivalents. And in a city where dependence on the car means one is constantly attending to road signs and highway exit information, it is impossible, even at the farthest Anglo corners of the Westside or the Valley, to move half a mile before encountering some resonant trace of the Southland's Hispanic core.

There is something problematic, after all, about living on a boulevard called La Cienega, Sepulveda, or Pico, or shopping on Rodeo, San Vicente, and Santa Monica—or even having voted for Ronald Reagan, whose country estate is called Rancho del Cielo and is located in Santa Barbara—while still believing that all this was just a lot of verbal fluff, a holdover from the region's previous incarnation. And if it was then all those nachos, jalapeño peppers, and guacamole that Anglos in the Southland had been serving their guests for generations, there in those adobe ranch houses with their Spanish red tile roofs, and a mariachi band playing somewhere in the background, had left the most unexpected after-taste. It turned out that these dishes meant more than the new Italian restaurant in Santa Monica or the new sushi bar in Carson City, and that their endogenous force was unmitigated even now. Nor were vacations exempt. The Hollywood scriptwriter Ben Stein might note in his amusing book of journals, *Hollywood Days, Hollywood Nights*, that "in the fall of 1981 I flew to San Jose en route to my dream town Santa Cruz on the Monterey Bay" and imagine he had written a jaunty lead to another of his accounts of his amorous conquests, but those casually dropped place names had their own resonance and were just as explosive a package, at least in the long run, as sexual desire ever was.

In retrospect, it was beginning to appear that all the frenetic activity that had accompanied the immediate post-World War II boom, all those freeways, shopping malls, and subdivisions stretching out to the mountains and beyond, had distorted the true picture of what had taken place in Los Angeles since the first Anglo settlers had arrived at the beginning of the nineteenth century. Mexican Southern California may, indeed, have receded as the Anglo migrants poured in, but it no more disappeared than the shoreline does when the waves wash over it at high tide. However often its neighborhoods were razed and its population pressed to relocate—from Olvera Street and the Temple-Beaudry area to Watts, from Watts to Boyle Heights—Mexican Los Angeles never failed to reconstitute itself. Its roots ran too deep, and what is more, those roots were constantly being watered by the nourishing flow of new immigrants.

Anglo Los Angeles soon lapsed into forgetfulness, the great drama of Anglo versus Hispano that had wracked the Southland during the nineteenth century temporarily overshadowed by the passions of suburbanization. But even the idyll wasn't all that idyllic. Hints of things to come came in the Zoot Suit riots of 1943, a virtual insurrection in East L.A. that erupted after brawls between Anglo sailors on shore leave and young toughs from the barrio known as Pachucos got out of hand, and in the early stirrings of the Mexican-American civil rights movement, mild by today's standards but radical enough at the time, under the leadership of an organization called LULAC (the League of United

Latin American Citizens). For its part, however, Anglo L.A., that metropolis of Greta Garbos, imagined itself to be alone.

As things turned out, however, out of sight *and* out of mind was not the same thing as out of the picture. Indeed, what took place in Los Angeles in roughly the period between the early twenties and the mid or late sixties consisted more of a spectacular occlusion of civic vision, or, it might be surmised, a collective act of wishful thinking, than any genuine diminution of the importance of Mexican L.A. In retrospect, the Chamber of Commerce version had far more in common with those football metaphors so beloved in American political and corporate life than it did with the real history of the Southland. It was a view that proffered the history of California and its supposed crowning achievement, the rise of Los Angeles, as nothing so much as an irreversible linear progress, a series of arcing forward passes from ethnic group to ethnic group. It was as if the missionaries had gotten the ball from the Indians (well, the less said about that the better, *Mission Play* or no *Mission Play*), and, in turn, had thrown to the Mexicans, whereupon the Anglo team had raced out under one final perfect spiral, snagged it, and raced triumphantly across history's goal line for the winning touchdown. That was always the American role, wasn't it, to bring history to an end? Americans had been engaged in the enterprise for more than two hundred years now, as Lincoln understood when he wrote about the country as representing the last, best hope of mankind, with emphasis presumably placed on the "last."

But what was even more interesting about this claim than its crude and distended sense of mission was the signal inability of most Anglo Californians to consider another, distressing possibility. Could it be that the gun whose report they had heard so clearly had not, in fact, signaled the end of the game at all—that is, the completion of the region's historic development, though not, God forbid, its ever-to-be-continued patterns of economic growth—but rather the conclusion of the first half of play? If so, that would have meant conceding that Los Angeles was not a metaphor or an incarnated myth after all, however elastic that metaphor had turned out to be, but a place, trapped in the continuum of its real history and the increasingly obvious limitations of its parched desert ecology. All past citizens of the city, the concluding sentence of the "L.A. 2000" report asserts, "made their Los Angeles dreams come true," so why should the present be any different? But into this reverie came Mexico, that reproachful canker, its renewed presence intimating that history was not a progress at all

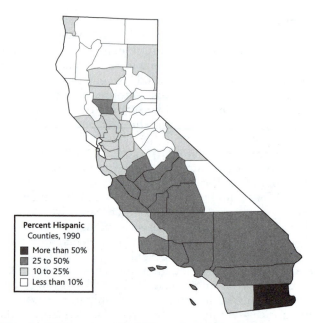

**Map depicting percent of Hispanic Population per county in 1990**

*Source*: U. C. Berkeley

but a cycle. The referee had thrown a yellow flag. The touchdown was being called back.

And it was only in a place that so obdurately construed itself as a dream that the change could have seemed like such a bolt from the sky.

## Questions for Discussion

1. Early in this selection, Rieff's tone suggests affinity with Anglo fears over Mexican immigration. Identify several places where this is so, and explain what you think his strategy is as he uses this tone. Is it parody? Is it to be taken seriously?

2. What is Rieff describing when he talks about "the centrality of the Mexican shadow world," in Southern California? Are there suggestions that people should see this as a threat, or is it merely stated as a fact of life?

3. What does Rieff mean when he uses the metaphor of the football game near the end of this selection? What is the difference between Los Angeles as

"incarnated myth" and as a real place, "trapped in the continuum of its real history," as Rieff says?

## Ideas for Writing

1. Walk or drive around the area where you live or work. Find as many clues of the "Mexican shadow world" as you can, if indeed there are any. Then write an essay in which you discuss the role of the Mexican past in the present situation of your region.
2. Research the Zoot Suit riots. What issues sparked the incidents? Who was involved? Did any change come as a result? Write a report in which you discuss the role of these events in the history of Los Angeles.

---

# The Third Border

## MIKE DAVIS

*Mike Davis is the author of a number of books of social commentary. A graduate of UCLA, he first came to prominence with his book* City of Quartz: Excavating the Future in Los Angeles *(1990). This was followed by* Ecology of Fear: Los Angeles and the Imagination of Disaster *in 1998. The book from which the selection here was taken,* Magical Urbanism, *won the 2001 Carey McWilliams Award presented by* MultiCultural *[sic]* Review. *Davis's articles appear in many publications, among them* The Nation *and* New Statesman.

---◆---

The first step in any Latino urban agenda must be to remove *La Migra* from the front yard. Visitors to Southern California are often shocked by the huge INS [Immigration and Naturalization Service] checkpoints—a veritable second border—that blockade the major Interstate freeways at San Clemente and Temecula, fifty to sixty miles north of Tijuana. Intended to intercept *coyotes* smuggling immigrants into Los Angeles and to reassure white suburbanites that Washington really is "in control," the controversial checkpoints have become for most Latinos hated symbols of an INS police state with sweeping powers far away from the border. They are blatant instances of racial profiling as federal policy. Even the

Chicano assistant district attorney, whose grandfather fought as a Marine at Guadalcanal, will tense a little and experience anew an ancient humiliation as he inches his shiny Lexus past the scrutiny of the Border Patrol in their sinister dark glasses. (Perhaps thinking to himself: "Goddamn Irish-Americans don't have to go through this.")

For those genuinely *sin papeles*, the checkpoints, especially at San Clemente (a stone's throw from Nixon's former "Western White House"), are often deathtraps. To avoid discovery, smugglers unload their cargo a mile or two before the checkpoint and order them to cross to the other side of the freeway and make their way along the beach (part of the vast Camp Pendleton Marine base) until they are safely north of the INS. Crossing ten lanes of high-speed Interstate freeway, congested until the early morning with heavy truck and tourist traffic, is a desperate gamble for anyone, but for tired and disoriented immigrants, many of whom have never seen a freeway before, it is often suicidal. Over the last fifteen years, more than a hundred people have been killed, including whole families mowed down while running hand-in-hand: at one point, there was a therapy group in San Diego for traumatized drivers who had accidentally hit freeway crossers. After spending a million dollars studying every option, except closing the San Clemente checkpoint, California's state transportation agency, Caltrans, created the world's first official "pedestrian accident zone" in the late 1980s, replete with bizarre warning signs that depict a frightened family bolting across the highway. It was a moral threshold in the naturalization of the daily violence of immigration.

But the border doesn't end at San Clemente. Indeed, as any ten-year-old in East L.A., or Philly's el Norte knows, borders tend to follow working-class Latinos wherever they live and regardless of how long they have been in the United States. In suburban Los Angeles and Chicago, for instance, the interface between affluent Anglo majorities and growing blue-collar Latino populations is regulated by what can only be typed a "third border." Whereas the second border nominally reinforces the international border, the third border polices daily intercourse between two citizen communities: its outrageousness is redoubled by the hypocrisy and cant used to justify its existence. Invisible to most Anglos, it slaps Latinos across the face.

Consider the San Gabriel Valley, just east of the City of Los Angeles. Once the center of the California citrus industry, the Valley, with nearly 2 million residents, is a mature, built-out suburban landscape politically fragmented into more than forty separate shards, ranging from large secondary cities like Pasadena and Pomona to unincorporated country "islands" and special-use incorporations like City of Industry and Irwindale. Although the great orchards were subdivided into tract homes a half-century ago, the fundamental division inherited from the citrus era between a Chicano/Mexican working class and an Anglo gentry continues to frame all social relations in the Valley. The traditional demographic balance, however, has been overturned, with roughly three Latino residents for every two Anglos by the early 1990s. Moreover, there is also a growing Chicano managerial-professional class, as well as a massive new Chinese immigration (approximately 250,000) that is all the more spectacular because it has taken the form of an eight-mile-long linear Chinatown extending eastward through Monterey Park, Alhambra and San Gabriel.

Although Anglo blue-collar residents have largely left the southern tier of Valley towns where they were formerly a majority, the wealthy foothill tier from La Cañada/Flintridge to Claremont remains highly attractive to young white professionals as well as to traditional elites. If the Valley floor has become the Chicano Democratic heartland, the foothill suburbs are still Reagan Republican and organized massively in support of anti-immigrant Proposition 187 in 1996. Here, amidst the sharpest ethnic and class tensions, a third border has arisen most obnoxiously to restrict the use of public space by poorer Latinos from nearby communities.

One example is the boundary between El Sereno and South Pasadena. El Sereno is an outlier of the City of Los Angeles in the western San Gabriel Valley. It is a well-groomed but aging blue-collar suburb, home to hardworking truckdrivers, medical secretaries and postal workers with last names like Hernandez and Rodriguez. South Pasadena, on the other hand, looks like Andy Hardy's hometown—big Midwestern-style family homes on quiet tree-lined streets—incongruously inserted into the Los Angeles urban fabric. Most importantly, its median home values are at least $100,000 higher than El Sereno's.

Some years ago when South Pasadena was still lily white, the city fathers decided that the twain must never meet and engineered the barricading of busy Van Horne Street. It may not be the old Berlin Wall, but to those on its "bad side" it insultingly stigmatizes their neighborhood as a violent slum. Serenos were especially incensed when South Pasadena justified the street closure in the name of "preventing drive-by shootings." Since many older Chicanos tell bitter stories of harassment by the South

Pasadena police, it is not surprising that they regard the barricade with the same fondness that Black southerners once felt about segregated drinking fountains.

San Marino, just to the east of South Pasadena, is one of the nation's wealthiest suburbs. It embalms ancient regional dynasties like the Chandlers of the *L.A. Times* and until recently provided a national headquarters for the John Birch Society. In recent years some of the Latino housecleaners and gardeners who keep its lush lifestyles scrubbed and pruned began to bring their own families on weekends to San Marino's beautiful Lacy Park. But the appearance of "aliens"—nannies pushing their own kids in prams not their mistresses'—in their cherished park incited near-hysteria, and the City Council obliged residents by imposing a weekend, nonresident use-fee of $12 per family—unprecedented in Los Angeles County. (Incredibly, the council justified the fee by claiming that the city was nearly broke.) Similarly, San Marino's crown jewel, the world-renowned Huntington Library and Gardens (built on the surplus value created by Henry Huntington's Mexican track laborers) changed its traditional free admission ("donation requested") to a strictly enforced $8 per head: another deterrent to diversity amidst the roses.

Arcadia, home of the famous Santa Anita racetrack (and Proposition 187's "godfather," State Senator Richard Mountjoy), has an even worse reputation among Valley Latinos. Historically it was one of the few citrus-belt towns that refused to allow its Mexican workers to live anywhere within the city limits, even on the other side of the tracks. In 1939, while Hitler was promulgating anti-Semitic laws, 99 percent of Arcadia's burghers signed a unique public "covenant," promoted by a local escrow company, that promised to keep their piece of paradise "Caucasian forever." They have never stopped trying. Thus when Arcadia's sprawling Wilderness Park became popular with Spanish-speaking families in the early 1990s, there was an even uglier uproar than in San Marino. "I've seen their graffiti," ranted a leader of the neighboring Highland Oaks Homeowner's Association. "I've heard their ghettoblasters . . . I don't want any riffraff coming into our city." The mayor agreed: "The park has been overrun with *these* people." As a result, Arcadia restricted public use of the park, now officially a "wilderness center," to a single eight-hour period on Fridays.

So far there has been little legal challenge to the foothill communities' legislation of exclusionary barriers, but in suburban Chicago, where Latinos are now the largest minority in 112 out of 149 incorporated communities, the Justice Department has had to file suit to prevent what critics have termed "city-sponsored ethnic cleansing." Thus in western suburban Addison, following a large Latino influx in the 1980s, the village purchased and destroyed most of a sprawling apartment complex that was the center of an immigrant community. In charging Addison with violating the Fair Housing Act, an assistant attorney general observed, "This is not urban renewal, it is urban destruction motivated by the national origin of the residents." Similarly, the Illinois Attorney General's Office denounced inner-suburban Cicero (whose Latino population exploded from 8.6 percent in 1980 to 37 percent in 1990) for using illegal occupancy ordinances to stop Latinization. "The town has made no secret that it wanted to limit the number of Hispanics." (The state pressed the same case against occupancy laws intended to limit the population of "La Selva" [the Jungle], an area of nearby Franklin Park.)

Northwest suburban Rosemont, on the other hand, has taken the extraordinary step of publically financing the walling-off of the affluent half of its population from poorer Latino residents. "Unlike the town's two apartment and condo neighborhoods, Scott Street has 24-hour, police-manned checkpoints and video cameras that record license plates—all paid for by the village. Although Rosemont is nearly 20 per cent Latino, the Scott subdivision is 95 per cent white." Supporters of the Rosemont *laager* point out that they have simply extended the regionally ubiquitous cul-de-sac (metropolitan Chicago has thousands of Van Horne Street-type barricades or cul-de-sacs demarcating racial and socio-economic borders) to its logical conclusion. Originally designed to wall-in Black residential areas, cul-de-sacs are now the first line of defense against Latino ethnic succession in Chicago's aging, inner suburbs. Roberto Suro's reassurance that Anglos nationally accept Latino immigrants "as an unobtrusive [and necessary] appendage to their new suburban culture" obviously applies only to the earliest stages of the relationship.

## Questions for Discussion

1. Davis begins his piece by talking at length about the INS checkpoint in San Clemente. What is his strategy in doing so?
2. What is Davis's tone as he discusses the examples of El Sereno/South Pasadena, San Marino, and Arcadia? Do the examples work to persuade readers of his argument?

3. The problem of the "third border," according to Davis, is not restricted to California. What is your reaction as a reader to his inclusion of suburban Chicago in his discussion?

## Ideas for Writing

1. Do some research on the current state of border enforcement in California. Then, write a report in which you explain whether you think the situation has improved or worsened since Davis wrote his analysis.
2. Survey the neighborhood or city where you live. Do structures exist to create a sense that outsiders are unwelcome? In an essay, explain whether you think people have a right to create such borders or whether doing so is simply a reaction of panic and racism toward others.

---

# Being Japanese Is Pretty Cool After All

## Machiko Yasuda

*Machiko Yasuda has written for* LA Youth, *a regional publication for LA area teens, as well as for Peninsula High School's* The Pen. *She has finished her studies at Palos Verdes Peninsula High School and now attends college at UCLA.*

———————— ✦ ————————

*My heritage and my parents' accents used to embarrass me, but now I have fun sharing my culture*

Growing up in the mostly white community of Palos Verdes, I was annoyed that my parents are Japanese immigrants. They stood out in public when they pronounced "work" and "walk" identically or said "Beverly Hills" more like "Bevaree Hiruzu."

In Palos Verdes, even though Asians are the predominant minorities, it still seemed like the Japanese immigrant parents were outcasts. Unlike other immigrant families, the majority of Japanese immigrants live here because they've been transferred as part of their jobs, and they know that they'll be here only about five years. So Japanese families often don't even try to interact with the locals.

My mom often asked me to help these new Japanese students adjust to my school, but I didn't even like associating with these people! I didn't want my classmates to think I, too, was a foreigner who couldn't speak English. My mom didn't care about that—she thought I was being a disrespectful brat for thinking that way.

What made the strain between my mom and me worse was being forced to go to Japanese school every week. My parents wanted me to be as "Japanese" as possible. I understood their reasoning, but I hated it. School was eight hours on Saturdays from first grade through 10th grade and all the weekly *kanji* (intricate Chinese characters used in Japanese) tests and pages of haiku poetry we had to write seemed pointless.

As I got older, my classmates and I sent a bitter message to the strict teachers at Japanese school and our unsympathetic parents. We refused to converse in Japanese outside the classroom. We didn't care about the rules anymore.

My hate for the weekend school torture in turn fueled my disgust for popular Japanese music and fashion. At Japanese school and in regular middle school, I'd see classmates with their backpacks and notebooks covered with "Engrish"—nonsense English phrases like "Always Rerax Panda." I always overheard some classmates talking about new hit singles with titles like "Locolotion" or "Serenade" (pronounced like say-ray-nah-day)! I usually never talked to these ESL (English as a Second Language) students because they didn't like mingling with the students born in the United States.

We used to nickname these students "fobs" (fresh off the boat). Even though I have the same kind of parents as the fobs, I was ashamed by the strange way these students dressed, with their blonde hair streaks and flashy clothes brands and obliviousness to American pop culture. In sixth grade, I didn't know where to start when a girl who sat next to me asked what, not who, N'Sync was. And how could they still wear that Brooklyn, I mean, "Blooklyn" jacket, and that T-shirt with the word . . . "enjordelicious?"

When I go to Japan I always see my cousins obsessing over new American clothing brands and TV shows like *Friends*, so why weren't the Japanese students trying to make the most out of living in the States? Weren't they embarrassed that Americans often associated Japanese people with socially oblivious, bad drivers with "Engrish" clothing and little understanding of the language?

Pointing out Engrish errors became a game for my brothers and me. To my parents though, our "game" was an insensitive assault on their culture. Maybe they were scared that we would grow up to be less "Japanese" and more "American." But none of us were even thinking about that. We just hated having to go school on Saturdays with our uncool, "fobby" Japanese counterparts.

As the oldest child, I had to teach my parents about American customs that don't translate well into Japanese culture: school dances, lockers on campus, drivers' permits before students graduate high school or tryouts for school sports.

For my eighth grade graduation dance my mom went all out. I'm not sure whether she thought it was going to be like a ballroom dance or a club rave, but she made it a family affair. The weekend before the dance, my mom and grandmother, who was visiting for the first time in five years, spent hours dressing me in my overly-expensive, way-too-long, fancy pink gown. The other girls wore knee-length cocktail dresses. And no, Mom, you really don't have to take so many photos and get them specially printed in large sizes!

## EVEN MY NAME HAS EMBARRASSED ME

Also, I have always disliked my name, Machiko (which is pronounced "Ma-CHEEK-oh"). Every year I brace for another creative, yet butchered pronunciation of my name during roll call on the first day of school. "Mockiko" and "Moshiko" are the most common ones. In sixth grade and 11th grade my name appeared as "MacHiko" in the yearbook. Why couldn't I have a name that didn't require a blank, puzzled look at Starbucks after I repeat it three times and then spell it out?

My resentment toward my Japanese background, however, started to change between my sophomore and junior years of high school. After three years of Spanish class, my parents let me participate in a Spanish immersion program at the Universidad de las Américas (UDLA) in Puebla, Mexico. I stayed in a college dorm for two weeks, right after school ended.

I had never been outside of the country besides Japan, and two whole weeks without any pushy parents or annoying brothers seemed like the perfect escape after a chaotic sophomore year. But I was scared that I wouldn't fit in.

Only a day after the school year ended, I was on a flight to Mexico City. The last thing I was expecting after my arrival was a kiss on the cheek from Tania and Pedro, the two UDLA students who were going to help me settle into the school. I never get kisses or hugs from my parents, and here were two strangers kissing me on the cheek. Japanese people are traditionally more reserved, so it's not common to show affection to your family like that. The way they were standing and talking SO close to me was different, too. It was such a contrast to the common Japanese greeting I'm used to—a bow from a respectful distance, not right in your face. After meeting a few more people I got used to it.

## SHE LIKED JAPAN MORE THAN I DID

During the bus ride, I sat next to Tania, a senior at UDLA studying Japanese and economics. She amazed me with her fluent Japanese and her knowledge of Japanese cities, even though she had never been there. She was able to talk to my dad, who was on his annual Puebla business trip, about what city she wanted to visit and what study program she wanted to participate in . . . and I didn't even know what area she was talking about. How could a Mexican student learn Japanese so well in just four years, and familiarize herself with the people and culture so quickly? When I found out that some college students were studying so hard, it made me feel lazy about how I treated Japanese school.

Some of my roommates asked about my background: When and why my parents came to the U.S.? Do all Japanese people have small, slanted eyes? How did I learn to speak the language? Do I eat sushi with chopsticks at home? Could I write their names or words like "love" and "hope" in Japanese for them?

I've always had people ask me about my parents and where I learned to speak Japanese, but not any of the other questions. I hated the weekly *kanji* tests at Japanese school, but here my roommates were so intrigued by my writing. I was beginning to realize that maybe I had been wrong hating Japanese school so much. Now I liked being able to write everyone's names in Japanese and teach them about the customs. Had I not spent my Saturdays with all those *kanji* tests I probably wouldn't have been able to do that for them—and how embarrassing would that have been?

As I walked around the town center I was paranoid about saying something that I didn't mean or doing something disrespectful. The students at my high school who had recently come from Japan probably felt the same way when they first moved to the United States. But, it seemed like everyone at UDLA, the cooks, security guards, students and my teachers, had at least a smile and a kind greeting for me. Even in the buses and around town the people seemed welcoming and didn't mind answering my questions for help. I started to think that I should be just as sympathetic to the fobs. Now I regretted not being more considerate and helpful before, especially because I already knew the language and their background.

One of my most memorable experiences in Mexico was visiting an orphanage called Viva Esperanza. Inside the tiny, crumbling ivy-covered building, I got to play basketball and jump rope with the kids. I was shocked to see everyone, from the youngest to the oldest, all wearing uniforms and credentials with their full names and birthdays around their necks. These tags were the only things that made one child different from the other, and it seemed like everyone was so proud of and attached to their names. Some girls gave me a full explanation of their first and last names. I used to be so embarrassed by mine.

While riding the bus one day I sat next to an elderly woman who was born in Oaxaca. She spoke Spanish and Zapotec, one of the numerous indigenous languages of Mexico. She taught me some words in Zapotec, which don't sound like Spanish at all. The way she was so determined about preserving her language, which is far less common in Mexico, was similar to what my parents wanted me to get out of Japanese school. They wanted me to be just like any other Japanese teen even if I lived in the United States.

## SHARING MY LOVE OF THINGS JAPANESE

Now that it's been a year since my trip, I've begun to look at my culture and background differently. The same things I tried to avoid talking about such as Japanese religious traditions or why my parents never hug me are things I don't mind taking an extra minute to explain. I love meeting people who are curious and intrigued by my culture, and introducing my friends to my Japanese CDs and DVDs is fun. I only wish I had studied enough in school to be able to translate song lyrics and movie titles better.

I realize how lucky I am to be able to learn the language of my relatives and taste my mom's authentic Japanese food, like her homemade California rolls. Now I listen to good Japanese music, too, minus the ridiculous "Engrish" lines. My iPod mini has more than a gig of Japanese music! It's been more than a year since I graduated from Japanese school, and I'm writing more e-mails to my cousins and watching my parents' television programs—two tasks I dreaded being forced to do in the past.

Now I don't mind helping my friend (who two years ago I would have mocked) with her ESL vocab homework or orchestra class directions. I'm obviously not friends with everyone, but now I'm anxious to see if there are any new Japanese students in my classes or clubs.

I'm also more appreciative of my name (although the Starbucks issue is still just as annoying). I still remember the vivid image of the children at Viva Esperanza in their uniforms with their name cards around their necks. The cards seemed to emphasize how much they valued their names, names their parents probably gave them. At least I have a proper first and last name and I know how to write it in proper characters, too. It's also nice to have an uncommon name that you don't always hear around school and on television.

## Questions for Discussion

1. In what ways did Yasuda find herself rejecting her primary (Japanese) culture as she was growing up? Identify the examples she gives in her piece.

2. Could you say Yasuda made peace with her heritage? In what ways does she support the statement of her title, that "Being Japanese is Pretty Cool After All?"

3. What did being away from the US, in what for her was the third culture of Mexico, teach Yasuda about her primary (Japanese) culture and its value?

## Ideas for Writing

1. Is it possible to retain a culture once you are geographically removed from its home? What elements are lost despite a person's best efforts not to change? What are the implications of this? Talk to someone who came to the US from elsewhere, or think about your own experience if you are an immigrant, then write an essay in which you discuss these issues.

2. Yasuda discusses the issue of one's name as a key factor in creating identity. Explain the examples she uses and why one's name has so much symbolic value. Then, offer some examples of your own to compare or contrast with her claims.

---

# Kids and Gangs: Seeking Solutions

## ALIZAH SALARIO

*Alizah Salario is a graduate of Pitzer College and a frequent contributor to the* Iranian Jewish Chronicle, Ostrich Ink, *and other online zines.*

---  ◆  ---

It's Thursday evening, and members of the Youth Leadership Council (YLC) crowd around a large rectangular table as though attending a policy conference.

Although this is Hathaway Children and Family Services, and members of the YLC are still in their teens, the meetings are treated with the seriousness and maturity of intense political discussions.

These middle and high school students might not be deciding foreign policy, but the issues they tackle are essential to the well-being of their community.

Today's topic? The local Dash bus route, which stops two blocks from Hathaway House.

That's two block too many for many who come to Hathaway, either for YLC meetings or just to chill. With poor lighting and a secluded staircase leading to the street, many students feel unsafe traveling even this short distance.

Mayoral candidates [in Los Angeles] highlighted "youth issues" as a major campaign bullet point. Improving education, increasing after-school programs, and decreasing gang activity are said to be among the top priorities for many politicians.

Yet with Northeast [Los Angeles] gang activity on the rise, climaxing in last month's gang-related shooting, many residents remain concerned about their children's safety. The reality is, they want real answers, not political speculation, and they want them now.

While leaders continue to debate what should be done about the issue of gang violence, those on the front lines offered some common sense solutions to a complex problem.

"People who are in gangs or crews or whatever, they think they're too cool to improve their community . . . all they care about is their rep," said Angie, a YLC member. Elsa Curyk understands this pressure to maintain one's reputation in gang culture. In her recent book *The Hard-Core Speak*, Curyk examines the complexity of gang-related issues through her experiences at a continuation high school for ex-gang members.

Through her own stories and those of her students, Curyk explores the appeal of gangs to youths who have yet to define their own identities. She shared an anecdote about one student sitting on the fence between socially acceptable choices, and the "hard-core" lifestyle.

"One day he was a perfect little kid, and the next he was so horrible. He kept going back and forth. So I said to him, 'How come one day you're so good, and next you're so horrible?' and he said, 'Well, Miss, because I don't know whether to be a good boy or a bad boy.' He put the conflict so clearly."

While gang members are often demonized by the media, Curyk explained the motivation behind joining a gang.

"If I'm a good boy, I'll be a momma's boy," the boy later explained to her. This student's experience epitomizes the internal conflict that many youths face when the incentives for being "bad" outweigh those for being good.

Members of the Youth Leadership Council agree, stating that gang members find satisfaction in "protecting" their turf.

"Tagging . . . it's disrespectful. There are walls for tagging, it's a turnoff, because you don't get that rush . . . our school has to be painted every single day . . . personally, I don't know how to prevent it. Maybe more things to do after school . . . I'm very involved in here [at Hathaway]," said Nadia, another YLC member.

Many gang members aren't thinking about long-term life goals. Gangs provide an instantaneous support network, personal validation, and much-needed attention. For some youths who can't find approval in typical situations because of the lack of opportunities, such as sports or the arts, it is easier to receive attention for being "bad."

Furthermore, explained Curyk, gang membership is for life. There are only three ways to get out of a gang: to get married and have a baby, move away, or join the army, she explained. If members choose to leave otherwise, they risk retaliation from their former cohorts.

While the students in the YLC have chosen a different path and spend their after-school hours at Hathaway, they understand why the structure and support that gangs offer appeals to many of their peers.

"There's not that much protection . . . look what happened at the park," said Angie, referring to the shooting. Ironically, members join gangs for their own protection.

"If we had more Hathaways, there would be less gang-related shooting . . . You're just here chillin'," said one member.

Despite this observation, there are few after-school options available for many middle and high school students.

While the proliferation of gang activity is a mystery to some residents, Curyk understands the appeal completely: She feels that gang activity has increased "because we're ignoring it . . . You need some kind of intervention . . . you're not going to save everyone, but I think a large percentage [can be saved]," she said.

But perhaps, this intervention should come in an unexpected form.

"It's important to find the right staff [for education and after-school programs] . . . You need to be yourself, and [kids will] connect with their higher selves . . . if it's really authentic, they'll listen . . . They can feel who cares. That can't be faked," she said.

For many, Curyk's approach is completely unorthodox. In a society that reserves tough-as-nails treatment for gang members, kindness and positive reinforcement may sound like an idealistic strategy. Yet Curyk feels that care, not criticism, is exactly what hard-core gang members need.

In fact, this is precisely what works with local youth at Hathaway House. Students receive positive attention for their efforts to shape up the community, and above all, they've found a safe space. Members of the YLC say they aren't tempted to join gangs because they've found a better alternative. As a result, many are frustrated and concerned with the negative choices of their peers.

Yet until there are more positive incentives for achievement and outlets for emotional support, Northeast youth will continue to turn to gangs to fulfill very human needs: support and positive attention.

Perhaps more foresight and community-wide discussions are needed to address the issue. Or maybe, as Nadia stated, it comes down to a simple question: "Do you want to do something [i.e. tagging one's territory] that's going to last maybe a couple of weeks, or do you want to do something that's going to last for generations?"

## Questions for Discussion

1. According to the article, what is the relationship between gang involvement and identity for young people?
2. In your opinion, do the young people Salario quotes as she explains the reasons for gang involvement make a convincing case? Does the methodology of Hathaway House sound like a reasonable approach to a solution?

3. Whose problem is this, really? Salario suggests several places where the responsibility might lie: the teens themselves, the parents, community leaders, and politicians. Which group do you think can and should do something to solve this problem, and what are the obstacles to success?

## Ideas for Writing

1. Find a gang intervention program through a local school, community center, or police department. Interview one of the people who runs the program, and one person who is being helped through it. Write an essay in which you evaluate both the mindset of the young person being helped and the approach which the program takes to the problem of gang violence.

2. Read further on the personal experiences of former gang members. (You might start with a book like *Always Running* by Luis Rodriguez.) Write a psychological profile of a person who becomes involved in such activity, and discuss whether you see his or her actions as choices or inevitabilities given the environment she or he lives in.

---

# The Anti-Heros: The LA4
## DONNA MUNGEN

*A naturalized Californian, Donna Mungen has published in* USA Today, Premiere Magazine, Daily Variety, LA Weekly, *and the* Los Angeles Times. *She is a former producer for* National Public Radio, *and her commentaries have aired on* All Things Considered *and* CNN-TV. *She was awarded First Place as Investigative Reporter from The Greater Los Angeles Press Club and covered the criminal O.J. Simpson trial for* The New York Times. *She is currently a professor of English at Pasadena City College.*

---
✦
---

While all eyes turned on the second Rodney King trial, others whispered and waited to see if Los Angeles would explode again should the verdict not be well received in certain neighborhoods.

Meanwhile, little media attention was being paid to the trial of the LA4: four young black men who made video history on the catastrophic afternoon of April 29, 1992 as truck driver Reginald

Denny made his ill-fated turn into the heart of South Central LA and the eye of a brewing social storm.

Even though most LA residents (both within and outside of the black community) reviled the actions of the young men known as the LA4, they still had a small faithful contingent of supporters who held a rally during the court proceedings. The event erupted into a near mini-riot before it was quickly extinguished by the forceful presence of the police, and I had the fortune to be there that day.

I stopped and queried a young female demonstrator regarding her reasoning and motivation for supporting the LA4's dastardly deeds. She turned to me with fiery eyes and barked back, "I don't think what the officers did to Rodney King was fair, and I don't think what these guys did is fair either. But if the white officers can get off, why can't these brothers get off? I feel there should be justice for black men as there is for white men."

For many Angelenos, the image of the televised dawn raid of Chief Darryl Gates, decked out in his warrior bullet-proofed vest, arresting the most notorious of the defendants: Damien 'Football' Williams remains singed to their eye filaments. According to the indictments served that day, Williams was charged with making an acrobatic fly-kick to the skull of the semi-conscious Reginald Denny who lay sprawled defenselessly in the middle of the street.

The four defendants later had the book thrown at them and were slapped with exorbitant bails. Legal tactics succeeded in getting some of the charges rescinded, but even the ones that stuck promised to keep all four of them on "ice" for the rest of their natural lives.

As an armchair attorney, I found the legal disparities between the treatment of the defendants in the King and Denny cases quite disturbing. From inception, the police officers were released on bail (which allowed some enough time to publish their own sensational accounts of the original Rodney King assault). And even during the most heated days of the King trial, the consequences of a guilty verdict for the police officers never included prospects that they would never see the light of day. However, all efforts at plea-bargaining in the LA4 case were rejected, and repeated accusations of racism reinforced by previous judicial decisions involving African-American defendants only served to compromise the public's perception of the government's case against the LA4.

Yet among most of my friends, few, if any, found much to champion in the LA4 case. This was no "Free Angela Davis" or "Down With the Pigs" political cause celebre. I'd go as far to say these young men were anti-heroes, or as the president of local branch of the NAACP announced at the time, "There are plenty of others you can find every day who are more appropriate to defend."

In a perverse way, the actions of the LA4 represented not only a lost generation, but also the worst that the African-American community had to offer. They were not the reason we marched on Washington in 1963, nor did their actions proclaim, "I am somebody." Rather 'they were the ones we wished to forget.'

Still they were our children, and we were forced to consider them and their actions. It has been said: You can't always love the deeds of your children. As much as I dislike the alleged actions of the LA4, I couldn't just completely dismiss the woman demonstrator's remarks. Certainly the actions of these young men were partially the manifestation of many of the problems brewing inside of our urban cookers. But the lingering question was how we could make succeeding generations of Black men feel it was not necessary to kick a White man in the head in order to obtain a measure of self-esteem.

The legal playing field must be leveled so that the reality of any case, including such high-profile cases as the LA4, Rodney King, or several years later the O.J. Simpson trial, demonstrates that everyone can obtain equal justice. I think it is no accident that both of these cases occurred at the same time. They served as a Yin and Yang influence in America—the ebb and flow—of life. We are forced, whether we like it or not, to look at the flip side of the coin and somehow, if we don't have to burn down and destroy the place we live to the essence of the truth, maybe we can be better from the process.

After 1992, the image of LA moved from one of the most desirable American cities to the home of increased unemployment, business flight, racial bigotry, drive-by shootings, and high foreclosure rates. And if that wasn't enough, we had the very dark apocalyptic concept further reinforced with the release of the movie *Falling Down*, the story of a mentally disturbed, unemployed engineer, played by Michael Douglas, who is mad as hell and isn't going to take it anymore, which visually translated into him going on a rampage kicking the asses of Koreans, Mexicans, women, and gays.

So little of these images reflect the love and beauty that has brought over 13 million residents from all corners of the world to live in LALA land. There's more to this city of rainbow faces, instant beach culture, constantly moving geography, and too often polluted vistas.

The other day I was thinking that when the East Coast seems like it would never surface from the "Snow of the Century," that I'd rather take my chances here with eighty-degree days. Indeed, LA's been bruised, scarred, and shaken to its roots, but we're only two hundred years old—sort of like a preteen with a major outbreak of acne. And in spite of the anti-heroes, there is still a lot of wonderful stuff here, and will continue to remain home for many angels.

## Questions for Discussion

1. Define the term "anti-hero." Then, explain whether it properly applies to these four young men. Use evidence from the reading to support your claim.

2. Mungen comes to express sympathy for the LA4, but she can only go so far toward offering her support. Describe her point of view, and explain where she pulls back from complete support of the four, and why you think this is.

3. Mungen suggests that the LA4 were treated differently by the legal system than were the defendants in the Rodney King case. Where does she express this, and what changes does she insist must take place?

## Ideas for Writing

1. Use your favorite search engine or library search tool to research "Rodney King," and "Reginald Denney." What do you find out about the two beating incidents? How are the perpetrators described or discussed in each case? What can you conclude as you set the depictions of each incident side by side? Write an essay in which you explain the contrasts as you see them.

2. Do some research on crime statistics and prison population statistics. What do you find regarding the ethnic profile of the people who are incarcerated in California? Does this surprise you, concern you, or merely confirm what you believed beforehand? Where were these values formed? Write an essay in which you explain your preconceptions, trace their origins as best you can, and discuss whether and why these notions are true or false.

---

# From *The Gangster We Are All Looking For*

### LÊ THI DIEM THÚY

*lê thi diem thúy (pronounced lay tee yim twee—wikipedia.org) was born in South Vietnam and immigrated to Southern California with her father amongst other refugees known as the "boat people" in the late 1970s. She left the state to complete her education at Hampshire*

College in Western Massachusetts, graduating in 1994. In addition to being a writer, she is an internationally known performance artist. Her novel The Gangster We Are All Looking For (2001), where this selection originally appeared, is based on her experiences growing up in California.

———————— ✦ ————————

We live in the country of California, the province of San Diego, the village of Linda Vista. We live in old Navy Housing bungalows built in the 1940s. Since the 1980s, these bungalows house Vietnamese, Cambodian, and Laotian refugees from the Vietnam War. When we moved in, we had to sign a form promising not to put fish bones in the garbage disposal.

We live in a yellow house on Westinghouse Street. Our house is one story, made of wood and plaster. Between our house and another one-story house are six two-story houses. Facing our row of houses, across a field of brown dirt, sits another row of yellow houses, same as ours, watching us like a sad twin. Linda Vista is full of houses like ours, painted in peeling shades of olive green, baby blue, and sun-baked yellow.

There's new Navy Housing on Linda Vista Road, the long street that takes you out of here. We see the Navy people watering their lawns, their children riding pink tricycles up and down the culs-de-sac. We see them in Victory Supermarket, buying groceries with cash. In Kelley Park they have picnics and shoot each other with water guns. At school their kids are Most Popular, Most Beautiful, Most Likely to Succeed. Though there are more Vietnamese, Cambodian, and Laotian kids at the school, in the yearbook we are not the most of anything. They call us Yang because one year a bunch of Laotian kids with the last name Yang came to our school. The Navy Housing kids started calling all the refugee kids "Yang."

Yang. Yang. Yang.

Ma says living next to Anh's family reminds her of Vietnam because the blue tarp suspended above Ahn's backyard is the bright blue of the South China Sea. Ma says, isn't it funny how sky and sea follow you from place to place as if they too were traveling.

Thinking of my older brother, who was still in Vietnam, I ask Ma, "If the sky and the sea can follow us here, why can't people?"

Ma ignores my question and says even Anh reminds her of Vietnam, the way she sets out for market each morning.

Ba becomes a gardener. Overnight. He buys a truck full of equipment and a box of business cards from Uncle Twelve, who is moving to Texas to become a fisherman. The business cards read "Tom's Professional Gardening Service" and have a small green picture embossed on them, a man pushing a lawn mower. The man has his back to you, so no one holding the card can tell it's not Ba, no one who doesn't already know. He says I can be his secretary because I speak the best English. If you call us on the business phone, you will hear me say: "Hello, you have reached Tom's Professional Gardening Service. We are not here right now, but if you leave us a message, we will get back to you as soon as possible. Thank you."

It is hot and dusty where we live. Some people think it's dirty but they don't know much about us. They haven't seen our gardens full of lemongrass, mint, cilantro, and basil. Driving by with their windows rolled up, they've only seen the pigeons pecking at day-old rice and the skinny cats and dogs sitting in the skinny shade of skinny trees. Have they seen the berries that we pick, that turn our lips and fingertips red? How about the small staircase Ba built from our bedroom window to the backyard so I would have a shortcut to the clothesline? How about the Great Wall of China that snakes like a river from the top of the steep hill off Crandall Drive to the slightly curving bottom? Who has seen this?[. . .]

Ma shaved her head in Linda Vista because she got mad at Ba for gambling away her money and getting drunk every week during *Monday Night Football*. Ba gave her a blue baseball cap to wear until her hair grew back and she wore it backward, like a real badass.

After that, some people in Linda Vista said that Ma was crazy and Ba was crazy for staying with her. But what do some people know?

When the photograph came, Ma and Ba got into a fight. Ba threw the fish tank out the front door and Ma broke all the dishes. They said they never should've got together.

Ma's sister sent her the photograph from Vietnam. It came in a stiff envelope. There was nothing else inside, as if anything more would be pointless. Ma held the photograph in her hands. She started to cry. "Child," she sobbed, over and over again. She wasn't talking about me. She was talking about herself.

Ba said, "Don't cry. Your parents have forgiven you."

Ma kept crying anyway and told him not to touch her with his gangster hands. Ba clenched his hands into tight fists and punched the walls.

"What hands?! What hands?!" he yelled. "Let me see the gangster! Let me see his hands!" I see his hands punch hands punch hands punch blood.[. . .]

When the eviction notice came, we didn't believe it so we threw it away. It said we had a month to get out. The houses on our block had a new owner who wanted to tear everything down and build better housing for the community. It said we were priority tenants for the new complex, but we couldn't afford to pay the new rent so it didn't matter. The notice also said that if we didn't get out in time, all our possessions would be confiscated in accordance with some section of a law book or manual we were supposed to have known about but had never seen. We couldn't believe the eviction notice so we threw it away.

The fence is tall, silver, and see-through. Chain-link, it rattles when you shake it and wobbles when you lean against it. It circles our block like a bad dream. It is not funny like the clothesline whose flying shirts and empty pants suggest human birds and vanishing acts. This fence presses sharply against your brain. We three stand still as posts. Looking at it, then at one another—this side and that—out of the corners of our eyes. What are we thinking?

At night we come back with three uncles. Ba cuts a hole in the fence and we step through. Quiet, we break into our own house through the back window. Quiet, we steal back everything that is ours. We fill ten-gallon garbage bags with clothes, pots and pans, flip-flops, the porcelain figure of Mary, the wooden Buddha and the Chinese fisherman lamp. In the arc of our flashlights we find our favorite hairbrushes behind bedposts. When we are done, we clamber, breathless. Though it's quiet, we can hear police cars coming to get us.

We tumble out the window like people tumbling across continents. We are time traveling, weighed down by heavy furniture and bags of precious junk. We find ourselves leaning against Ba's yellow truck. Ma calls his name, her voice reaching like a hand feeling for a tree trunk in darkness.

In the car, Ma starts to cry. "What about the sea?" she asks. "What about the garden?" Ba says we can come back in the morning and dig up the stalks of lemongrass and fold the sea into a blue square. Ma is sobbing. She is beating the dashboard with her fists. "I want to know," she says, "I want to know, I want to know . . . who is doing this to us?" Hiccupping she says, "I want to know, why— why there's always a fence. Why there's always someone on the outside wanting someone . . . something on the inside and between them . . . this . . . sharp fence. Why are we always leaving like this?"

Everyone is quiet when Ma screams.

"Take me back!" she says. "I can't go with you. I've forgotten my mother and father. I can't believe . . . Anh Minh, we've left them to die. Take me back."

Ma wants Ba to stop the car, but Ba doesn't know why. The three uncles, sitting in a row in the bed of the truck, think Ma is crazy. They yell in through the rear window, "My, are you going to walk back to Vietnam?"

"Yeah, are you going to walk home to your parents' house?"

In the silence another shakes his head and reaches into his shirt pocket for his cigarettes.

Ba puts his foot on the gas pedal. Our car jerks forward, and then plunges down the Crandall Drive hill. Ma says, "I need air, water . . . " I roll the window down. She puts her head in her hands. She keeps crying, "Child." Outside, I see the Great Wall of China. In the glare of the streetlamps, it is just a long strip of cardboard.

In the morning, the world is flat. Westinghouse Street is lying down like a jagged brushstroke of sun-burnt yellow. There is a big sign within the fence that reads

COMING SOON:
CONDOMINIUMS
TOWN HOUSES
FAMILY HOMES

Below these words is a copy of a watercolor drawing of a large pink complex.

We stand on the edge of the chain-link fence, sniffing the air for the scent of lemongrass, scanning this flat world for our blue sea. A wrecking ball dances madly through our house. Everything has burst wide open and sunk down low. Then I hear her calling them. She is whispering, "Ma/Ba, Ma/Ba." The whole world is two butterfly wings rubbing against my ear.

Listen . . . they are sitting in the attic, sitting like royalty in the dark, buried by a wrecking ball. Paper fragments floating across the surface of the sea.

There is not a trace of blood anywhere except here, in my throat, where I am telling you all this.

## Questions for Discussion

1. How does the neighborhood described appear to outsiders, and what does the piece reveal about its real qualities?

2. What does the selection say that might explain the authorities' willingness to flatten the neighborhood? What could people like Ma and Ba offer that might convince these outside observers to see the place they live in differently?

3. What do the "sea" (the blue tarp), the "Great Wall," and the lemongrass signify, and why are they so important to the narrator, Ma, and Ba in confirming their identity? Do they help you to sympathize with the family's situation?

## Ideas for Writing

1. Do some research on refugee groups from Vietnam, Cambodia, and Laos. What help did they get from the US government as they resettled? What became of communities like the one in Linda Vista? As you write about them, consider whether you agree with lê's tone, which seems to suggest that the displacement of the people from their first settling point is tragic. In the case of the people portrayed here, should the government have allowed them to live on indefinitely in the old Navy housing in Linda Vista?

2. The piece describes the gardening enterprise as something Ba bought, complete with business cards, almost like a franchise. Talk to some people who work in a freelance business like gardening or pool maintenance, and find out what rules, formal or informal, govern their trade. Are there territories they observe? Who's in control? Write up a business plan for a gardening service in which you describe it as if it were a franchise like a Subway restaurant or a McDonald's.

# My Oakland: There Is A There There
## ISHMAEL REED

*Ishmael Reed was born in 1938 in Chattanooga, Tennessee. He is a novelist, poet, and professor at UC Berkeley, and has lived in and written about Oakland since 1979. His many books and anthologies include* From Totem to Hip-Hop: A Multicultural Anthology of Poetry Across the Americas, Blues City: A Walk in Oakland, Mumbo Jumbo, *and* The Reed Reader. *In addition to his international recognition as a writer, Reed has worked to reduce drug dealing in his neighborhood and helped to organize a neighborhood watch program. The Ishmael Reed Papers (1964–1995) are housed at the University of Delaware.*

---◆---

On New Year's Eve, famed landscape architect John Roberts accompanied me on my nightly walk, which takes me from Fifty-third Street to Aileen, Shattuck, and back to Fifty-third Street.

He was able to identify plants and trees that had been imported from Asia, Africa, the Middle East, and Australia. On Aileen Street he discovered a banana tree! And Arthur Monroe, a painter and art historian, traces the "Tabby" garden design—in which seashells and plates are mixed with lime, sand, and water to form decorative borders, found in this Oakland neighborhood and others—to the influence of Islamic slaves brought to the Gulf Coast.

I won over my neighbors, I think, after I triumphed over a dozen generations of pigeons that had been roosting in the crevices of this house for many years. It was a long and angry war, and my five-year-old constantly complained to her mother about Daddy's bad words about the birds. I used everything I could get my hands on, including chicken wire and mothballs, and I would have tried the clay owls if the only manufacturer hadn't gone out of business. I also learned never to underestimate the intelligence of pigeons. Just when you think you've got them whipped, you'll notice that they've regrouped on some strategic rooftop to prepare for another invasion. When the house was free of pigeons and their droppings, which had spread to the adjoining properties, the lady next door said, "Thank you."

Every New Year's Day since then our neighbors have invited us to join them and their fellow Louisianans for the traditional Afro-American good-luck meal called Hoppin' John. This year the menu included black-eyed peas, ham, corn bread, potato salad, chitterlings, greens, fried chicken, yams, head cheese, macaroni, rolls, sweet potato pie, and fruitcake. I got up that morning weighing 214 pounds and came home from the party weighing 220.

We've lived on Fifty-third Street for three years now. Carla's dance and theater school, which she operates with her partner, Jody Roberts—Roberts and Blank Dance/Drama—is already five years old. I am working on my seventh novel and a television production of my play *Mother Hubbard*. The house has yet to be restored to its 1906 glory, but we're working on it.

I've grown accustomed to the common sights here—teenagers moving through the neighborhood carrying radios blasting music by Grandmaster Flash and Prince, men hovering over cars with tools and rags in hand, decked-out female church delegations visiting the sick. Unemployment up, one sees more men drinking from sacks as they walk through Market Street or gather in Helen McGregor Plaza on Shattuck and Fifty-second Street, near a bench where mothers sit with their children waiting for buses. It may be because the bus stop is across the street from Children's

Hospital (exhibiting a brand-new antihuman, postmodern wing), but there seem to be a lot of sick black children these days. The criminal courts and emergency rooms of Oakland hospitals, both medical and psychiatric, are also filled with blacks.

White men go from door to door trying to unload spoiled meat. Incredibly sleazy white contractors and hustlers try to entangle people into shady deals that sometimes lead to the loss of a home. Everybody knows of someone, usually a widow, who has been deceived into paying thousands of dollars more than the standard cost for, say, adding a room to a house. It sure ain't El Cerrito. In El Cerrito the representatives from the utilities were very courteous. If they realize they're speaking to someone in a black neighborhood, however, they become curt and sarcastic. I was trying to arrange for the gas company to come out to fix a stove when the woman from Pacific Gas and Electric gave me some snide lip. I told her, "Lady, if you think what you're going through is an inconvenience, you can imagine my inconvenience paying the bills every month." Even she had to laugh.

The clerks in the stores are also curt, regarding blacks the way the media regard them, as criminal suspects. Over in El Cerrito the cops were professional, respectful—in Oakland they swagger about like candidates for a rodeo. In El Cerrito and the Berkeley Hills you could take your time paying some bills, but in this black neighborhood if you miss paying a bill by one day, "reminders" printed in glaring and violent typefaces are sent to you, or you're threatened with discontinuance of this or that service. Los Angeles police victim Eulia Love, who was shot in the aftermath of an argument over an overdue gas bill, would still be alive if she had lived in El Cerrito or the Berkeley Hills.

I went to a bank a few weeks ago that advertised easy loans on television, only to be told that I would have to wait six months after opening an account to be eligible for a loan. I went home and called the same bank, this time putting on my Clark Kent voice, and was informed that I could come in and get the loan the same day. Other credit unions and banks, too, have different lending practices for black and white neighborhoods, but when I try to tell white intellectuals that blacks are prevented from developing industries because the banks find it easier to lend money to Communist countries than to American citizens, they call me paranoid. Sometimes when I know I'm going to be inconvenienced by merchants or creditors because of my Fifty-third Street address, I give the address of my Berkeley studio instead. Others are not so fortunate.

Despite the inconveniences and antagonism from the outside world one has to endure for having a Fifty-third Street address, life in this neighborhood is more pleasant than grim. Casually dressed, well-groomed elderly men gather at the intersections to look after the small children as they walk to and from school, or just to keep an eye on the neighborhood. My next-door neighbor keeps me in stitches with his informed commentary on any number of political comedies emanating from Washington and Sacramento. Once we were discussing pesticides, and the man who was repairing his porch told us that he had a great garden and didn't have to pay all that much attention to it. As for pesticides, he said, the bugs have to eat, too.

There are people on this block who still know the subsistence skills many Americans have forgotten. They can hunt and fish (and if you don't fish, there is a man who covers the neighborhood selling fresh fish and yelling "Fishman," recalling a period of ancient American commerce when you didn't have to pay the middleman). They are also loyal Americans—they vote, they pay taxes—but you don't find the extreme patriots here that you find in white neighborhoods. Although Christmas, Thanksgiving, New Year's, and Easter are celebrated with all get-out, I've never seen a flag flying on Memorial Day, or on any holiday that calls for the showing of the flag. Blacks express their loyalty in concrete ways. For example, you rarely see a foreign car in this neighborhood. And this Fifty-third Street neighborhood, as well as black neighborhoods like it from coast to coast, will supply the male children who will bear the brunt of future jungle wars, just as they did in Vietnam.

We do our shopping on a strip called Temescal, which stretches from Forty-sixth to Fifty-first streets. Temescal, according to Oakland librarian William Sturm, is an Aztec word for "hothouse," or "bathhouse." The word was borrowed from the Mexicans by the Spanish to describe similar hothouses, early saunas, built by the California Indians in what is now North Oakland. Some say the hothouses were used to sweat out demons; others claim the Indians used them for medicinal purposes. Most agree that after a period of time in the steam, the Indians would rush en masse into the streams that flowed through the area. One still runs underneath my backyard—I have to mow the grass there almost every other day.

Within these five blocks are the famous Italian restaurant Bertola's, "Since 1932"; Siam restaurant; La Belle Creole, a French-Caribbean restaurant; Asmara, an Ethiopian restaurant;

and Ben's Hof Brau, where white and black senior citizens, dressed in the elegance of a former time, congregate to talk or to have an inexpensive though quality breakfast provided by Ben's hardworking and courteous staff.

The Hof Brau shares its space with Vern's market, where you can shop to the music of DeBarge. To the front of Vern's is the Temescal Delicatessen, where a young Korean man makes the best po'boy sandwiches north of Louisiana, and near the side entrance is Ed Fraga's Automotive. The owner is always advising his customers to avoid stress, and he says good-bye with a "God bless you." The rest of the strip is taken up by the Temescal Pharmacy, which has a resident health adviser and a small library of health literature; the Aikido Institute; an African bookstore; and the internationally known Genova Deli, to which people from the surrounding cities travel to shop. The strip also includes the Clausen House thrift shop, which sells used clothes and furniture. Here you can buy novels by J. D. Salinger and John O'Hara for ten cents each. (Of all the establishments listed here, only the Siam restaurant, the Aikido Institute, and the Genova Deli remain.)

Space that was recently occupied by the Buon Gusto Bakery is now for rent. Before the bakery left, an Italian lady who worked there introduced me to a crunchy, cookielike treat called "bones," which she said went well with Italian wine. The Buon Gusto had been a landmark since the 1940s, when, according to a guest at the New Year's Day Hoppin' John supper, North Oakland was populated by Italians and Portuguese. In those days a five-room house could be rented for forty-five dollars a month, she said.

The neighborhood is still in transition. The East Bay Negro Historical Society, which was located around the corner on Grove Street, included in its collection letters written by nineteenth-century macho man Jack London to his black nurse. They were signed, "Your little white pickaninny." It's been replaced by the New Israelite Delight restaurant, part of the Israelite Church, which also operates a day-care center. The restaurant offers homemade Louisiana gumbo and a breakfast that includes grits.

Unlike the other California neighborhoods I've lived in, I know most of the people on this block by name. They are friendly and cooperative, always offering to watch your house while you're away. The day after one of the few whites who lives on the block—a brilliant muckraking journalist and former student of mine—was robbed, neighbors gathered in front of his house to offer assistance.

In El Cerrito my neighbor was indeed a cop. He used pomade on his curly hair, sported a mustache, and there was a grayish tint in his brown eyes. He was a handsome man, with a smile like a movie star's. His was the only house on the block I entered during my three-year stay in that neighborhood, and that was one afternoon when we shared some brandy. I wanted to get to know him better. I didn't know he was dead until I saw people in black gathered on his doorstep.

I can't imagine that happening on Fifty-third Street. In a time when dour thinkers view alienation and insensitivity toward the plight of others as characteristics of the modern condition, I think I'm lucky to live in a neighborhood where people look out for one another.

A human neighborhood.

## Questions for Discussion

1. What are the "inconveniences and antagonism from the outside world" which a person with an address on Fifty-third Street has to endure, according to the article?
2. What are the benefits of living there, as Reed outlines them?
3. Reed talks about the neighbors helping others in times of tragedy, and he contrasts that with the distance between people in his old, more affluent, neighborhood. What set of cultural values does he suggest may differentiate the two places? Is this the same conclusion you would come to if you looked at each neighborhood from an outsider's point of view? What in his piece leads you to this conclusion?

## Ideas for Writing

1. Find a neighborhood in your city or town which has strong community bonds, formal or informal. (Hint: ask some people who have lived where you do for a long time to point you in the right direction if you don't know where to look.) Interview some residents there, then write about their experiences. Be sure to explain and analyze the reasons they offer you for why their neighborhood has strong ties amongst residents.
2. Research the lending policies of the bank where you or your family does business. Don't just look at what the bank says—talk to people, do some research online, and search old newspaper articles in your library database. Is there any disparity that you can find between what the bank says and what it does? How does this confirm or deny Reed's assertions about unfair lending practices in minority communities?

## Thinking and Writing about Chapter 2

### Connecting the Essays

1. Both Salario and Yasuda speak about the problems of young people in California, though Yasuda comes from a much more economically privileged background than the young people Salario speaks of. Compare the way each depicts the emotional content of the issues facing young people. Are the problems depicted in one article more profound, more important, or more difficult than those portrayed in the other?

2. Yasuda and lê talk about people who in many ways are as different as they can be—in where they are from, and in their economic status in California, to name just two. Yet in both cases, family is central in their thinking. Write an essay explaining the ways in which the two pieces might be seen as united in their emphasis on the family as a central aspect of one's identity.

3. McWilliams speaks in a sometimes-panicky voice about the immigration that he sees as California's future. Rieff might be seen to mirror this tone as he talks about people's perception about Latin American immigration to the state over the past twenty years or so. Compare and contrast the two men's points of view by focusing especially on the tone of each essay.

4. Mungen, you might say, invents an identity for the young men accused in the Reginald Denney incident, calling them the "LA4" and labeling them "anti-heroes." The young people Salario speaks of seek to resolve conflicts about who they are by creating gangsters of themselves. Contrast the situation of creating one's own identity versus having one created for you by someone else. Do you believe it is more satisfying to seize one's own identity than to accept an identity offered by an outsider?

5. Reed discusses the fact that despite the middle-class's inability to imagine a meaningful culture existing in the cities, there is vibrancy in the community there. Davis, by contrast, seems to see the city as a place of divisions (of course, he is talking about Southern California, whereas Reed discusses Oakland, in the North). Could Reed's point of view be read as supplementing Davis's by giving a picture of one intimate aspect of the large urban landscape, which Davis reads as hostile and fearful?

### Extending the Theme

1. During the mid-1990s, there was a genre of LA disaster film that in some respects might be called a reflection of the chaos going on in the real world of Los Angeles. *Falling Down* and *Escape from LA* are films representing this group. Watch one of these, or a similar movie, and write about its presentation of community, or the lack of it.

2. Watch a couple of films which depict gang life in one of California's cities. What do you think the message of these movies is, and for whom is that

message intended? Write an essay in which you discuss what might be the reaction of the gangsters themselves if they were to view such a movie.

3. Go online and look up the official city website of Oakland, Los Angeles, or San Diego. How does what you find there reflect, or fail to reflect, the reality of life as explained by an author from this chapter who talks about one of these cities? Write an essay in which you compare and contrast one selection with one site.

4. Visit an area of the city where you live which is considered an ethnic enclave. Notice the ways in which this is signaled, both officially through signage or unofficially through a preponderance of a certain type of business. Research the history of the area either formally or through talking to people there. Write an essay in which you explain the circumstances that led to the area being populated as it is and describe or invent an official plan to shape the future of the area.

5. Research California's population demographics. What can you conclude about the trends as they exist now? What will the state look like in another fifty years? Write an essay with the tone of Rieff or McWilliams, but set your piece in 2050.

# Getting Our Fair Share

People seek their dreams through sacrifice and struggle. The history of California involves people seeking opportunities for a better life, often pushing against established rules in order to realize the promises of California. Before recorded history, native peoples lived relatively peaceably on the land now called California. Once the Europeans arrived, the cultures of the tribes were destroyed, leaving Spain in charge. Californians, a melting pot of ethnicities since the beginning, have lived under the rule of Spain, Mexico, and the United States, with each historic transition bringing new challenges and profound change.

When the Spanish era ended due to the Mexican revolution in 1821, California became part of the nation of Mexico. The language of daily activity, Spanish, remained the same, but other social and political traditions changed, partially due to the influx of immigrants from around the world, many drawn by the lure of gold. Not long after, the United States went to war with Mexico and through military victory gained not only California, but the land that would become Arizona, New Mexico, Colorado, and Texas—about one-fourth of the modern U.S. was Mexico until 1848.

During the transition from Mexican rule to American hegemony, 1848 until the 1860s, Californians needed to figure out their roles and relationships, as well as adjust to a new political system and language. People weren't sure who was in charge and who owned the valuable land. However, as a preview of today's focus on personal freedom, the state of California never permitted the enslavement of African-Americans. When California became a state in 1850, the nation gained another "free" state and kept its delicate balance for another decade until the slavery issue tore the country into the Civil War.

Chapter 3 tries to capture the complexity of politics and social change throughout the 150-plus years since California became a state. From the early years to the present, Californians' endless search for innovative solutions to their problems has often started trends that ripple across the nation and the world. Like today, social and economic progress came through complex human activities, often motivated by strong leaders with a vision of social change.

Tim Hodson's essay captures the political, social and economic diversity of the 1800s and explains how the roots of today's apparent "instability" actually have existed for centuries. Ethnic struggles in that era mostly involved Chinese immigrants brought to build railroads, then pushed aside when the work was done. The anti-Chinese vigilantes of the 1860s were perhaps very similar to today's anti-immigration "Minute Men" who insist on creating a nonofficial response to immigration. Hodson looks at history to help explain much more recent events, such as the recall of Gray Davis and the election of Arnold Schwarzenegger.

Peter Schrag looks at the ways that direct democracy, the California method of allowing "the people" to decide how the state should run, affects the political landscape. He explores even more controversial issues such as eliminating representative democracy and having everyone vote on everything. Could California voters do more than they already do? Would people be better served if all laws were made by voters and we had no representatives at all?

Speaking of elected representatives, Heather Barbour asks if 120 legislators represented one million Californians in 1879, does that number of elected state officials still adequately represent 36 million residents? Barbour asks if legislative size matters, and explains how other states handle the proportion of elected representatives to the number of residents.

Issues which might be resolved very differently if we had more or different legislators include the enormous problem of California's uninsured residents. About 20% of Californians have no medical insurance and rely on hope, prayer, herbs, and ultimately tax-funded public health care to survive. John and Judith Glass discuss the ongoing struggle to develop universal health care in the most populous state, a combination of legislation and ballot measures that continues to motivate thousands of health care activists.

Battles such as the effort to change our health delivery system are always built on those who came before. In a similar struggle to change public policy, Ken Burt tells the story of California's Fair Employment Practices Commission, created first at the federal level, but then also signed into law in California by Governor Pat Brown in 1959. This law protects all of us from discrimination in hiring, and it took a broad coalition of blacks, Jews, Catholics, Latinos, and labor activists to get the law passed.

And finally, the struggle to get an education, the key to most of the economic opportunities available, is discussed in Linda Darling-Hammond's "Lesson One: Training Counts" and William Piland's "College in California: Options Reduced?" Darling-Hammond explains the problems for California's K-12 public schools when too many teachers are underpaid and underprepared. Piland takes a concerned look at rising fees for public colleges and universities. Both researchers note that California has the resources to provide high quality education but needs the political will to do so. The dream of the Master Plan for educational access and opportunity has been shattered, and today's Californians face the challenges of re-invigorating that promise.

Human progress requires human activism. As you read these essays, you might think about your role in making California (or your home state) a better place for all. In fact, just by reading this book and being better informed, you are already taking a step towards doing your share. Congratulations, and enjoy.

# History, Myth, and Political Instability in California
## TIM HODSON

*Tim Hodson is a product of California's higher education system, earning his B.A. at CSU Fullerton, then his M.A. and Ph.D. in Political Science from the University of California, Santa Barbara. He has served as an assistant professor at Claremont McKenna College and visiting professor with CSU Sacramento and the University of Southern California. Dr. Hodson is currently Executive Director of the Center for California Studies at CSU Sacramento.*

✦

The recall of Gray Davis and election of Arnold Schwarzenegger reinforced the image of California politics as peculiarly unstable and unpredictable. Indeed, the recall, with its infamous 135 candidates, prompted State Librarian Kevin Starr to lament "[t]his confirms everybody's worst suspicion about California" (Arrillagaap, 2003).

The recall, however, was neither unique nor a function of la-la land celebrity mania. It was quite consistent with 150 years of California politics and mythology. The years following the Conquest, the Gold Rush and statehood were so pervasively and persistently chaotic that it has shaped California politics every since. This historical tendency for unstable politics has been reinforced by an equally persistent belief in California as a promised land, a new land and a land of tomorrow. History and mythology both made the recall possible and help explain it.

California's reputation for unstable politics is as old as the state. In 1850 Bayard Taylor (2000) wrote ". . . the results of the gold discovery produced a complete revolution in society . . . and for a time, completely annulling the Government" (p. 118). In the 1930s President Roosevelt's political guru Louis Howe regarded California politics as crazy. In the 1950s Theodore White declared that California politics defied reasonable analysis (Hill, 1968). Cary McWilliams (1976), perhaps California's finest interpreter, summed it up: "California is a state without a political gyroscope, a state that swings and sways, springs and turns in accordance with its own peculiar dynamics" (p. 192).

If California ever had a gyroscope (a debatable proposition given the instability of Spanish and Mexican California, the latter once having 14 governors in one five year period), it went missing with the Mexican-American War (Rawls & Bean). After the American conquest, California would have five different military governors, sometimes two at once (Rawls & Bean). The military tried to administer California through existing Mexican laws and town *alcaldes*. These efforts failed because of inadequate military forces, the lack of a clear legal mandate after the Treaty of Guadalupe Hidalgo was signed and, most important, the avalanche of gold-seekers hostile to a "foreign" system.

Conditions were approaching anarchy when word arrived that the South had blocked California becoming a non-slave state or even a territory. Refusing to wait until Congress reconvened, General Bennet Riley ordered a constitutional convention be held and a state government be elected. This was accomplished in November 1849, nearly a year *before* California was officially admitted as a state. In the first ten years as a state, the pattern of instability would continue with California averaging a new governor every two years (Walker, 1999).

During California's birth as a state, the structure and basic authority of government was thus conflictual and chaotic. As President John Tyler said, California was "left without any regularized organized government" (Royce, 2002). In contrast Colorado, which was ceded to the United States at the same time as California, experienced a major gold rush in 1859 but did not achieve statehood until 1876.

Chaos inevitably produces drives for order and stability. In post-conquest California, this was reflected by both official and unofficial efforts. The later included the Committees of Vigilance, which appeared regularly throughout the state in the 19th century.

Traditionally, vigilantism has been portrayed by historians and Hollywood as necessary efforts to confront lawlessness in the absence of official law enforcement (Royce, 2002; McGrath, 2003). The necessity of vigilantism can be debated, but what cannot be debated is the fact that California vigilantism typically took place in *defiance* of legally constituted government authority. The most prominent vigilante movements, the San Francisco Committees of Vigilance, exemplify this fact.

To illustrate, the most prominent and oft-celebrated vigilante movements were the 1851 and 1856 San Francisco Committees of Vigilance. Both Committees arose in response to specific crimes that were heralded as proof that law and order had collapsed. Both committees organized armed militias, arrested and executed alleged criminals. The problem was that law and order had not broken down. The 1851 Committee lynched one man and arrested two others. The Sheriff, with a writ of *habeas corpus* signed by the state Governor, moved the two men to the city jail. The Committee promptly stormed the jail and lynched the two prisoners. The 1856 Committee was even more contemptuous of government. When two alleged murders were arrested and jailed, the vigilantes decided the courts were too slow. They marched to the jail, brushed aside the Sheriff, the Mayor, the Governor and the commander of the state militia (William T. Sherman, later of Civil War fame) and lynched the accused men. Later the vigilante committee put the Chief Justice of the state Supreme Court on trial for the "crime" of having resisted them (Burns, 2003; Royce, 2002).

The California committees of vigilance of the 1850 to 1870s shared three basic characteristics. First, most were created not in the absence of but in defiance of legitimate constitutional authorities. This contempt for legitimate civil and military authority was justified by invoking the "higher law" of the people and claiming that they, and not elected officials, were the people's real representatives. For example, when the leader of American miners who attacked Chilean miners in the "Chilean War" of 1849 was served with an arrest warrant, he threatened to execute the court official, proclaiming, "The people are sovereign . . . we are the people and as such we have our own . . . judge and we recognize only his authority" (McGrath, 2003). Second, vigilante movements fiercely attacked anyone who opposed them, often threatening opponents with physical harm and economic ruin. They thus scorned the core democratic freedom to hold and express differing opinions. Third, many vigilante movements had significant class and political overtones. The 1856 Committee, for example, was also a political effort by largely Protestant, nativist, and wealthy groups determined to crush a political machine that was disproportionately Catholic, immigrant, and working class.

James J. Rawls (Rawls & Bean, 1998) summarized the consequences of vigilantism in a phrase that could apply to the legacy of California's political birth: "a vicious, dangerous and persistent tradition of contempt for the normal processes of democratic government" (p. 127). The patterns established in this period (i.e., intense, disruptive but transient political uprisings; a belief that government and constitutional structures and procedures could and should be ignored, and that certain groups hold a monopoly on the will of the people) can easily be seen in the Workingmen's Party and the constitutional convention of 1879, the Progressive movement of 1910–11, and the 2003 recall.

California political instability is a matter of historical record but also a function of the mythology of California. California is a place that exists first and foremost in the imagination and thus holds a place in Western and global culture as compelling as it is unparalleled. Real and mythological, California embodies three remarkably constant themes: California as the Promised Land, as a New Land, and as the Land of Tomorrow.

Western culture identified California as a Promised Land decades before the first European ever got to California. A Spanish romance written in 1500 proclaimed there was "an island called California, very close to the side of the terrestrial Paradise . . ." (Rawls & Bean, p. 21).

Paradise is, by definition, someplace exotic, distant, and nearly inaccessible. California, for most of its history, was geographically inaccessible and thus exotic. California was so inaccessible that 227 years passed between the first European landing (1542) and the first permanent European settlement (1769). There is simply no parallel in the European settlement of the rest of North America. Advances in transportation made California accessible, but the finality of the Pacific coast keeps intact the notion of the state being the edge of geography. Lord Bryce (1897) wrote, "What America is to Europe, what western America is to eastern, California is to the west . . . California is the last place before you come to Japan" (p. 426). Others have written about the meaning of *El Norte* and the Golden Mountain, but whether seen as the farthest edge or the first gateway, California still connotes something unique and special.

The idea of the Promised Land was given reality by the Gold Rush, "the beginning of the nation's and the world's fascination with California and things Californian as the embodiment of the American Dream" (Rohrbough, 2002, p. 55). The Gold Rush created astonishing, unprecedented, and democratic wealth. Between 1848 and 1854, an estimated $345 million came out of the Sierras. Because gold was placer (i.e., found near the surface) and the land public, it could be mined easily with no need of royal decrees or corporate funding. It was the first time in history when technology, geology, and politics made it possible for ordinary people to become immensely wealthy by their own means.

The Gold Rush was followed by many other rushes and booms, from land to oil to silicon chips, all of which promised, and frequently created, the reality of fabulous wealth. The belief of California as a Promised Land continues today, as evidenced by Governor Arnold Schwarzenegger's description of California as an "empire of hope and aspirations" (Schwarzenegger 2004).

Promised lands, however, can prove ordinary. Dreams of wealth and happiness come true for some, but not all. Failed dreams can produce bitterness and failed booms, economic busts. Both can create political upheavals and scapegoating. The Chilean War of 1849 and the Foreign Miners Tax were motivated by resentment of non-Americans in the gold fields. The Workingman's Party was motivated by anti-Chinese feelings born, in part, by the economic collapse of the 1870s. The economic dislocations of the Great Depression triggered wholesale deportations of California-born Latinos, as well official and vigilante actions against Dust Bowl refugees from Okalahoma, Texas, and Arkansas. From the Gold Rush on, California has also been seen as a new land with a "society more mobile and unstable, less governed by fixed beliefs . . ."

than any other (Bryce, p. 428). Generations of new arrivals and natives have viewed California as unencumbered with conventional thinking and social expectations; the expectations of Des Moines, Guadalajara, or Taipei simply do not matter here. Moreover, regarding the state as a sociological and psychological blank slate allows Californians and California to reinvent and redefine as they chose. This helps explain why California boast more plastic surgeons per capita than other state as well as Californians' disinterest if not denial of their history. Visitor bureau websites for Savannah or Austin extol their cities' history; San Diego's barely mentions it is the oldest city in California, having been founded in 1769.

California as a new land stems from Spanish and American conquerors regarding all that came before them as unimportant. But population growth makes it persist. Between 1850 and 1860, the state grew by more than 300 percent and has essentially never stopped. Successive, massive influxes of people simply overwhelmed existing political and social establishments. Once newcomers established roots and the normal accruements of stable society, a new wave would arrive, submerging stability and reinventing society. This, in turn, reinforced political instability. A new land can be an essential precondition for innovation and growth, but it can also lead to knee-jerk rejections of the exactly the things that foster political stability.

California as the Land of Tomorrow flows from the mythology of the Promised Land and the New Land. If a promised land can be found today, by definition, it will be found where tomorrow has already arrived. Moreover, if California is a new land without the restrictive conventions of old lands, it is also a place where the norm is experimentation, innovation, and change.

In myriad ways, California has been the land where tomorrow came first. Innumerable technological, industrial, and societal developments either began in or took off in California, including freeways, computer technology, genetically engineered foods, aviation, massive water transfer systems, and the whole range of entertainment industries from talkies to Industrial Light and Magic. A state economic development brochure unconsciously reflected the mythology by boasting that, "The first fact about California is change. Swift, revolutionary, breath-stopping change," and proclaiming Californians as the "People From Somewhere Else" united in the "shared belief that tomorrow will be better than today and the absolute knowledge that tomorrow comes first" to California (*Welcome to the Californias*, 1989).

The Land of Tomorrow can also have a darker side. Societal change is always disruptive. When a people and a polity embrace change as a defining characteristic, political instability becomes the norm. Public policies can be discarded simply because they're old and not because they failed. Public servants can be forced from office by term limits, in part, because their experience was seen as worthless and more of the past than the future. It is not coincidental that California was the first state to adopt term limits and did so by an initiative the proponents of which invoked the higher law of the "people" and had an unmistakable political agenda (Schrag, 2004).

Support for a Davis recall was widespread but generally unexpected. Although conservative and Republican operatives began planning a recall within weeks of Davis' re-election, the result of these insider machinations was a genuine popular upheaval. The historic and mythic fluidity of California politics clearly enabled the recall and the rapid transformation of Arnold Schwarzenegger from celebrity to Governor echoed similar events in 1966, 1934, 1910, and 1879. The political upheaval of 2003 echoed the patterns set in the 1850s: intense, disruptive, but transient; motivated by a belief that the results of a legitimate election be ignored because the will of the "people" trumps democratic processes and structures.

California's political explosions, for example, have consistently regarded democratically established structures, procedures, and authority as disposable by any person or group proclaiming to be the "true" voice of the people. The recall is a legitimate constitutional process, but the Davis recall was driven by an eagerness to reject the normal processes of democratic elections. Californians reelected Gray Davis in November 2002. The honesty of that election has never been questioned. The arguments of recall proponents, including the extent of the budget deficit, merely echoed issues and criticisms raised in the 2002 campaign and rejected by the majority of voters. Fundamentally, recall proponents denied the legitimacy of the 2002 election, just as the Committees of Vigilance denied the legitimacy of elected officials they opposed. Recall leaders echoed the vigilante belief of moral superiority over existing democratic structures. Recall leader Howard Kaloogian (2003) denounced the decision of an appellate court to stay the election pending resolution of a voting machine dispute saying, "To deny the two million Californians who signed recall petitions a timely and fair election is irresponsible and unacceptable." Thus, Mr. Kaloogian criticized the court not on grounds of legal precedent or logic but rather by attacking the legitimacy of a court that failed to heed the "people."

Finally, California's political outbursts have often been fed by a sense of anger and impatience consonant with the myths of California. Certainly, recall supporters were impatient and demanded immediate change. Mr. Schwarzenegger echoed this sentiment with his pledges of action, action, action. The recall was an expression of anger by many Californians who felt frustrated with budget crises and what many perceived as a dysfunctional state government. But fundamentally, the anger was also generated by a fear that the promises of California's mythology were endangered.

In summary, the political disruptions of 2003 were neither unprecedented nor explainable by a collective obsession with celebrities. Instead, the Davis recall and Schwarzenegger election were consistent with more than 150 years of California politics and resonated with a longer tradition of California mythology. History and myth provide the context in which more immediate explanations and causes can be best understood. Whether the remedy will prove more or less perilous than having done nothing remains to be seen, but Lord Bryce's (1897) observation of the upheavals of his time seems particularly apt today: "The masses are impatient, accustomed to blame everything and everyone but themselves for the slow approach of the millennium, ready to try instant, even if perilous, remedies for a present evil" (p. 426).

## References

Arillagaap, P. (2003, August 27). California Inspires Pride and Puzzlement. Retrieved September 11, 2008, from http://www.kansascity.com

Bryce, J. (1897). *The American Commonwealth*. New York: Macmillian.

Burns, J. F. (2003). Taming the Elephant: An Introduction to California's Statehood and Constitutional Era. *California History, 8*, 1–26.

Hill, G. (1968). *Dancing Bear: An Inside Look at California Politics*. Cleveland, OH: World Books.

Kaloogian, H. (2003, September 17). Retrieved January 7, 2004, from http://www.recallgraydavis.com

McGrath, R. D. (2003). A Violent Birth: Disorder, Crime, and Law Enforcement, 1849–1890. *California History, 81*, 27–73.

McWilliams, C. (1976). *California: The Great Exception*. Santa Barbara, CA: Peregrine Smith.

Rawls, J. J., & Bean, W. (1998). *California: An Interpretative History* (7th ed.). New York: McGraw-Hill.

Rohrbough, M. J. (2002). We Will Make Our Fortunes—No Doubt of It: The Worldwide Rush to California. In K. N. Owens (ed.), *Riches for All: The California Gold Rush and the World* (pp. 50–70). Lincoln: University of Nebraska Press.

Royce, J. (2002). *California: A Study of American Character*. Berkeley, CA: Heyday Books.

Schrag, Peter (2004). *Paradise Lost: California's Experience, America's Future*. Berkeley, CA: University of California Press.

Schwarzenegger, A. (2004, January 6). State of the State Address. Retrieved January 26, 2005, from http://www.governor.ca.gov/state/govsite/gov_speeches

Taylor, B. (2000). *Eldorado: Adventures in the Path of Empire*. Berkeley, CA: Heyday Press.

Walker, D. L. (1999). *Bear Flag Rising: The Conquest of California, 1846*. New York: Forge Books.

*Welcome to the Californias*. (1989). Sacramento: California State Department of Trade and Commerce.

## Questions for Discussion

1. Hodson makes the argument that instability is an ongoing part of California's history. What examples bolster his argument? Are there particular periods of California history that especially demonstrate instability? Does he imply several kinds of instability or use any words with similar meanings to convey his point?

2. What role does Hodson give to human innovation in creating California? What historic moments and examples does he use to convey the importance of technology in the state's development? How does he refer to innovation and creativity as having both positive and negative potential?

3. What is the role of human emotion in California's political system? How does public outrage translate into political action or policy changes? What examples of current emotional/political events can you find to explain Hodson's views of such "political explosions"?

## Ideas for Writing

1. Hodson uses phrases such as "Land of Tomorrow" and "promised lands." Create your own brief phrase, such as "hometown life" or "a better way," to write about places, either real or imagined, that illuminate your concept of California. Be creative in developing a phrase on which to build your essay.

2. Hodson talks about "rushes and booms" in California's economy. Research some of the current economic trends in California and describe where the "booms" of today might exist. (Hint: check current employment data for California to find where the jobs are.)

# California, Here We Come

## PETER SCHRAG

*Peter Schrag writes regular columns for the* Sacramento Bee *as well as many other publications.* He is the author of numerous books, including Final Test: The Battle for Adequacy in America's Schools *and* Paradise Lost: California's Experience, America's Future *and is currently a visiting scholar at the Institute for Governmental Studies at UC Berkeley.*

———————— ✦ ————————

This June [1998] marks the twentieth anniversary of the passage of Proposition 13, the California voter initiative that has in many respects had a political and social impact on this era—not just in California but across much of the nation—almost as profound and lasting as that of the New Deal on the 1930s, 1940s, and 1950s.

The effect on California—which had been well above the national average in what it spent to educate its children, to provide free or nearly free higher education to every person who wanted it, for highway construction, and for a range of social services for children and the needy—was traumatic. Cutting local property taxes by more than 50 percent and capping the tax rate at one percent, Proposition 13 and the various initiatives that followed in its wake forced California to a level of spending far below the national average for such things as K-12 schooling, public library services, the arts, and transportation. The respected journal *Education Week* said last year of California schools, "a once world-class system is now third-rate." Even with a booming economy, California remains in the bottom third among the states, and far below the other major industrial states, in what it budgets per pupil.

Just as important, the march of ballot initiatives, the attack on legislative discretion, and the related acts of "direct democracy" that Proposition 13 helped to set in motion—involving taxes and spending, affirmative action, immigration, school policy, environmental protection, three-strikes criminal sentences, term limits, campaign reform, insurance rates, and virtually every other public issue—continue with unabated force, in California and beyond. In November of 1996 voters in twenty-three states were polled on a total of ninety initiatives, the most in more than eighty years (a decade ago there were forty-one), on everything from hunting rights to gambling to logging regulations to sugar production to the legalization of medical marijuana use (which was approved in Arizona and California).

This June, as if to honor the anniversary of Proposition 13, Californians will again confront a large array of sometimes nearly incomprehensible ballot measures, among them yet another one on term limits and one that would all but end bilingual education. Each proposed reform further restricts the power of the legislature and local elected officials to set priorities, respond to new situations, and write budgets accordingly. When half of the state's tax-limited general fund must, under the terms of one initiative, be spent on the schools; when a sizable chunk must, under the mandate of the state's three strikes measure, be spent on prisons; and when lesser amounts must, under the terms of still other initiatives that have been approved in the past decade, be spent on the repayment of bonds for parkland and transportation projects, the amount left over for everything else shrinks with Malthusian inevitability—as does the state government's capacity to cope with changed circumstances. When cities and counties are prohibited from raising property-tax rates beyond Proposition 13's one percent, and when it is difficult to raise other revenues without a vote of the electorate (in many instances a two-thirds vote) or of the affected property owners, local control is drastically reduced.

Just as inevitably, public policy is increasingly distorted by the shifting of costs from the general fund to the Byzantine system of fees, assessments, and exactions that local governments have devised in their attempts to get around tax limits and other restrictions. This reinforces the larger shift from a communitarian to a fee ethic—in the support of parks and playgrounds, in the construction of new schools, and in financing a range of other services that used to be funded entirely from general taxes. As one California letter writer complained to a newspaper, why should citizens contribute to "the methodical pillaging and plundering of the taxpayer, forcing those who have no kids to pay through the nose for someone else's"?

Direct democracy is an attractive political ideal, as close to our own experience as the New England town meeting. It has never worked, however, in large, diverse political communities, and the belief that electronics, direct mail, and televised slogans can replace personal engagement has so far looked far more like fantasy than like anything derived from hard political experience.

In the case of the initiative, the new populism—unlike the reform movement that wrote the initiative into the constitutions of nineteen states around the turn of the century—seems to want greater engagement in government less than it wants an autopilot system to check government institutions with little active involvement by the citizenry beyond occasional trips to the polls to vote on yet more initiatives.

California sparked the anti-government, anti-tax mood that has gripped the nation for most of the past two decades, and it remains the most extreme illustration of that mood, a cautionary tale for those enamored of plebiscitary democracy. But it is now hardly unique. Virulent anti-institutionalism, particularly with respect to government, has become a prevailing theme in our national political discourse. A decade after Ronald Reagan left office, his facile dismissal of government as "the problem," not the solution, remains a talk-show staple, a posture that serves to exonerate both civic laziness and political ignorance. And this attitude, which has become banal toward representative government, now also encompasses the related institutions of constitutional democracy: the courts, the schools, the press. Voting and serious newspaper readership are declining together. The communitarian civic ideal that they represent is giving way to "markets," a fee-for-service ethic, and the fragmented, unmediated, unedited exchange of information, gossip, and personal invective.

The media—new and old alike—may ensure against the power of Big Brother to dominate communications, but they also proliferate shared ignorance at an unprecedented rate: what used to be limited to gossip over the back fence is now spread in milliseconds to a million listeners during the evening commute, and to thousands over the Internet. And at the fringes are the militias and the "patriots," collecting weapons and supplies, training in the hills, and hunkering down against the black helicopters and the coming invasion of United Nations troops. That kind of ignorance and extremism, the new media, and the surrounding paranoia about government have all become commonplace in the past decade. Oliver Stone's *JFK* and the videos promoted by Jerry Falwell about the alleged murder of Vincent Foster work the same territory.

Tracy Westen, the president of the foundation-funded Center for Governmental Studies, in Los Angeles, has constructed a "digital scenario" for the election of 2004—a not altogether wild fantasy about thirty-five California voter initiatives on various subjects, all of which have been circulated for "signatures" online, along with a spectrum of arguments pro and con, available at the click of a voice-activated mouse, from every conceivable source. In combination with a number of new elective offices, including drug commissioner and gay-rights commissioner, those measures contribute to a total of 200 ballot decisions for each voter to make.

Among Westen's futuristic initiatives is one urging Congress to approve an amendment to Article V of the U.S. Constitution such that the language guaranteeing every state a "Republican form of government" is modified to permit the states to replace representative democracy with direct democracy. Westen points out that most of the technology for this politopia—individually targeted campaign ads, interactive "discussions" with candidates, electronic voting—already exists. Since "state legislatures seem to be fighting more and doing less . . . and leaving the real legislation to the people," the scenario continues, "it seems the trend toward 'democracy by initiative' is inevitable." A few years ago the Canadian fringe Democratech Party wanted to submit all government decisions to the public through electronic referenda. An official Democratech statement said, Representative government assumes that the people need to elect someone to represent them in a faraway legislative assembly. But with modern, instantaneous communications, the people can directly make their own decisions, relegating politicians to the scrap heap of history.

Three years ago *The Economist* mused about the possible benefits of replacing representative democracy with Swiss-style direct democracy, in which the voters "trudge to the polls four times a year" to decide all manner of plebiscitary questions. This process would prevent lobbyists and other special interests from buying the outcome, because "when the lobbyist faces an entire electorate . . . bribery and vote-buying are virtually impossible. Nobody has enough money to bribe everybody."

California shows that the process of bedazzling voters with sound bites, slogans, and nuanced bias works as effectively in the initiative process as it does in electoral politics. Offers that sound like something for nothing (a 50 percent property-tax cut, or a guaranteed level of education funding, or a state lottery offering a payoff for schools as well as for the lucky winners) may not be bribes, but they are the nearest thing to them. And when they work at the ballot box, their effects may last far longer than those of conventional legislation.

The larger danger, of course, is precisely the nondeliberative quality of the California-style initiative, particularly in a society that doesn't have the luxury of slow alpine trudges during which to reflect on what it's about to do. Nothing is built into the process—no meaningful hearings, no formal debates, no need for bicameral concurrence, no conference committees, no professional staff, no informed voice, no executive veto—to present the downside, to outline the broader implications, to ask the cost, to speak for minorities, to engineer compromises, to urge caution, to invoke the lessons of the past, or, once an initiative is approved by the voters, to repair its flaws except by yet another ballot measure (unless the text of the initiative itself provides for legislative amendment). Indeed, if the past decade of initiatives in California demonstrates anything, it is that the majoritarianism essential to the ethos of direct democracy almost inevitably reinforces an attitude of indifference if not hostility toward minority rights. All these dangers would be exacerbated, of course, by electronic or other forms of absentee balloting, whereby voters would no longer be required to go to the local school or church or social hall and encounter their fellow citizens participating in the same civic ritual—and thus be reminded that they are, after all, part of a larger community.

To say all that, probably, is merely to say awkwardly what the Framers of the Constitution said better in Philadelphia, what Hamilton, Madison, and Jay said in *The Federalist*, and what scores of delegates said in 1787–1788 at the various state conventions leading up to ratification, even before the terror of the French Revolution: unchecked majorities are a danger to liberty almost as great as oligarchs and absolute monarchs.

Among the most common measures, put on the ballot by the organization U.S. Term Limits in fourteen states and passed in 1996 by voters in nine, is the "Scarlet Letter" initiative, also known as the "informed voter" initiative, which instructs a state's elected officials to support a constitutional amendment limiting members of the House of Representatives to three two-year terms and members of the Senate to two six-year terms, and which requires state election officials to indicate on the ballot next to the name of each congressional incumbent and each member of the legislature whether he or she "disregarded voters' instruction on term limits." It also requires nonincumbents to indicate whether they have signed a pledge supporting the amendment; those who have not will be similarly identified on the ballot. For Paul Jacob, who heads U.S. Term Limits, no compromise is acceptable.

The watchword is "No Uncertain Terms" (which also happens to be the name of the organization's newsletter).

Jacob's very inflexibility helped to derail a more moderate term-limits amendment when it came up in the House (for the second time) early last year. It would have allowed six two-year terms in the House and two six-year terms in the Senate. By denouncing it as a sellout, U.S. Term Limits helped to ensure that no term-limits amendment was approved, and thus that the organization would enjoy a long, healthy life. The large turnover in Congress in 1994 probably took enough steam out of the movement to reduce its chances of success, but not enough to end it.

The Scarlet Letter initiative is probably unconstitutional. (U.S. Term Limits is now asking individual candidates to pledge to serve no more than three terms in the House or two in the Senate.) In Arkansas, one of the nine states that passed it in 1996, the state supreme court struck it down, as a violation of the procedures set forth in the U.S. Constitution for amendment. Because the drafters of the Constitution, in the words of the Arkansas court, "wanted the amending process in the hands of a body with the power to deliberate upon a proposed amendment . . . all proposals of amendments . . . must come either from Congress or state legislatures—not from the people." The U.S. Term Limits measure was "an indirect attempt to propose an amendment . . . [that would] virtually tie the hands of the individual members of the legislature such that they would no longer be a deliberative body acting independently in exercising their individual best judgements on the issue."

There are scattered indications that the rabid anti-government fervor of the early nineties may have peaked. (One of those indications, in the view of Nancy Rhyme, who tracks the issue for the National Conference of State Legislatures, is that only nine states passed the Scarlet Letter initiative.) Certainly, term limits are not likely to be written into the Constitution any time soon.

But the issue will not go away, either in national politics or in the eighteen states that now have term limits for their legislatures written into their constitutions or otherwise written into law. On almost the same day that term limits failed (again) in the House early last year, the Scarlet Letter, funded largely by U.S. Term Limits and a handful of out-of-state term-limits organizations, qualified for the next California ballot. (U.S. Term Limits kicked in about $300,000 to the campaign to qualify the California "informed voter" measure but won't, of course, disclose where its money comes from. The organization is willing to provide a list of its National Finance Committee members, all of whom are said to have contributed more than $1,000, but will not specify which among them are its largest contributors.) A few months later the long-established California organization Field Poll reported that voter support of term limits, which stood at roughly two thirds, remained just as strong as it had been in 1990, in the months before California approved term limits for legislators and other state officials.

Nor has the initiative process lost its allure. Twenty-four states have some form of initiative in their constitutions, most of them dating from the Progressive Era. Recently there have been moves in a number of other states—including Rhode Island and Texas—to write the initiative process into their constitutions.

The pressure does not come from Hispanics or other newly active political groups, who tend to vigorously oppose these constitutional changes as openings to yet more measures like California's Proposition 187—which, until it was blocked by a federal court, sought to deny schooling and other public services to illegal immigrants. Rather, the impetus is from Ross Perot's United We Stand America and other organizations that are overwhelmingly white and middle-class. And in the states that already have the ballot initiative, there is increasing pressure to use it, sometimes generated by the dynamics of political reform itself. In California, political officeholders, from the governor down, have become initiative sponsors as a means of increasing name recognition and raising or stretching political campaign funds. And as initiatives circumscribe the power and discretion of legislatures, often the best way of responding to new circumstances—and sometimes the only way—is through yet another initiative. The result, for better or worse, is an ongoing cycle of initiative reform, frustration, and further reform.

Yet despite all the unintended consequences and the inflexibility of the initiative and other devices of direct democracy, they seem to have one thing in common, whether they are used by liberal environmentalists or by tax-cutting conservatives: they are the instruments of established voter-taxpayer groups, particularly the white middle class, against urban politicians and political organizations that represent the interests and demands of minorities, immigrants, and other marginal groups. At the turn of the century the Yankee establishment in Boston and other cities sought to create political institutions and devices to dilute the power of the upstart Irish. In its impulse and spirit the current pressure for plebiscitary solutions driven by the general electorate, in which the white middle class can still dominate, is not all that different.

The celebratory history of direct democracy centers on its inclusiveness, but in our politically more sophisticated (and no doubt more cynical) age there is a need to understand that defense of the initiative may be less disinterested than it seems. The groups that embrace and cheer it are not just "the people" fighting "the interests" or "the politicians," much less battling "Satan" and "Mammon," as the editor of the *Sacramento Bee* put it in the heyday of the Progressives. They are often established political interest groups trying by extraordinary means to further a cause or repulse the advances of other groups. More important, each initiative reduces the power and accountability of legislatures—and thus the general ability to govern, meaning the ability to shape predictable outcomes. And whereas the initiative may well further the Jeffersonian objective of tying government down, and thus preventing mischief, it also vastly reduces the chances that great leaders, and the visionary statecraft with which they are sometimes associated, will arise. In the battle over the initiative the Framers would be the first to recognize that our politics, rather than being too conservative, are in the Burkean sense not nearly conservative enough.

## Questions for Discussion

1. Define and give examples of direct democracy as mentioned by Schrag. What issues have been presented to voters through the ballot? What tone does Schrag take as he describes this process in California?
2. Schrag contrasts a market approach with a communitarian civic ideal. What does he mean by these terms? What examples of this dichotomy can you describe from the reading or other sources?
3. How does Schrag convey his personal views in his essay? What words and themes let the reader know his position on the issues he describes?

## Ideas for Writing

1. Think of an issue you want changed. Write an essay describing the problem and proposing solutions. Develop your theme as if you were going to put your idea on the ballot for voters.
2. Do some research about term limits. What is the apparent intention of term limits? What are some unintended consequences? Does your city or other local government have term limits for elected officials?

# Battles for Fairness: California's Unions Fight Discrimination

## KENNETH C. BURT

*Kenneth C. Burt is political director of the California Federation of Teachers and author of* The Search for a Civic Voice: California Latino Politics. *He has worked for a number of elected officials, including former California Assembly Speaker Willie Brown. Burt is a product of Harvard University's John F. Kennedy School of Government and the University of California, Berkeley, where he returned as a Carey McWilliams Fellow. Burt has published articles in many anthologies and academic journals, winning the Historical Society of Southern California's Doyce B. Nunis award.*

———————— ✦ ————————

Work is arguably the single most important part of people's lives. It consumes more than a third of the average day, plays a major role in defining who we are and how we relate to the larger society and, most importantly, provides the means to support both life and leisure for our families and ourselves. It is therefore not surprising that in a world filled with inequality, fair employment—the ability to get a job without facing discrimination—became the great mid-century domestic cause.

## EXECUTIVE ORDER 8802

Anti-Semitism, anti-Catholicism and racism were once pervasive in California in the first half of the twentieth century. Employers freely discriminated. Sometimes this pattern penetrated whole industries. Want ads and employment agencies sought "white" workers—or "Protestants."

All of this became less tenable on the eve of the United States' entry into World War II. Victory in the epic struggle against Adolf Hitler and his theories of racial purity required homefront unity. The U.S. also needed to avoid handing Hitler a propaganda victory.

So, in 1941, when A. Philip Randolph and C.L. Dellums of the Brotherhood of Sleeping Car Porters threatened to organize a

"Negro March on Washington," President Franklin D. Roosevelt signed Executive Order 8802, prohibiting discrimination in the defense industry and establishing the federal Fair Employment Practices Commission (FEPC). The FEPC included prominent labor and religious leaders, and the board established a presence in California; the small staff included a Latino, Ignacio Lopez.

Randolph was closely allied to the Jewish Labor Committee (JLC), and to David Dubinsky, president of the JLC's largest constituency group, the International Ladies Garment Workers Union (ILGWU), through their civil rights advocacy within the American Federation of Labor (AFL) and political ties dating back to the old Socialist Party.

The FEPC had an uneven but marked effect in California. In Northern California, a large number of African Americans faced challenges finding work in the shipyards of Richmond, across the bay from San Francisco. In San Diego, Latinos fought to gain jobs in the shipyards and airplane factories. The war created the greatest number of opportunities in Los Angeles. The city's auto, rubber, and steel factories retooled, and the nascent airplane industry expanded rapidly, as did shipbuilding.

Minority workers got some of these new jobs. Garment worker Hope Mendoza, for example, became a "Rosie the Riveter" in an airplane factory. Assemblyman Augustus Hawkins, the lone African American state legislator, obtained a job building ships. Others obtained positions in light industry, such as furniture, which opened up when other workers took defense jobs or went into the armed service.

## AUGUSTUS HAWKINS

In 1943, Assemblyman Augustus Hawkins sought to extend the protections of fair employment to all sectors of the economy by introducing the first state Fair Employment Practices (FEP) legislation. In the part-time legislature, Hawkins represented an increasingly African American section of South-Central Los Angeles; the city's black population swelled during the war as families left their homes in the southern states in search of employment and freedom from Jim Crow segregation.

Hawkins personified the confluence of minority voters and organized labor. He won his seat with labor's help. He left the shipyard to accept a position with the Congress of Industrial Organization's Political Action Committee (CIO-PAC). In California, the CIO was smaller but more militant than the more established AFL.

Hawkins reported to Sidney Hillman, president of the Amalgamated Clothing Workers, the second largest predominately Jewish union, and a Roosevelt confidant. He worked with Harry Bridges, CIO Western Director, and the head of the International Longshoremen's and Warehousemen's Union (ILWU), which led the 1934 San Francisco General Strike that led to the rebirth of organized labor on the west coast.

As World War II wound down, a coalition of national labor, minority, and religious organizations pushed Congress to enact a permanent FEPC. The coalition and its local affiliates also pushed to enact FEP laws in five states, including California, where Hawkins reintroduced his measure during the 1945 legislative session.

Judge Isaac Pacht, long-time head of the Jewish Federation of Los Angeles, chaired the Southern California Committee for a State FEPC. Daniel Marshall from the Catholic Interracial Council served as vice chair. A number of prominent African Americans and Latinos also participated.

The FEP drive succeeded in four states, including New York, but failed in Congress (where U.S. Senator Dennis Chavez, of New Mexico, authored the bill) and in the Republican-controlled State Capitol in California. The 1945 campaign in California, however, served an important function because, according to Assemblyman Hawkins, "That is when we began to form these coalitions."

## PROPOSITION 11

Frustrated by legislative inaction, Hawkins partnered with the CIO and the National Association for the Advancement of Colored People (NAACP) to place Proposition 11 on the ballot in 1946. The voter initiative was modeled after FEP measures in other states. To pass the voter initiative Hawkins worked with both the CIO, which had long championed civil rights as central to organizing minority workers, and the larger AFL, which (with the exception of groups like the Garment Workers and Sleeping Car Porters) traditionally focused more on wages and benefits.

In 1946, the AFL California Federation of Labor endorsed Proposition 11, and the Los Angeles Central Labor Council established a Labor Committee to Combat Intolerance at the request of the ILGWU Pacific Coast Manager Louis Levy. To ensure the committee's vitality he arranged for the Jewish Labor Committee, which he also headed in the state, to hire a full-staff person dedicated to civil rights. Zane Meckler, a labor journalist and member of the American Federation of Teachers, staffed the committee and helped coordinate AFL participation in the Proposition 11 campaign.

"All Americans are from minority groups and each one of these groups is vulnerable to attack from a combination of other groups," Meckler told a labor audience. "The ranks of labor comprise members of all these minorities. Therefore bigotry and bias is a gun held at the head of labor."

The measure failed two-to-one in a year that saw Republicans retain control of the governor's office and huge majorities in the state legislature. It became clear that a great deal of public education was needed on the issue and that the campaign would take several years. A consensus also emerged that advocates should refocus their attention on city councils and the state legislature.

To advance this goal in California and other states, the national AFL and CIO bodies decided to organize civil rights committees in every municipal council and designated the Jewish Labor Committee as the group responsible for providing staff, as was the case in Los Angeles, starting in 1946. Over the next couple of years the JLC, operating in its own name and as the voice of organized labor, helped keep the idea of fair employment alive by providing speakers for union meetings and community groups. The JLC also organized special visits to California for A. Philip Randolph.

## LOS ANGELES 1949

While Hawkins reintroduced the FEP bill in the state legislature, the forces for fair employment focused their attention on local government, particularly in Los Angeles and San Francisco.

The 1949 election of Los Angeles City Councilman Edward Roybal provided a boost for the FEP. The first Latino on the council in modern history, he joined a body where thirteen of his colleagues were Protestant men and one was Irish Catholic. Roybal immediately assumed the role as civil rights advocate and spokesman for working families and for Latino, African American, Asian, and Jewish voters.

Roybal introduced an FEP ordinance and the liberal civil rights coalition went to work lobbying the fifteen-member council.

Religious and labor leaders joined leaders from a number of Jewish groups (American Jewish Committee, Anti-Defamation League, Jewish Labor Committee) and the Mexican American-oriented Community Service Organization, the Japanese American Citizens League, and the NAACP.

Despite the all-out push, the proposed ordinance lost 7 to 8. Subsequent efforts to pass a comprehensive ordinance likewise failed, but the council did vote to prohibit discrimination by companies doing business with the city. Meanwhile in Northern California, the San Francisco Board of Supervisors enacted a comprehensive fair employment ordinance in 1957.

## CAL COMMITTEE

In the early 1950s the statewide civil rights organization came together under the banner of the California Committee for Fair Employment. C.L. Dellums from the Oakland-based Sleeping Car Porters chaired the group and worked closely with the NAACP, where he held a leadership post. Co-chairs included Rt. Rev. Msgr. O'Dywer, Judge Isaac Pacht, and Los Angeles Councilman Edward Roybal. Steelworker John Despol represented the California CIO Council, and construction worker Neil Haggerty represented the AFL California Federation of Labor. The Cal Committee worked closely with Assemblymen Augustus Hawkins and Byron Rumford (D-Oakland), who alternated sponsoring the measure in the legislature.

The Cal Committee was organized out of the California Federation of Labor headquarters in San Francisco and the Jewish Labor Committee office in Los Angeles. The JLC's Bill Becker, who had organized farmworkers with Ernesto Galarza, served as the bill's principal lobbyist because of his proximity to the State Capitol in Sacramento. The JLC's Max Mont organized for the Cal Committee in Southern California while also staffing the Los Angeles Central Labor Council's anti-discrimination committee. Much of the committee's resources came from the labor movement. "It wasn't just the ILGWU and the United Auto Workers, the liberal unions, but also the Carpenters, and others in the Building Trades," recalled Becker.

The Cal Committee galvanized support throughout the state. Labor conducted petition drives and encouraged members to write their legislators. Protestant, Catholic, and Jewish religious leaders preached from the pulpit and participated in community coalitions. Minority groups likewise mobilized their members, working through entities such as the Community Service Organization and the Japanese American Citizens League, and, most notably, the NAACP.

"They'd come up and lobby in Sacramento. They'd send people into the offices to talk to legislators, and there was gradually a general change in sentiment. You could see less opposition coming," Rumford recalled. Each legislative session the measure would get further through the process.

## 1958 ELECTIONS

In 1957, conservative U.S. Senator William Knowland threatened the Republican dominance of state government when he announced plans to run for governor despite the desire of the popular and moderate Republican Governor, Goodwin Knight, to run for reelection. Then, in an effort to mobilize conservative voters, Knowland and his anti-union allies placed Proposition 18, a so-called Right-to-Work Initiative, on the ballot. It would make union membership voluntary.

After months of vacillating, Governor Knight decided to run for the U.S. Senate to avoid a bitter primary battle. However, the public conflict soured swing voters to both men in a state where Democrats held a three-to-two registration advantage. At the same time moderate blue-collar Republican union members abandoned the GOP, and the California Democratic Council, comprised largely of college educated suburbanites, aggressively pushed to elect Democrats statewide.

To rally the civil rights community, the labor movement brought in A. Philip Randolph, the "father of the FEPC" during World War II. Randolph keynoted a two-day Labor Conference on Human Rights at the Statler Hotel in downtown Los Angeles in early October 1958. The CSO, NAACP, and the JLC co-sponsored the conference with the Central Labor Council. JLC Executive Director, Max Mont, coordinated the event. Speakers included Jewish garment union officials, Assemblyman Hawkins, Councilman Roybal, and many others, including representatives of the co-sponsoring organizations. The labor-minority coalition reaffirmed their commitment to defeating the anti-labor initiative and to enacting fair employment legislation after the election.

The campaign also organized rabbis, priests, and ministers to oppose Proposition 18, making it a moral imperative. The JLC's partner in the Catholic community, the Catholic Labor Institute, played a key role. Gubernatorial candidate Pat Brown joined Bishop Alden Bell and hundreds of Catholic trade unionists at the annual Labor Day Mass and Breakfast, where the church's pro-labor social gospel was reiterated. The group's patron within the hierarchy was Monsignor Thomas O'Dwyer, a California Commit-tee for Fair Employment co-chair, who collaborated with the Jewish and Latino garment workers to elect Roybal to the Los Angeles City Council.

Such relationships paid multiple dividends. Organized labor formed the Eastside Committee to Save Our State to fight Propo-sition 18. Latino labor leader James Cruz, from the AFL Brick and Clay Workers, headed the committee; Dave Fishman, from the Jewish Painters in Boyle Heights, served as the coordinator. The No on 18 group kicked off its election outreach with a Saturday afternoon caravan that snaked through the working class neigh-borhoods of Boyle Heights and Lincoln Heights to raise aware-ness of the election. They stopped at major shopping centers to distribute information to voters. Three days later, the group sponsored a rally at the Carpenters Hall at Brooklyn (now Cesar Chavez) and Soto Streets.

The JLC also reached out to the Jewish business community, which still suffered the sting of discrimination. Some law firms in Los Angeles, for example, still recruited young associates solely from the ranks of Protestant graduates. And, outside of their sig-nificant presence in Hollywood, Jews remained a rarity in the pri-vate sector unless self-employed. Jewish entrepreneur Benjamin Swig, proprietor of San Francisco's Fairmont Hotel, signed the statement against the Right-to-Work Initiative in the ballot pam-phlet along with the AFL and CIO leaders. Swig's prominence in the fight underscored the linkages between labor and civil rights in California in the 1950s.

## LABOR AND CIVIL RIGHTS

On Election Day in 1958 the voters trounced Proposition 18, the Right-to-Work Initiative. Strongest opposition came from unionists, African Americans, Latinos, and Jews. The massive turnout by labor and minority voters contributed to Pat Brown's million-vote margin and swept Democrats to power in the state legislature.

Assemblyman Byron Rumford reintroduced fair employment legislation. The civil rights coalition pressed for rapid passage and continued to underscore its broad support. Hawkins recalled a key meeting with Brown. "We had labor people, Catholics and Jews; we had them all, to show that it was not just a Black issue," stated Assemblyman Hawkins.

Governor Brown and organized labor kept their commitment to make fair employment a top priority. The Governor stated in his inaugural address that "Discrimination in employment is a stain upon California" and urged the legislature to act.

External pressure for the long-sought measure came from the California Committee for Fair Employment and its constituent groups, particularly the AFL and CIO unions that enjoyed enormous influence given the lopsided defeat of Proposition 18 and their support for the new Democratic legislative majority.

According to William Becker, the bill's chief lobbyist, a number of legislators, particularly rural Democrats, remained nervous about supporting the bill. (This is significant because the agriculturally oriented rural areas dominated the State Senate due to apportionment of the upper house by county and not by population.)

Becker emphasized the importance of the liberal-labor-religious coalition in passing the landmark civil rights bill in what was then an overwhelmingly white, Protestant legislature in an overwhelmingly white state. The legislature contained only two African Americans, and not a single Asian or Latino member.

The legislators ultimately voted for it, according to Rumford, "because it was part of the platform" on which they had run—and it was the governor's top priority.

Governor Brown appointed former Los Angeles Supervisor John Anson Ford, an elder statesman and respected liberal, to chair the commission responsible for overseeing the implementation of the controversial new law. Brown then named C.L. Dellums, chair of the California Committee for Fair Employment, to the commission along with Carmen Warshaw, a Los Angeles-based Jewish businesswoman and civil rights supporter. He used the other two seats to reward friends of the legislative leaders who helped pass the measure through their respective bodies.

The commission soon hired Spanish-speaking staffers to facilitate enforcement of the fair employment law among the Latino community. Later in his administration, Brown followed this up with the appointment of the first Latino Commissioner.

## A CHANGED SOCIETY

The FEPC so fundamentally altered employment patterns in the state that few remember the era when whole industries openly discriminated and newspaper want ads and employment agencies recruited people by race, ethnicity, and religion.

"There was a time a black person couldn't get a job in a service station. You never saw a black face work for, say, Shell Oil or any of those stations. I mean an ordinary manual job, no particular skill, no particular profession," stated Rumford, looking back to the pre-FEPC period. "When we got the Fair Employment Practices Act the whole thing changes completely! You see [black] clerks in stores; you see them filling prescriptions. Nobody thinks anything about their color."

As the new law reduced racial and religious barriers to employment, other barriers became more obvious, and movements developed to pressure the legislature to expand the scope of the law. Today, the California Department of Fair Employment and Housing (DFEH) recognizes fourteen categories of discrimination: Age (40 and over), Ancestry, Color, Creed, Denial of Family and Medical Care Leave, Denial of Pregnancy Disability Leave, Disability (mental and physical) including HIV and AIDS, Martial Status, Medical Condition (cancer and genetic characteristics), National Origin, Race, Religion, Sex, and Sexual Orientation. Originally part of the Department of Industrial Relations, the DFEH is now its own department, with fifteen offices around the state. It reports to the state's Consumer Services Agency.

Despite the dramatic expansion in worker protections, more subtle forms of discrimination continue to exist, and California is not yet fully integrated culturally or economically. The income gap is growing based on immigrant status, level of education, and role in the economy. Still, it is important to recognize these civil rights pioneers and the pivotal role of the liberal-labor-minority-religious coalition and the women and men who labored for sixteen years, from 1943 to 1959, to outlaw racial discrimination on the job in California. Together, they overcame significant obstacles in the challenge to create a more just society.

### Questions for Discussion

1. What examples does Burt give of racism and other forms of bigotry in California? When did public attitudes begin to change and why?

2. What was the role of ethnic organizations, labor unions, and elected officials in creating the Fair Employment Practices Commission in California? Does Burt convey any value judgment of the process he describes? Explain how you know his viewpoint about fair employment.

3. Describe some of the ethnic organizations Burt mentions. How did Jewish, Latino, and African-American people work within their own communities? How did they unite to develop the policies that improved equal opportunity in California?

### Ideas for Writing

1. Research the history of California's laws that pertain to race or ethnicity. What historic examples explain past forms of discrimination? How do fairness and anti-discrimination laws motivate changes in human behavior? Write an essay about the evolution of fairness and equality in California.

2. Burt writes about individual leaders who made a difference. Find out who is making a difference today in your community. Who are they? What issues are they tackling? What motivates them? If you can, interview some community leaders and tell their story.

---

# Super-Sized Legislators: Should California Downsize its Districts?

## HEATHER BARBOUR

*Heather Barbour served in state government as Assistant Secretary at the California Technology, Trade, and Commerce Agency and principal consultant to the Legislature's Joint Committee on Preparing California for the 21st Century. She graduated Phi Beta Kappa from U.C. Santa Cruz with a B.A. in anthropology. She also earned her MA in Public Policy from Pepperdine University. More than anything, she enjoys teaching community college students.*

———————— ✦ ————————

In November 2004, many California voters went to the polls and chose a state senator for themselves and nearly 900,000 of their closest neighbors. In practical terms, this meant working-class Californians living in small, rural, mountainous towns near the Oregon border are represented by the same person advocating on behalf of voters living in wealthy Sacramento suburbs. Can this one legislator truly be accountable to the needs and interests of hundreds of thousands of people living in such disparate circumstances?

Of course not. California's legislative districts are too big and their unwieldy proportions seriously obscure the real diversity in California's lifestyles and politics.

When America's founders devised our republic, they envisioned districts that each contained around 30,000 people. There was no magic to this number. Even the architect of the U.S. Constitution, James Madison, recognized the hopelessness of imposing science on such schemes. He recommended only that legislative districts should be neither too big nor too small. He also assumed they would be augmented from time to time.

California, however, has not augmented the number of representatives in its Legislature since 1879, when its total population was about 1 million. Now, a single state Senate district contains nearly this number.

California has the largest legislative districts in America. The state's 80 Assembly districts each average a whopping 423,000 people. And there are twice as many constituents in each of the state's 40 Senate districts. By comparison, lower house districts in other states range from 3,000 people in New Hampshire to 139,012 people in Texas.

California's upper house districts, by population size, are nearly seven times the national average. If California's Senate districts matched just the large-state average, its Senate would have 94 members instead of 40.

Further, while no state compares to California in population size, the populations of Texas and Florida combined are a rough equivalent. The Legislatures in those states contain 341 members; nearly triple the 120 serving in California. Citizens in Illinois, Pennsylvania and Ohio—again, a combined population approximately equal to California—are represented by 562 state legislators. In fact, if you tally up the 21 smallest states, the number of residents is roughly equal to California's population. Residents of those states, however, are represented by a combined total of more than 3,000 state legislators.

California's super-sized districts are not just harmless mathematical curiosities; they contribute to political alienation, a fatal condition for representative government. Voter turnout has been on the decline for the past 40 years, and polls show three-quarters of Californians think the state Legislature is doing a fair or poor job when it comes to working for the "best interests of people like you." The gap between representative and represented is dangerously wide in California, which limits the authority and vision of officeholders and causes voters to turn to ballot box policymaking or disengage altogether.

The idea of curing California's political ills by decreasing the size of legislative districts inevitably elicits howls from political insiders. They know smaller districts mean more legislators in Sacramento. The objection is obvious: How will more politicians solve our problems?

But Madison anticipated the need for such adjustments more than 200 years ago. The performance of the California Legislature today affirms his predictions. "Too big," legislatures, he noted, will succumb to confusion and the "intemperance of a multitude." With a "too small" legislature, Madison warned of a lack of diversity in policy discussions and the ease of "combination for improper purposes."

California's Legislature clearly exhibits the symptoms of a governing body that is too small, both in its lack of diversity in policy discussions and the so-called ease of combination for improper purposes. In other words, purposes that put special interests over the public's interest.

Only two voices count in the California Legislature: Republican and Democrat. This is outrageously narrow representation in a state where nearly 21 percent of the population declines party affiliation. Further, there's little diversity of opinion even within party ranks. In 2003, 21 of 25 Senate Democrats voted with labor unions over 90 percent of the time. All 15 Senate Republicans, on the other hand, unanimously backed 100 percent of the legislative positions of the California Taxpayers' Association, an anti-tax group, in 2004. How's that for diversity?

As for the "ease of combination for improper purposes," examples of this kind of malady are common in Sacramento. One example is the disastrous vote in 1996 to deregulate the state's energy market. Key stakeholder groups and a small group of legislators quietly crafted the bill, then passed it through the Legislature without a single "no" vote. The subsequent energy crisis jeopardized the state's business climate, bankrupted its public utilities, sent electricity bills soaring and, eight years later [2004], is still unresolved. If the Legislature contained a greater quantity and diversity of voices, it is logical to assume the chances of heading off this foreseeable crisis would be greatly improved.

As it is California's Legislature is clearly not working as it is currently structured; so, what size should the Legislature and its districts become?

California is far too big to accommodate districts approaching the national average. Even matching Texas, with the nation's second largest districts, would more than triple the size of the California Assembly to about 252 seats.

Some have suggested merging the Legislature's two chambers into one body of 120 districts in a unicameral arrangement. This option has the benefit of decreasing the size of districts without changing the size of the Legislature. Bills would also pass more efficiently because they would only go through one chamber and one set of committees. Unicameralism, however, was rejected by the state Constitution Revision Commission about a decade ago for reasons no less relevant now. Bicameralism is critical to maintaining checks and balances.

The best design for the California Legislature would be to retain the bicameral structure while reasserting the original conception of the two chambers. Let the Senate be the smaller, deliberative body, and the Assembly be the larger house, where the passions and will of the people are expressed. This means Assembly districts should be as small as possible and Assembly seats most susceptible to challenge and competition. Senators, on the other hand, must be able to withstand unpopular votes, which means they need larger districts and longer terms. These conditions can be met by expanding the ratio of senators to Assembly members from the current 1-to-2 distribution to a 1-to-3 relationship.

Under this model, for example, the Assembly might have 150 members representing 233,000 persons each, while the Senate would have 50 members, representing 700,000 persons each. These dimensions are consistent with the recommendations of a 1970s study of state legislatures by the non-partisan Citizens Conference on State Legislatures.

So, what do citizens get from this design? A lot. For starters, citizens will have better access to legislators who are more interested in their concerns. A lawmaker representing urban, suburban, and rural communities is forced to consider a myriad of often conflicting needs for schools, health care, public safety, and other services. Many interests are left out without ever being heard in the Legislature. A lawmaker focused on a more concentrated population can be a better advocate.

Smaller districts will also improve the representation of moderate and third party voters. Independent candidates have a greater chance of winning a smaller district, and independent voters are more likely to be heard in a district where they make up a greater share of the electorate.

More citizens will be able to take part in government, too—both because there will be more seats available and because campaign costs will be more manageable. Campaign costs in California's Senate districts currently hover around $600,000. By comparison, the average campaign in a Massachusetts state Senate district—containing around 160,000 people—costs about $120,000.

Inside the Capitol, smaller districts would also cause dramatic change. Lobbyists and special interests would lose power since they would be forced to persuade more lawmakers with closer ties to their voters. Leadership power, diminished by the restrictions of term limits, may also grow as the voice of each individual lawmaker assumes a smaller share of the total body.

With more eyes watching and questioning government decisions, Californians could also expect better oversight and higher quality legislation. As president Woodrow Wilson noted, "it is not far from the truth to say that Congress in session is Congress on public exhibition, whilst Congress in committee rooms is Congress at work." The same can be said of the state Legislature. The real work occurs in committees where legislators develop bills, study issues, and make law.

Yet, committees produce good policy only when legislators have the time to become experts in the issues or there are many hands to manage the workload. Prior to term limits, committee members had years to gain expertise. Since term limits, however, studies have shown a drop in work quality. Most legislators now have a broad, but usually shallow, understanding of policy. A larger Legislature will mean more people to do the people's business, mitigating one negative impact of term limits.

In recent decades, Californians have adopted increasingly stringent political reforms in an effort to curtail corruption and increase accountability in government. But even after dramatic changes, such as term limits and budget mandates for taxes and schools, polls indicate that confidence in California government continues a dangerous decline.

With frustration growing, voters may be ready to consider even more aggressive change.

A recent opinion poll found most voters don't think smaller districts will make a difference, but 40 percent believe they would be "better represented."

Ultimately, Californians cannot manage the direct democracy our state is fast becoming. Californians must restore their trust in government and turn over the vast majority of policy decisions to elected representatives.

It is time to think creatively and boldly about new designs for a government that will reflect the new generation of California's diversity of ideas. The changes must make our representatives more accountable to voters and reflective of their ideas. That is only possible when the governed are closer to their government.

## Questions for Discussion

1. Explain Barbour's argument that California's legislature is too small to serve the state's people. What other states have a more appropriate ratio of residents to elected representatives?
2. Explain Barbour's bicameral solution, including the differences between the two houses as she envisions them. Could this modification make a difference in how people connect to their representatives?
3. Discuss the issue of government functionality: do fewer constituents create better representation? How does this happen?

## Ideas for Writing

1. Imagine yourself running for political office. Would you prefer to run in a smaller or larger district? Write a speech about your goals and ideas.
2. In an essay, develop the themes Barbour mentions about length of political terms and the roles of lobbyists. In order to improve political representation, what other reforms may be needed in addition to her proposal for larger legislative bodies?

---

# Unprotected Californians: Health Care as the New Civil Rights Issue

## JOHN AND JUDITH GLASS

*John F. Glass earned his Ph.D. in sociology at UCLA. He has served on the faculty of California State University, Northridge and several other colleges and universities in the Los Angeles area, teaching applied and clinical sociology. For the past decade he has been an active member of Health Care for All, promoting single-payer health insurance as the best solution for California's health care crisis.*

*Judith Glass has a Ph.D. in economics from UCLA. She was for-*
*merly the chair of the Social Relations Department at Immaculate*
*Heart College and Director of the MBA Program in not-for-profit*
*management at the University of Judaism. Her current focus is on*
*the connections between ethics and economics.*

———————— ✦ ————————

*"Of all the forms of inequality, injustice in health care is*
*the most shocking and inhumane."*

MARTIN LUTHER KING, JR.

## I. INTRODUCTION

We are the only modern industrial country without universal
health care, a singularly unenviable position. According to the
World Health Organization, we rank 37th in quality of health care,
yet we spend more per person than any other country. Cutbacks in
funds and services plus rising costs for medical services, insurance,
and prescription drugs are the order of the day. Hospitals are closing, and emergency rooms are overwhelmed. Prescription drug
prices are far higher in the US—a third to a half more than in other
industrialized countries. Unpaid medical bills account for over half
of all personal bankruptcies. California's health care system, too, is
clearly broken. One out of 5 Californians is uninsured. Los Angeles
County alone has almost 300,000 uninsured children and 2 million
uninsured non-elderly adults. Some 85% of these belong to working families, mostly those with low and moderate income who do
not have access to affordable insurance through their employers.

Longtime California farm worker organizer Dolores Huerta
reports that her own hospitalization and home health care for an
abdominal aortic fistula in 2000 cost more than $250,000. If she
did not have insurance through her union and Medicare, the burden on her family would have been catastrophic (*San Jose Mercury
News*, June 3, 2005).

A Los Angeles public school teacher with multiple leg fractures
and "full" health insurance was told, in an emergency room, that
no orthopedic surgeon at that hospital would take her case because
her insurance did not pay enough! The doctor admitted that she
would have been better off without health insurance, because then
they would have had to admit her to a costly emergency room.

This essay will detail the unique history of health care coverage in the United States and what is now happening in California, discuss the conflicting philosophical positions on providing health care, and assess the difficulties of making reforms to correct this enormous problem.

In 1935, old age (social security), and unemployment insurance were enacted which provided a safety net to millions of workers and their families against loss of income. Proposals for national health insurance failed at this time. Our reliance on employer-based health insurance began during World War II when prices and wages were frozen. Employers began to offer health insurance as a benefit to recruit scarce workers, a practice that continues today. As Daniel Akst wrote in the *New York Times* (11/03/03) "Nobody expects employers to provide groceries, housing, or clothing, but for odd historical reasons American employers have evolved into providers of health insurance."

Employer discontent is now increasing as health care costs rise, often in double digits each year, far outrunning inflation. In California, as in all other states, most group health insurance is employment-based. Some employers are passing more of their health costs to employees or dropping coverage altogether; only 60% of businesses offer health insurance to their workers, down from 66% in 2003 and 69% in 2000. Some wish to cover their employees but simply can't afford it. Some large employers such as Wal-Mart don't provide insurance to many of their employees, thus lowering their own costs, but this practice encourages their uninsured employees to seek public assistance, thus transferring health care costs to the community at large.

Additional drawbacks of maintaining an employer-based system is that the unemployed or self-employed are not included, and employees are restricted to the plans and benefits their employers offer. Changing or losing a job may mean having to change doctors at best, losing coverage altogether at worst. It is also a burden on employers who have to compete with those not paying health insurance.

## II. PROBLEMS OF COVERAGE AND COSTS

There is a crisis in coverage. California as well as the rest of the nation is struggling to resolve this shameful situation: some 45 million persons in the US are without health insurance, 7 million in California alone.

Buying health insurance is often not an option because of pre-existing conditions. The problem is not limited to these individuals and families. We are all affected when we live in a state where 20% of the population is sicker, less productive, and less financially secure than the rest. Those without insurance rely on expensive emergency rooms for acute or primary care; 15% of emergency rooms closed in the last decade for running in the red.

There is also a crisis of escalating cost. State Senator Sheila Kuehl has reported that there are some 9000 health plans in California and that more than 30% of the $150 billion spent on health care in California goes for administrative costs, marketing, advertising, and salaries. In contrast, Medicare, our federally funded health insurance for those 65 and older, has an overhead of some 3–4%. We waste huge amounts of money by having different health insurance coverage depending on whether injuries happen at work, at home, or in a car.

## III. PHILOSOPHY: ASSUMPTIONS AND VALUES

There are some fundamental assumptions and value judgments that underlie conflicting views of our health care system and the efforts to reform it. Is health care a right or a privilege? Who is responsible for paying for health care? What insurance model should be utilized?

If people are sick and need medical care, is there a right to treatment at a reasonable cost, or is it the responsibility of the individual to provide and pay for his/her health care? The predominant view in the US favors leaving responsibility with individuals for providing for their own care through ordinary market mechanisms. The familiar phrase that sums up this approach is "freedom of choice." A free market approach is contrasted with "socialized medicine," big government and bureaucracy. Assistance, when called for, therefore takes the form of legislative efforts to provide private health savings accounts, tax breaks, and other means by which some individuals are helped to enter the market for insurance and health care.

But others are critical of market approaches. They raise questions about the extent to which service to the sick is compatible with making money for stockholders or corporate owners. There is much evidence that for-profit insurance companies selling health insurance to individuals or employers is not only wasteful, but inherently in conflict with providing the best care to the most. The less service doctors provide, the more money insurance companies make. Screening out the sickest people, denying coverage to those with current or past illnesses—called "pre-existing conditions"—and charging more to those who can least afford it, are some examples of this.

In a social insurance model, such as Medicare, risk is shared by all, rates are lower because of a large pool of insured, and more people can be insured at a lower cost per person. Social insurance, unlike experience-based insurance (e.g. auto insurance where rates are based on driving records), is the appropriate model when health care is considered a social good, not a private one.

Critics of the market approach claim that health care is a fundamental right like having clean water, public education, and safe streets, and governments—federal and state—have a responsibility to insure that quality, affordable, and reliable health care is available to all. Equal access to health care is analogous to equal access to voting and protection against discrimination. A poor person's pneumonia is the same as a rich person's, and each should have access to the same quality treatment. The free market does not allow this, since ability to pay is a key factor in obtaining care.

This criticism extends to the often-proposed expansion of health savings accounts, which simply encourage high-deductible plans from employers and insurers, shift costs from insurers to individual consumers, starve public health programs for resources, and further undermine traditional insurance pools, making health care less affordable overall. Such savings accounts also do nothing to address quality of care, adequate coverage, or cost control.

## IV. CONTEMPORARY RECOGNITION OF THE PROBLEM AND SOLUTIONS

In 1994, the year that President Clinton's national health care plan was defeated by Congress, California advocates of universal health care proposed a state financed single payer system through Proposition 186. Single payer means that the state acts as the insurance company, collecting all the money and paying public and private providers of medical services, be they individual doctors or an HMO (Health Maintenance Organization) such as Kaiser.

A combination of employer, doctor, labor, and insurance interests poured money into a huge media campaign to soundly defeat this proposition, likening it to socialized medicine, higher taxes, loss of choice, and increased governmental bureaucracy. But single payer plans are not socialized medicine, since health care providers are not employees of the state.

Universal single payer bills, such as those introduced by State Senator Sheila Kuehl in 2003, 2005, and 2007 would replace all public and private insurance plans and cover all California residents with comprehensive insurance, including dental, vision, and prescription drugs with little or no co-payments or deductibles, saving an estimated $8 billion the first year alone according to the Lewin Group, an independent health care cost analysis firm. Rational planning, simplified administration, cost controls, and bulk purchasing of drugs and durable medical equipment account for some of the savings.

Several other efforts to increase the number of insured revolve around requiring employers to cover their workers or pay into an insurance pool. A limitation of these and other incremental reforms is the loss of statewide purchasing power, no control of health care costs, and lack of continuity of health care. Other limitations of employment-based health insurance have already been discussed.

Poll after poll shows that over 80% of the American people favor some kind of national health insurance. Yet, the current wasteful, inefficient, and unfair system is difficult to change. Perhaps the biggest obstacle to reforming our health care system is fear of change and mistrust of government. A single payer system in California or nationally would mean a major structural change affecting everyone. There are some 200,000 licensed insurance agents in California at risk of losing employment. Powerful lobbies of business, insurance, and drug companies generate enormous opposition to changing the current system. They believe their profits depend on it.

In California there are two ways to pass real health care reform: convincing the 90% of voters who already have insurance that they will be better off with universal coverage by passing an initiative, which requires a majority vote, or going through the legislative process where any bill with new taxes requires a two-thirds vote of the Senate and Assembly and the Governor's signature.

Financing health care is now definitely high on the state and national agenda. Many incremental plans have been proposed; covering all children, expanding Medicare, providing state-funded insurance for low-income people, requiring employers to provide insurance or pay into a state fund. These plans are provoking debate in the legislature and among voters. The bottom line will continue to be whether or not we are willing to pay for comprehensive coverage for all.

## Questions for Discussion

1. How do the authors set a tone of crisis about our health care system? What examples and terms do they use to convey the depth of the problem?
2. Analyze the differences presented in the essay between private health care (provided by employers or purchased by individuals) and public health care systems for the uninsured provided through tax dollars.
3. Explain the "free market" approach to health care. Do you agree with this approach? Why or why not?

## Ideas for Writing

1. Find out what health care options exist in your community. How many choices do people have if they are employed? Does being employed guarantee health insurance? What happens to those without insurance?
2. Explore the concepts of "free market" vs. "social insurance" approaches to health care. Is health care a public good, like education, that should be available to all? Or is it a privilege earned by those who can afford to obtain it? How do other nations handle the health needs of their people?

# Lesson One: Training Counts
## LINDA DARLING-HAMMOND

*Linda Darling-Hammond is the Charles E. Ducommun Professor of Education at Stanford University, where she has launched the Stanford Educational Leadership Institute and the School Redesign Network. Professor Darling-Hammond has also served as faculty sponsor for the Stanford Teacher Education Program. She was the founding Executive Director of the National Commission for Teaching and America's Future and has written numerous books and articles about how to achieve quality education.*

✦

As children across California strap on their backpacks and return to school, parents are crossing their fingers. They know intuitively what numerous studies have shown: The single most important influence on a child's achievement is the teacher. And in our state, these days, a child's chance of encountering a highly skilled, well-trained, and caring teacher is a lot smaller than it should be.

In a 2001 poll, 87% of Californians identified well-qualified teachers in every classroom as the key to raising student achievement, far ahead of reforms like vouchers or testing. When asked what makes a good teacher, they listed knowledge about teaching and learning first, followed by knowledge of classroom management and subject matter.

But in California schools, more than 40,000 teachers—nearly 15% of the total—lack these basic qualifications. California has more emergency-credentialed teachers than in 25 other states combined. Last year, in addition to 37,000 teachers working on emergency permits, who had not met the state's standards for content knowledge or teaching skills, about 2,500 teachers were working on waivers without having passed even the state's basic skills test. Others are teaching on "intern" or "pre-intern" credentials while they finish their training. These teachers make up well over half the staff in some schools serving large concentrations of low-income and minority students. These are often the same schools that lack textbooks, supplies, adequate facilities, and decent working conditions.

The reasons for this situation are now familiar. Proposition 13 led to reduced funding to schools while enrollments were growing. Salaries slipped, and class sizes grew. Then, state law requiring smaller class sizes increased demand for teachers and led rich districts to raid poor districts for qualified teachers.

Less acknowledged is how much these disparities affect learning. At least four recent studies in California have found that, after controlling for student poverty and conditions like class size, the proportion of emergency-credentialed teachers in a school significantly lowers student achievement on state tests. As student promotion and graduation are now tied to these tests, requiring higher standards for kids without requiring any standards for their teachers threatens to leave more and more children behind.

No Child Left Behind—the federal law passed last year [2001] to improve education for underserved students—was intended to remedy this situation. It not only requires states to test every child every year, with rewards and sanctions attached to the scores, it also requires that states provide all children with "highly qualified" teachers by 2005–06. It defines these teachers as being fully certified by the state and having demonstrated competence in the subjects they teach. Funds are provided to states to help them implement plans to reach this goal.

Seems like a sensible idea. But rather than formulate a plan to get qualified teachers into all the state's classrooms, the State Board of Education instead tried to define away the problem by proposing to set the standards for "highly qualified teachers" at the level currently required of those who enter teaching on emergency permits. The U.S. Department of Education said it could not accept this definition, and California is back at the drawing board.

Although the situation looks daunting, it is fixable, as other states and districts have shown. The problems in staffing California schools are not caused by shortages of qualified individuals in the state or the nation. Nationally and in California, there are two to three times as many certified teachers in the population as there are in the schools. Many states in the Midwest and New England have teacher surpluses. Most of the "shortages" exist because people are unwilling to work in cities and poor rural districts that pay less than those in the suburbs and have larger classes and fewer resources.

Such disparities plague California. In 2001, beginning teacher salaries ranged from $23,000 to $45,000. After adjusting for cost of living, there was a 3-1 ratio between the starting salaries offered by Vallecito Union, a high-achieving Calaveras County district with no uncertified teachers, and Alum Rock Union, a low-performing San Jose district where 34% of all teachers are not fully certified. Economist Michael Pogodzinski found that California districts offering lower salaries than others in their county have more emergency hires.

Other studies have found that teachers who are underprepared leave their jobs at much higher rates than those who are fully certified. About 35% of emergency-credentialed teachers leave within the first year, and more than 60% never receive a credential. Teachers who are unprepared are typically shocked by the number of things they don't know how to do; feel inadequate in meeting the needs of the wide range of students in their classes; and experience more stress and less success than teachers who have learned how to organize a classroom, motivate and engage students, and plan curriculums. By contrast, at least 70% of prepared teachers generally remain in the profession after five years. Mentoring also matters. Teachers who receive intensive one-on-one classroom mentoring during their first year also stay at much higher rates.

Reducing attrition is one of the most important ways to meet the demand for teachers because it accounts for most of the supply problem and wastes precious resources. According to the Texas Center for Educational Research, it costs about $8,000 to recruit, hire, and orient a replacement teacher—money that could be better spent helping teachers become more effective in the first place.

When conditions improve, qualified teachers appear and stay. The recent experience of New York City is instructive. A state mandate that uncertified teachers could no longer be placed in low-performing schools—along with the requirements of the new federal law—led to improvements in hiring practices and a 16% increase in teachers' salaries to make them more comparable to the surrounding suburbs. The coming school year's vacancies were filled by July, and 90% of the new hires are fully certified, in contrast with only 60% the year before. The remaining 10% will be certified within the year.

Some California cities serving large proportions of low-income and minority students have done the same. New Haven Unified, which serves Union City in Alameda County, has long been known for having surpluses of teachers because of its single-minded focus on getting and keeping those who are well-qualified. Anaheim and San Diego have recently turned the corner, hiring almost all certified teachers last year by combining aggressive recruitment from local colleges and out-of-state with increased salaries, improved working conditions in high-need schools, and mentoring supports. These initiatives benefited from policies recently enacted to help recruit and retain qualified teachers in high-need schools—even if these are not yet on a scale sufficient to solve the problem.

When purpose is joined with persistence, these problems can be solved. Connecticut is a case in point: It went from 20 years of teacher shortages in its major cities to surpluses statewide within three years by increasing salaries until it was the top-paying state in the nation and equalizing the pay across districts. At the same time, the state improved teacher education and mentoring, provided scholarships for teaching candidates in high-need fields, and eliminated emergency credentialing. Connecticut's schools became among the best in the nation, even as they served a growing share of students from low-income and immigrant families.

California—the largest and wealthiest economy in the nation and the fifth-largest in the world—can and should do the same. A high-tech economy like ours cannot run well without a highly skilled labor force. In the poll mentioned earlier, eight out of 10 Californians agreed that "we should ensure that all children, including those who are economically disadvantaged, have teachers who are fully qualified, even if that means spending more money to achieve that goal."

Education can be a strong weapon in the fight against crime. Most prison inmates are functionally illiterate, and 40% of adjudicated juveniles have learning disabilities that were not diagnosed in school. From the mid-1980s to the mid-1990s, criminal justice expenditures in California grew by 900% while spending for education grew by less than 25% in real-dollar terms. A year

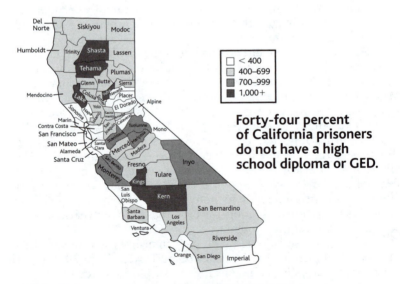

Legend:
- □ < 400
- ▨ 400–699
- ▦ 700–999
- ■ 1,000+

**Forty-four percent of California prisoners do not have a high school diploma or GED.**

## California Incarceration Rates per 100,000 Adults, by County, 2005

*Source:* California Department of Corrections data, Dept. of Finance 2005—in Public Policy Institute, *California Counts,* vol. 8, no.1, August 2006, p. 7.

Note: Incarceration rates by country are not age-adjusted.

**Map of Campus Locations for California State University (CSU)**

*Source:* California State University website, www.calstate.edu/datastore/campus_map.shtml.

in prison for one inmate costs taxpayers up to $30,000. Average costs per pupil in grades K-12 are now less than $6,000. We can pay for qualified teachers now or for prisons later. It's California's choice.

## Questions for Discussion

1. What is the relationship between education funding, teacher salaries, and teacher preparation? How do all of these factors influence student learning?
2. Describe the role of teacher preparation in retention of teachers and quality of education. How do other school systems (outside of California) handle this challenge?
3. What connections does the author make between education and prisons? How does she compare the two in terms of their cost and impact on society?

## Ideas for Writing

1. Recall your own elementary school teachers. Which ones are most memorable and why? What do you know (or can you surmise) about their educational preparation for teaching? Write an essay about what you remember as "quality teaching."
2. Research the most current data in your local school district regarding teacher salaries, teacher preparation, student test scores, and general reputation of the school district. Write an essay about how you would improve the schools in your area.
3. Visit a local school and interview teachers about their background, preparation, and experiences. Write an essay based on their stories.

# College in California: Options Reduced?

## WILLIAM E. PILAND

*William E. Piland is a product of community college, then went on to get his BS, MS, and EdD degrees at Northern Illinois University. He is the author of numerous articles and books about community college leadership development, and serves as Professor of postsecondary Education at San Diego State University. He serves as the Director of the Graduate Institute of the San Diego and Imperial Counties Community College Association (SDICCCA) Regional Faculty Internship Program.*

━━━━━━━━━━ ✦ ━━━━━━━━━━

Higher education, the California dream for well over 2 million undergraduate students, is turning into a nightmare. The Golden State's promise of unparalleled access to community colleges and universities is becoming a tarnished relic of the past. And this state of affairs is occurring at a time when the demand for higher education has never been greater. Increasingly it is coming from segments of society that have historically been shut out for a variety of reasons. Students of color, low income students, first-generation college students, immigrants, and special needs students—the very future of California—are primarily the ones being turned back from the citadels of higher learning. California, with its once proud heritage of free or very inexpensive education, a community college or state university within driving distance of the overwhelming majority of its population, and a world-class research university system, is rapidly turning its back on its future.

The problem of access cuts across all segments of higher education, but by far, most students affected are enrolled in the state's community colleges. The Community College League of California (CCLC) estimates that more than 175,000 students were denied access to the state's 108 community colleges during the 2003–04 academic year. About 90,000 of these reflect an actual enrollment decrease caused by budget reductions that forced colleges across the state to cancel thousands of class sections. The remaining 85,000 represent the expected demand based on increases in high school graduates and the adult population who would otherwise have attended community colleges but were similarly shut out. Adding to this, the California State University (CSU) system announced that its campuses will not admit over 20,000 students who are identified as qualified. These students are to be "redirected" to the community colleges.

Leticia is a 20-year-old Latina who is the first person in her nuclear family to enter higher education, and only the second in her large, extended family. Both her parents are legal immigrants from Mexico. Leticia could not get a full course load in fall 2003 because her college reduced its offerings and because of high student demand. What makes her case so interesting is how intertwined her life is with her schooling. Her enrollment fees were covered by financial aid, and she made just enough with her job as a college mentor to cover books, transportation, and other incidental expenses. Because she lost her full-time status, she will lose her father's medical insurance. It only covers her if she is a full-time student. She will also lose her mentor job which is also contingent on full-time status. She will be forced to either get a full-time job with benefits or perhaps simply turn to some other form of state assistance. And she will be forced to delay or terminate her educational plans. Unfortunately, Leticia is only one of a long, long list of students who share her fate.

These statistics demonstrate that the state is moving backwards when it comes to providing students with access to its comprehensive community college system. In the light of the governor's budget for 2004–05, the CCLC anticipates that an additional 100,000 students will not take part in community college education in 2004–05. These numbers are staggering. Longer-range projections are even more disheartening. But the numbers alone do not reflect the whole story. Many more students have had to delay accomplishing their educational goals because they can't get the courses they need in a reasonable time frame.

## CALIFORNIA'S HISTORIC COMMITMENT TO ACCESS

The 1960 California Master Plan for Higher Education, which became a model for many other states, promised that every student who wanted to pursue a college education would be able to do so at a public college or university. By 2005, this promise was ultimately realized in ten University of California (UC) campuses enrolling slightly over 200,000 students, CSU with twenty-three campuses and over 333,000 students, and the California Community Colleges (CCC) with 108 campuses and over 1.6 million students in the year 2005. According to the Master Plan, UCs enroll the top 12% of high school graduating classes, CSUs the top 33%, and the CCCs all high school graduates and non-graduates past a certain age. This system became the envy of the higher education establishment across the country.

The state also chose to foster access through low tuition policies. In fact, the term "tuition" is not even used in California; "fees" are assessed instead. In 2002, fees were $11 per credit—only 22% of the national average for community college tuition. University fee rates were comparably low. For example, 2002 fees at CSU campuses were $888 for a full-time student per semester, also substantially below the national average for similar universities. To sustain low fees the state made a commitment to substantially subsidize higher education through tax support. In non-recession years, California has a history of being generous with its higher education systems. But state support has been steadily declining. In 1971, 16.8% of the total state budget was allocated to the three segments of higher education. By 2003, that allocation had declined to 11%. Clearly in recent years the state has placed other priorities well before its commitment to access embodied by the 1960 Master Plan.

## TIDAL WAVE II

Tidal Wave II, sometimes referred to as the "Baby Boom Echo," portends an enormous upsurge in the number of recent high school graduates who will enter California higher education institutions—if there is space available. The tidal wave has already begun and will peak in 2015–16. Because the number of students seeking to enroll in public colleges and universities already exceeds the capacity of the system, the problem will grow worse each year unless decisive action is taken. A staff analyst at the California Postsecondary Education Commission (CPEC) has estimated that by 2013, 1.8 million eligible students will have been turned away from California higher education institutions, 1.35 million of whom would otherwise have attended a community college. Despite repeated pleas to respond to the challenge of Tidal Wave II, the State of California has no plan to do so.

Who are the students being shut out of higher education opportunities? Unlike the first Tidal Wave of students, who were largely white with a large proportion coming from families with a tradition of college-going, students in this second wave will be largely first-generation college students, students from low-income families, and students of color. In 1999, the California Citizens Commission on Higher Education projected that by the year 2010 the number of Latinos graduating from high school would almost double, with increases from 30 to 45% of all high school graduates, to become the largest ethnic group in California. Another rapidly growing group, Asian Americans, will have increased to 16% of total public high school graduates by 2010. It is telling that the state appears to be losing its commitment to access at precisely the time when the majority college population will comprise people of color.

Obtaining a college education has always been viewed as a way up for Americans trying to climb the socioeconomic ladder. Graduating from college has become essential to getting and keeping high-paying jobs, jobs that make it easier to raise healthy families. California stands to lose extraordinary contributions if it turns its back on the next generation of students. To ignore them would put the state's civic unity at grave risk. Individual opportunity, the watchword of today's policy makers, is becoming a hollow phrase.

California's economy is built upon education and advanced skills. The state depends on an educated work force now, and it will need an even more educated work force in the future. Business leaders know that a skilled and employed citizenry also provides the paying customers for goods and services needed to drive the economy forward. Abandoning the educational aspirations of state residents because of neglect or unsound fiscal policies will harm the state's economy and imperil a way of life that has benefited so many members of Tidal Wave I.


## THE CURRENT SITUATION IN CALIFORNIA

Oh what a difference a few years make! Community college fees had risen to $18 a unit, an increase of 64%, and they stood at 35% of the national average. Then the governor increased fees to $26, an increase of 44%. Thus in two short years, community college fees could increase by 136%. These steep, last-minute increases had severe effects on access, because community college students tend to come from the lowest income groups. This is another case of budget balancing on the backs of the poor. Huge fee increases, coupled with drastic cut-backs in the numbers of course offerings, were slamming the open-door on students who are in dire need of higher education opportunities to better their lives and their communities. Suddenly fees, in 2007, were lowered to $20 a unit, a decline of 23%. This "yo-yo" effect is particularily unsettling for low-income families. It is almost impossible to plan for financing a college education with this schizophrenic fee policy.

The halcyon days of state support for higher education have also ended. State aid for community colleges in 2002 averaged $4,321. This figure placed California 45th among states in financial support for its community colleges. At the same time, local tax support has been greatly reduced for most community colleges thanks to the passage of Proposition 13, which shifted revenue from taxes from the local to the state level during the 1970s. From 2001–03 there were 74,000 unfunded FTEs in California's community colleges—students who were being educated with no state support. By 2002, class size had risen to an average of 28.5—the highest in the nation—and by 2003 "fill rates" (the percentage of seats taken in a class) were running between 90 and 95%, making California community colleges the most efficient higher education institutions in the country from a classroom utilization perspective. This lack of support by the state for its community college system has devastating impacts. One out of every four community college students in the nation is enrolled in California.

Sarah is a 20-year-old white female who is the first in her family to attend college. As a second year Anthropology major with 61 units completed, she has had direct experience with the frustrations of registering for classes in California's community colleges. Sarah is part of a transfer guarantee program with one of the UC campuses, and had been planning to transfer in the fall semester. Unfortunately she had to postpone her plans because of the difficulties she faced in getting needed classes.

In Sarah's own words: "To complete the transfer contract I would have needed a Biology class, a very impacted class. I was registered for four other classes to complete the contract. I attended two full class sessions of Bio and still was far down on the wait list. I went through every option to try to find a way in. After seeing about four walk-in counselors, they gave me little more than tired looks and advice to take the class at another college. The classes were impacted all over the county anyway. Plus without my own vehicle that wasn't an option. I could not take a night course because I work at night to support myself so I can attend college."

California colleges and universities have become competitors who vigorously fight for ever-decreasing financial scraps thrown from the budgetary table. These days, in too many cases, they would just as soon attack each other—behind the scenes of course—than join forces to form a united front to advocate for the entire system. Meanwhile, the layers of distrust between the three segments on budgetary matters couldn't be cut with a Bowie knife. Since so much of the State budget is already spoken for through voter initiatives, what remains to fund higher education constantly shrinks. The community colleges in California, interesting enough, fall under Proposition 98, passed in the late 1980s to guarantee that at least 40% of the state budget goes to K-14 education. But they have only received their legislated share of that 40% pie once in fifteen years. Here community colleges are trumped by the power of the K-12 system as well as the two university systems. And as the resources for the entire state shrink with a falling economy and tax cuts enacted during better times, the acrimony ratchets higher and higher. The result is a "zero sum game" where the higher education segments are distracted by internal fighting or don't care enough to take an active role in changing the system. In light of health care and other social needs, higher education lacks a compelling argument for better budgets right now. As a result, coordination of higher education interests to undertake effective action has not occurred and "outside" interests like influential community members, unions, the business community, and others have not been systematically solicited for support.

The California Legislature recently conducted another study of the Master Plan for Higher Education. These studies are not new, and in fact occur every few years. Except for a revision to the community college system in the late 1980s, which emanated from a Master Plan review, nothing has come of them. The two university systems and their lobbying groups fight any attempts at meaningful reform. Yet each of these studies continues to support the basic tenants of the original Master Plan, with its boldly stated commitment to access. The latest time around the legislature wanted to create a new plan for all of education in the state, pre-K through 20. The bills that were introduced to codify the study's recommendations became immersed in contentions about governance, while ignoring needed finance remedies or the fundamental changes involved in rethinking the missions, purposes, operations, and relationships of the three higher education segments.

## RECAPTURING THE SPIRIT: THE CAMPAIGN FOR COLLEGE OPPORTUNITY

Against this backdrop of minimal state action to reaffirm the Master Plan for Higher Education, a new initiative is attempting to energize the citizens of California to support student access. This initiative is being referred to as the Campaign for College Opportunity. Only time will tell how effective it becomes.

The public will—and, by extension, the political will—to recapture the spirit of educational opportunity for all Californians has up to now been lacking in California. A sour economy, coupled with strong and enduring anti-tax sentiments, has paralyzed the state. Individual interest, short-sighted thinking, a "we can't do that attitude," and a lack of true understanding of the crisis being faced in the community college sector have all eroded college access. Yet the impending denial of meaningful access to hundreds of thousands of students ranks at the top of the list of current problems. This problem has thus far resisted an effective response because of a number of factors:

- The problem is large and expensive to solve.
- A feasible solution requires changes that will anger and displease a variety of constituencies.
- The families and students who will be most affected by the shortage of college opportunities don't yet know that the problem exists.
- Even if these families and students knew about the problem, they are not politically influential, particularly in terms of campaign contributions.
- The largest impact falls upon community colleges, the segment least well understood and most ignored in Sacramento.

Restricting access is an extraordinary problem that requires an extraordinary response. The Campaign for College Opportunity is attempting to reaffirm the Master Plan promise of access for all eligible students to a quality education in both California's community colleges and its universities on the grounds that it is a) in the economic self-interest of the state and its citizens, and b) morally right.

There are some positive signs that California's citizens support their higher education institutions—and especially their community colleges. Virtually all of the state's 109 colleges enjoy broad and deep support in their local communities. Huge numbers of California citizens have attended community colleges and have been touched by the excellent instruction offered there, by the diverse set of important academic programs available, and by the responsive student services offered to them, that there is a deep reservoir of good will for this segment of higher education. A clear demonstration of this goodwill is the fact that during a recent two-year period, 39 out of 40 local bond measures were passed by the citizens in community college districts, yielding a total of $8.4 billion to go toward construction, remodeling, and equipment. This represents a deep wellspring of support on which to build a viable campaign.

The keystone of the Campaign for College Opportunity is a broad coalition of important constituencies that can create a political environment in which elected officials can and will take necessary actions. The three co-founders of the Campaign are the heads of the Mexican American Legal Defense and Educational Fund, the California Business Roundtable, and the Community College League of California. The Campaign has begun to reach out to leaders of both public and private higher education, business, taxpayer groups, communities of color, civic groups, religious organizations, labor unions, elected officials from both parties, public school constituencies, and education reform groups. Unlike past efforts at serious problem-solving in higher education in California where either a group of academics talked a problem to death without ever taking action or special-interest groups pushed their own agendas while resisting any type of change which might have the slightest impact, the Campaign for College Opportunity intends to a) conduct a sustained and effective public information initiative that will inform the public about the nature and consequences of Tidal Wave II and the necessity of sustaining the Master Plan, and b) develop consensus about the steps to be taken to reaffirm access.

In order to move a solution forward, agreement must be reached on several highly controversial issues. Three are fundamental:

- *The Magnitude and Nature of State Support.* There is simply no way to educate the massive numbers of additional college students on the horizon without a dramatic increase in state support. But the issues here go beyond simply increases in state spending to include such matters as disparities in funding among districts, financial incentives to produce more graduates in high-demand fields like nursing, the ratio of full-time to part-time faculties, and categorical funding for programs that address the needs of special groups of students.

- *Student Fees.* If large increases in state financial support are needed to accommodate larger enrollments, it is reasonable to ask whether students and their families should be expected to pay more of the cost of higher education. A discussion of student fee increases would benefit from agreement on the following points. First, income from student fees should go directly to the colleges themselves. In California, this is currently not the situation. Fees collected by the colleges flow to central state budget coffers and are placed in the General Fund. Second, increases in student fees should be moderate and predictable. And third, student financial aid should be increased to meet the full financial need of low income students. Tuition has been a highly emotional issue in California, and since state government had enacted massive increases some sanity needs to be brought to bear on this issue.

- *College Priorities and Management.* If the California electorate is to be persuaded to provide substantially more funding for community colleges, stronger assurances are needed that state money is being used in the most efficient and effective ways possible. The search for greater efficiency will have to become intense. Even more difficult struggles will arise over issues of college educational priorities like the open-door policy and the question of who can benefit from instruction, the priority given to recent high school graduates versus returning adults, and the colleges' missions in relation to student goals of transfer, degree completion, certificate completion, and life-long learning. These are tough issues that will divide the public, elected officials, and college leadership. But they cannot be ignored.

## CONCLUSION

California stands at a crossroads linked by demography, scientific and technological advances, economic transformation, and the basic principles of democracy. Wonderful achievements were underwritten by previous generations that committed themselves to providing college opportunity for all students, regardless of wealth or family background. The people of California have benefited from their sacrifice. For the future, however, these benefits can only be realized if California citizens have the wisdom and the determination to keep the historic promise of college opportunity for the generations now coming of age.

### Questions for Discussion

1. Describe California's Master Plan for Higher Education. What are the three segments of higher education, and how do they provide maximum opportunities to Californians?

2. Analyze Piland's statement, "the state appears to be losing its commitment to access at precisely the time when the majority college population will comprise people of color." What does he imply?

3. Describe the issues identified by the Campaign for College Opportunity, and the plans for solving them. Explain your views of the solutions offered by this organization.

### Ideas for Writing

1. Research some of the current legislation that affects public higher education in your state. What are the issues facing lawmakers? How do they respond to public needs and to various interest groups?

2. Write an essay about the cost of higher education and the long-term financial burdens many young people must handle in order to attend college. What political changes could make the situation better?

## Thinking and Writing about Chapter 3

### Connecting the Essays

1.  What is the role of trust between people and their government? Using Schrag, Barbour, and Hodson, comment on how people lose faith in government. How might trust in government be restored?
2.  Explain your definition of the political terms "conservative" and "liberal." Analyze the underlying political perspectives (ideologies) of Hodson, Barbour, Burt, and Glass and Glass. Can you figure out who is more conservative? More liberal? What clues can you find in their essays and their ideas?
3.  Compare the political changes proposed by Barbour and in the Glass essay. Of the two issues (expanding the Legislature or universal health coverage) which one seems most important for the long-term improvement of California? Make a clear argument for your choice.
4.  Many of the authors (Schrag, Hodson, Barbour) seem discouraged about California's current situation. If you could bring them together for a dialogue, how might they prioritize the changes each one recommends? How could their solutions interact, either in conflict or harmony?

### Extending the Theme

1.  Develop the concepts of the words "minority" and "majority." Do these terms have new meanings in light of population changes? In an essay, discuss the future in regards to ethnic diversity. How could prejudice and discrimination disappear eventually? Is this a desirable goal?
2.  Research how other states handle higher education. Is there the same kind of open access that California strives for? What is the role of government in providing higher education? What is the role of private business or nonprofit organizations in providing or funding education? Write an essay about educational opportunities.
3.  Research how other states fund their public schools and pay their teachers. How does California rank in K-12 education, in terms of student performance, teacher satisfaction, and general quality of education?
4.  Research the health care system in Canada, England, or some other nation that has universal health care. What are some criticisms or problems with national universal health care? How does the Glass essay respond (if at all) to the problems of universal care? Develop your own creative system for providing health care.
5.  Using some of the approaches of Hodson and Burt, analyze the historic and economic circumstances of your area. What challenges does your community face due to its particular history of ethnic relations, past discrimination, etc? What about the role of economic change, such as the movement of jobs from the United States to other nations? What are the future employment prospects in your community, and how should young people prepare for them?

# Safety, Security, and Sustainability

People, people, everywhere. The perception that California is full is probably most acute in Los Angeles, which seems to stretch endlessly in every direction from no matter where you are. San Francisco features a different type of crowdedness, not one which spreads laterally, but one which feels more dense. Drive out of either city, however, and you're struck by a different impression. Space.

Some of it is wild, like the national forests near LA and the redwood forests in the north of the state. Much of it is farmed, either for grapes as in the Napa Valley, or fruits and vegetables as in the Central Valley, the self-proclaimed "salad bowl of the world." But while rolling farmland is an image much used to suggest peace and tranquility, in fact, there's more to these parts of California than meets the eye. With farming come other issues, including the effects on both land and people of industrial agriculture's use of pesticides and the question of labor itself—who does it, where do the workers come from, and what rights do they have?

In the cities, the relationship of people to the environment sometimes takes second place to the relationships between people, period. Dreams come in different forms, and California cityscapes often reflect a version of paradise which current residents have inherited from those who came before. Hence the classic Midwestern "picket fence neighborhoods" in much of greater Los Angeles. The trouble comes when people try to squeeze tighter than the designers allowed for, which can lead to conflicts of values over things as simple as building fences and as complicated as how to design new urban landscapes with greater density as the goal.

All of this leads to an important question, one being asked every day by a variety of people with a related spectrum of concerns: How long can this continue? Is California as residents currently "do" it sustainable? Each essay in this chapter takes up this question from a different viewpoint. And while the writers don't always say it, their concern is essentially the same—to figure out how California's people and environment interact, and whether it is possible for the current interrelationship to continue as growth brings even more people with dreams of their own.

Joan Didion poses the question of sustainability in specific terms of why so many California cities are clamoring to have prisons built within their boundaries. Reading this as a new version of the same old phenomenon of "selling the future of the place to the highest bidder," Didion offers a poignant beginning to a series of essays which try to figure out whether there's life left in the state yet.

The chapter's next selection starts where, in a sense, California starts—with the question of water use and politics. Wade Graham tries to sort out the complicated history of how the state came to enjoy the benefits of cheap imported water and to explain the effects of water use on growth in the state.

Water plus labor in California is an equation adding up to only one thing—agricultural production, and the next essay in this chapter talks about the impact of corporate farming on people. Marc Cooper discusses the progress, or lack thereof, that farm workers have seen in their attempts to be properly treated and compensated for their work.

Heng L. Foong continues the focus on the human element of the growth of California. Her concentration is on access to medical care, and she explains the problems that ensue when immigrant families find themselves in the unfamiliar situation of having to understand complicated medical discourse spoken in a language not familiar to them.

The final three essays in this chapter also talk about growth. Randall Lewis offers a remedy for urban overcrowding. The 2% solution he describes is designed to use urban land in the most effective way, making it possible for people to afford housing within reasonable distance of the city's culture and opportunities.

Greg Goldin complements Lewis's point of view as he debates the symbolic effect of fences in reconfiguring urban space. Both would agree, most likely, that life in the larger cities of California is not going to be the same fifty years from now as it was fifty years ago, with single-family houses adorning green lawns which invite neighbors up for a chat because of their open design.

To finish off the chapter, Chris Thompson takes us up north, to Oakland, as he discusses the merits and problems inherent in development of an area that had established itself for its funky charm and is now threatened by the possibility of redefinition in the form of two giant condo buildings.

Each article in this chapter takes up a different issue, though in the end, all of them are related to the same thing—the fact that California exists as many people's dream-place, and so is attracting more and more newcomers every day. What to do with them, how they can live with each other and in harmony with the environment which is the staging ground for their dreams, and the place of government in forging, or forcing, the compromises necessary to keep peace; these are the questions addressed by each writer.

---

# The Promise of the Prison
## JOAN DIDION

*Joan Didion was born in Sacramento and lived her early life in California. After graduating from UC Berkeley, she went to New York to work for* Vogue. *She returned to California eight years later and embarked upon a freelance writing career which has produced novels and screenplays as well as essays. The latter, particularly her collections* Slouching Toward Bethlehem *(1968) and* The White Album *(1979) created her reputation as one uniquely capable of portraying life in California in words. She now lives in New York once again.*

---  ◆  ---

For most of my life California felt rich to me: that was the point of it, that was the promise, the reward for having left the past on the Sweetwater, the very texture of the place. This was by no means to say that I believed all or even most Californians to be rich, only to suggest that the fact of having no money seemed to me to lack, in California, the immutable gravity that characterized the condition elsewhere. It was not designed to be a life sentence. You were meant, if you were a Californian, to know how to lash together a corral with bark, you were meant to know how to tent a raft and live on the river, you were meant to show spirit, kill the rattlesnake, keep moving. There were in California a lot of "dead brokes," Henry George had pointed out in 1868, in a passage from "What the Railroad Will Bring Us" that got read to me (rather selectively, in retrospect) by my grandfather, "but there never was a better country to be 'broken' in, and where almost every man, even the most successful, had been in the same position, it did not involve the humiliation and loss of hope which attaches to utter poverty in older and more settled communities."

That I should have continued, deep into adult life, to think of California as I was told as a child that it had been in 1868 suggests a confusion of some magnitude, but there it was. *It's not a word we use,* my mother had said about class. *It's not the way we think.* Only in the 1980s did certain facts—two of them, not unrelated—manage to penetrate what was clearly a fairly tenacious wish not to examine whatever it was I needed to believe. The first fact, which entered my attention as an almost personal affront, was that California no longer felt rich enough to adequately fund its education system. The second, or corollary, fact was that there seemed to be many towns in California—including towns I knew, towns I thought of as my own interior landscape, towns I had thought I understood, towns in the Sacramento and San Joaquin Valleys—so impoverished in spirit as well as in fact that the only way their citizens could think to reverse their fortunes was by getting themselves a state prison. Since the building and staffing of new prisons were major reasons why California no longer felt rich enough to adequately fund its education system, this second fact initially presented itself as an even deeper affront than the first, evidence that a "new" California had finally and fatally sold out the old.

Then I remembered, then I realized.

We were seeing nothing "new" here.

We were seeing one more version of making our deal with the Southern Pacific.

We were seeing one more version of making our bed with the federal government.

We were seeing one more enthusiastic fall into a familiar California error, that of selling the future of the place we lived to the highest bidder, which was in this instance the California Correctional Peace Officers Association.

The California Correctional Peace Officers Association is the prison guards' union, a 29,000-member force that has maintained for some years now the most effective lobbying operation in Sacramento. In the 1998 election cycle, for example, the union funneled over two million dollars to Grey Davis's gubernatorial campaign and another three million dollars to various other candidates and propositions. "All I've ever asked is that we get to play in the ballpark with all the big guys and gals out there," Don Novey told *The Los Angeles Times* in 2000. Don Novey is the former guard at Folsom State Prison who became in 1980 the president of the California Correctional Peace Officers Association. "They call us the 800-pound gorilla. But we're just taking care of our own like everybody else." Don Novey refers to those who consider the need for new prisons an arguable proposition as "the other element." He gave $75,000 to the opponent of a state senator who had once spoken against a prison bond issue. "If Don Novey ran the contractors' union," a Republican strategist told the *Times*, "there'd be a bridge over every puddle in the state." The prison guards were in California the political muscle behind the victims' rights movement. The prison guards were in California the political muscle behind the 1994 "three strikes" legislation and initiative, the act that mandated a sentence of twenty-five years to life for any third felony conviction, even for crimes as minor as growing a marijuana plant on a windowsill or shoplifting a bottle of Ripple. The prison guards were the political muscle that had by the year 2000 made the California corrections system, with thirty-three penitentiaries and 162,000 inmates, the largest in the western hemisphere.

Incarceration was not always a growth industry in California. In 1852 there was only San Quentin, by 1880 there was also Folsom. During the 104 years that followed, a century during which the population of California increased from 865,000 to 25,795,000 people, the state found need for only ten additional facilities, most of them low or medium security. It was only in 1984, four years after Don Novey took over the union, that the new max and supermax prisons began rolling online, Solano in 1984, "New Folsom" (a quarter mile removed from "Old Folsom") in 1986, Avenal and Ione and Stockton and San Diego in 1987, Corcoran and Blythe in 1988, Pelican Bay in 1989, Chowchilla in 1990, Wasco in 1991, Calipatria in 1992, Lancaster and Imperial and Centinela and Delano in 1993, Coalinga and a second prison at Blythe in 1994, second prisons at both Susanville and Chowchilla in 1995, Soledad in 1996, a second prison at Corcoran in 1997.

Delano, the town in the San Joaquin between Tulare and Bakersfield that became synonymous outside California with Cesar Chavez's farmworkers' union, still yearns for its own second prison, "New Delano," to be built just across the road from what is already called "Old Delano," the ten-year-old North Kern State Prison. Mendota, west of Fresno and south of Chowchilla, still waits for what was to have been its privately built and operated prison, on which construction was begun and then postponed by the Nashville-based Corrections Corporation of America, which had hit a snag trying to contract with the state for prisoners to fill the $100 million maximum-security prison it had already built in the Mojave desert. "They can build whatever prisons they want," Don Novey had said to this point. "But the hell if they're going to run them."

That these prisons should remain the objects of abject civic desire is curious, since they have not actually enriched the towns that got them. A new prison creates jobs, but few of those jobs go to local hires. The Department of Corrections allows that it imports half the "corrections workers" in any new prison, but "tries" to hire the rest from the community. Opponents to "New Delano" point out that only seven to nine percent of the jobs at these new prisons have typically been local hires, and that the local hires get the low-paid service jobs. Of the 1,600 projected jobs at "New Delano," only 72 would be local hires. There are, moreover, costs, both economic and social: when the families of inmates move into a prison town, they not only strain the limited resources of local schools and social service agencies but bring emotionally stressed children into the community and school system. "The students are all very high risk," a school official in Lassen County, where Susanville is located, told *The Los Angeles Times*. "They come from single-parent homes. They're latchkey kids, often on AFDC. It's very obvious they're from a whole different area. It creates societal conflicts. The child does not fit in."

It was 1993 when the California Department of Corrections activated its first "death fence," at Calipatria. It was 1994 when the second "death fence" was activated, at Lancaster, carrying a charge of 650 milliamperes, almost ten times the voltage required to cause instant death. "What the fence does is take out the human-error part," the warden at Lancaster was quoted as

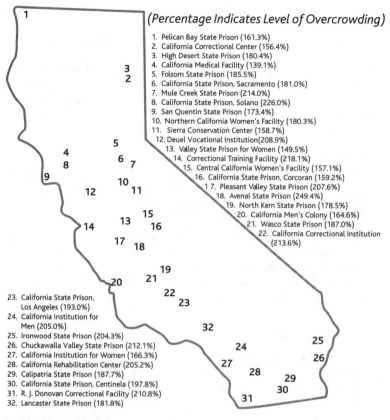

*(Percentage Indicates Level of Overcrowding)*

1. Pelican Bay State Prison (161.3%)
2. California Correctional Center (156.4%)
3. High Desert State Prison (180.4%)
4. California Medical Facility (139.1%)
5. Folsom State Prison (185.5%)
6. California State Prison, Sacramento (181.0%)
7. Mule Creek State Prison (214.0%)
8. California State Prison, Solano (226.0%)
9. San Quentin State Prison (173.4%)
10. Northern California Women's Facility (180.3%)
11. Sierra Conservation Center (158.7%)
12. Deuel Vocational Institution(208.9%)
13. Valley State Prison for Women (149.5%)
14. Correctional Training Facility (218.1%)
15. Central California Women's Facility (157.1%)
16. California State Prison, Corcoran (159.2%)
17. Pleasant Valley State Prison (207.6%)
18. Avenal State Prison (249.4%)
19. North Kern State Prison (178.5%)
20. California Men's Colony (164.6%)
21. Wasco State Prison (187.0%)
22. California Correctional Institution (213.6%)

23. California State Prison, Los Angeles (193.0%)
24. California Institution for Men (205.0%)
25. Ironwood State Prison (204.3%)
26. Chuckawalla Valley State Prison (212.1%)
27. California Institution for Women (166.3%)
28. California Rehabilitation Center (205.2%)
29. Calipatria State Prison (187.7%)
30. California State Prison, Centinela (197.8%)
31. R. J. Donovan Correctional Facility (210.8%)
32. Lancaster State Prison (181.8%)

## California State Prisons

*Source:* California Department of Corrections, www.fdungan.com/map

having said, explaining that the million-dollar fences would save money in the long run because armed officers could be removed from prison gun towers. "The fence never goes to sleep. It doesn't go to the bathroom. It doesn't do any of those things. It's always working." It was also 1994 when standardized testing of reading skills among California fourth-graders placed them last in the nation, below Mississippi, tied only with Louisiana. It was 1995 when, for the first time, California spent more on its prisons than on its two university systems, the ten campuses of the University of California and the twenty-four campuses of California State University.

Through most of my life I would have interpreted the growth of the prison system and the diminution of the commitment to public education as evidence of how California had "changed." Only recently did I come to see them as the opposite, evidence of how California had "not changed," and to understand "change" itself as one of the culture's most enduring misunderstandings about itself.

## Questions for Discussion

1. Didion suggests that the desire of a town to have a prison is both a depressing reality and a reinvention of the survival mentality which has always allowed people to cope with California's realities. How does she define and explain the California mindset in this selection?
2. Does it surprise you to learn that initiatives like "three strikes" came through the lobbying efforts of the prison guards' union? Why do you think Didion includes this information in the piece?
3. According to the reading, are the costs of having a prison in one's community worth the benefits, when it's all totaled up?

## Ideas for Writing

1. Do some research on prisons and politics in California. Who has been behind recent ballot initiatives related to crime and punishment? What issues currently face the system? You might start your investigations with the California Department of Corrections and Rehabilitation website, www.cya.ca.gov.
2. Choose one of the new prisons Didion mentions and find out more about life in the town by looking online or using your library's search tools to check out the local newspaper. What place does the prison play in the life of the community? Write an essay in which you evaluate its impact on the area, whether economically, socially, or psychologically.

---

# A Hundred Rivers Run Through It
## WADE GRAHAM

*Wade Graham is an environmental writer and activist who has written for the* Los Angeles Times, The New Yorker, Harper's Magazine, Outside, *and other publications. Born and raised in*

*Santa Barbara and now living in Los Angeles, he is a trustee of Glen Canyon Institute, based in Salt Lake City, Utah, dedicated to restoring the canyons of the Colorado River, and editor of* Hidden Passage, The Journal of Glen Canyon Institute. *He holds a PhD in American history from UCLA.*

—————————— ✦ ——————————

In California, people like to say that water flows uphill to money, and by that measure there is a hell of a lot of money in California. Every year the state moves 14 trillion gallons of water, in directions mostly south, capturing it behind 1,200 dams on every river and stream of any size before fluming it hundreds of miles, lifting it over some mountain ranges and pumping it under others, fitting the sere landscape with a caul of pipes, ditches, and siphons that irrigates an agricultural empire far greater but not unlike the one that bloomed in the deserts of Babylon and ancient Egypt. And if wealth has tamed the water, then the water has made California wealthier still. The state's $1 trillion economy ranks it seventh among the earth's nations, and in addition to providing 55 percent of America's fruits, nuts, and vegetables, California has managed to become the sixth-largest agricultural exporter in the world by intensively farming a region that receives less than twenty inches of rain per year. The confluence of wealth and water has made the state populous as well—32 million thrive where nature herself would tolerate far fewer—and has rewarded its luckiest residents, the majority of whom have always come from somewhere else to this "last best place to start over," with a style of life so gratifying, so bountiful and gentle, as to seem like an afterlife. "Eureka," the state motto says: I have found it.

But for all its plenty, California is a land of great inequity. Seventy-five percent of its available water originates north of San Francisco Bay, while 75 percent of its water demand lies south of the bay. The agricultural interests that founded the state—and, in the first-come-first-served tradition that built the West, provided the basis for the tangle of water rights and laws that both state and federal governments must live by—today account for 80 percent of California's yearly consumption of water while providing just 2 percent of its total economy. For years California's farmers have used their vast allotment of water to grow such absurdly water-intensive and low-yield crops as rice in the north and alfalfa in the southeastern desert, in some areas paying a mere $3 an acre-foot[1]—far less than the cost of delivery to the taxpayer who financed the dams and the ditches—for water that can cost urban users in Los Angeles as much as $780 an acre-foot. Even at these prices, the same amount of water that would support 8 jobs growing grass for cattle might provide 16,000 jobs manufacturing silicon chips. Economists have pointed out that since urbanites and industry use far less water than does irrigated agriculture, all urban needs well into the future could be satisfied by shifting just 10 percent of agriculture's water to the cities—an increment easily absorbed by adopting standard conservation practices on the farm. But agriculture remains an enormously powerful lobby in California, and it has shown little inclination to surrender such a large part of its birthright in the name of efficiency.

And so the cities, generally in the south and generally under Los Angeles's flag and thumb, have obtained water wherever and however they could, most famously in the 1907 Owens Valley water grab that is the theme of Roman Polanski's 1974 film *Chinatown* but most successfully by looking east, first to the desert-bound Colorado River and then, beyond it, to the headwaters of federal subsidy in Washington. Of the water California uses each year, 12 percent descends from the 1,400-mile-long Colorado River, which provides water for 9 percent of the U.S. population and which seven Western states—California, Arizona, Nevada, Utah, Colorado, Wyoming, and New Mexico—divvy up with Mexico to meet their widely varied needs. Who is allowed to take what from the Colorado was codified in 1922 with the signing of a compact made from a hodgepodge of existing local laws, treaties, and contracts. Then, as now, the rules were improvised by those who got there first. The other basin states had barely awakened from the slumber of their territorial days before California reached out and secured for itself an outsized share of the stream: 4.4 million acre-feet as opposed to 3,881,250 for Colorado, 2,800,000 for Arizona, 1,725,000 for Utah, 1,500,000 for Mexico, 1,050,000 for Wyoming, 843,750 for New Mexico, and 300,000 for Nevada. Although the total claims on the river's water are greater than its 15 million acre-foot average annual flow, only California and Nevada use their full entitlements, and it is generally assumed that the four upper-basin states, which have no

---

[1]One acre-foot is enough water to cover an acre of land to a depth of one foot: about 326,000 gallons, or roughly enough water to last two average households one year.

major cities near the river's deep canyon, never will; even with Phoenix, air conditioned with power from the Colorado and growing at the giddy rate of an acre every hour, Arizona will not soon need all the Colorado River water to which it holds rights. This fact, and a bit of legerdemain with the water levels behind the northern dams, has allowed urban southern California, in the form of the gargantuan Metropolitan Water District (of which both L.A. and San Diego are members), to continue to divert an extra 500,000 acre-feet of its neighbors' unused entitlements through its aqueducts, paying no more than the standard 25 cents an acre-foot. The Bureau of Reclamation, a division of the Department of the Interior, has traditionally played the role of permissive parent—nudging California to move water from its huge irrigation projects, which clamor for it, to its proliferating cities, which need it; gently chastising the state for taking more than its share year after year; but generally devoting most of its attention to the environmental damage caused by half a century of federal dam building in the West. There has been no pressing need to do otherwise.

Over [several years in the 1990s], however, Secretary of the Interior Bruce Babbitt has taken to strolling along the Colorado's banks with a large stick in his hand and news photographers in tow, referring to himself as the "River Master" and vowing to make the system make more sense. He made a great noise, and he has made it at the behest of the other six river states, which, all grown up [by that time had], together and separately, pressured Babbitt and California for assurances that California could stay within its entitlement should the need arise. Eager Southern California developers, in other words, should not be allowed to take the extra water for granted. In 1996, for the first time, Arizona began claiming its full entitlement and pumping it into holes in the desert, in effect storing enormous amounts of groundwater and pushing the entire lower basin over its 7.5 million acre-feet apportionment. At that year's annual meeting of the Colorado River Water Users Association, it was clear that California had still made no progress toward coming up with an enforceable plan to satisfy its neighbors.

To keep the peace, Babbitt started attaching carrots to his ever-present stick in an effort to encourage the antagonists to reach an amicable and mutually profitable agreement. But eventually he realized that the only carrot he really had to dangle in front of the southern California cities was more water, which they would likely find a way to take with or without his help. And so in

December, at another meeting of the Colorado River Water Users Association, Bruce Babbitt finally did what all involved expected of him: on behalf of the United States government, he gave up. Abandoning the long-established policy of providing the greatest good to the greatest number, Babbitt announced plans for a regional market for water in the West, beginning with the legalization of interstate sales of Colorado River water. Plainly put, this was the largest deregulation of a national resource since the Homestead Act of 1862; the only thing that could have topped it would have been a privatization of all federal lands. The deals would be small at first (Nevada and the Metropolitan Water District have already arranged to pay Arizona to store water for future use), but in the long run the fast-growing southern states, and especially California, would be able to obtain, for a reasonable fee, vast quantities of water from a virtually limitless source.

Babbitt had delivered the carrot. More importantly, he had handed over the stick.

The notion that prices [would] do the work that Babbitt and the courts could not has been met with the sort of can-do optimism one still tends to associate with the Golden State when pollution, crime, and congested motorways are factored out. Even the Environmental Defense Fund has lent its support to the market idea, saying that market-based transfers are the best way to forestall the building of more dams. Many well-intentioned people also hope that the environmental lobby will emerge as a buyer of water, supported by government as it struggles to restore such damaged ecosystems as the Sacramento-San Joaquin Delta.[2] Most economists believe that the market will finally give agriculture the right incentives (that is, enough money) to sell the magic 10 percent of its water to the cities.

---

[2]The Delta, just east of San Francisco—the focus of the state's major watershed, through which drinking water for 20 million people and irrigation water for half the nation's fruits and vegetables passes—is on the verge of physical collapse: The levees and ancient peat islands that hold back the salty water of San Francisco Bay are crumbling. Huge batteries of federal and state pumps suck water from every source available through a tumult of islands, levees, and channels before jacking it up into twin aqueducts and exporting it to the fields and cities of central and southern California. At times of low river flow and high demand, the pumps pull so hard that the Bay's poisonous salt fingers come close to being sucked into the intakes. Three of the state's four races of chinook salmon are on the brink of extinction. It is also worth noting that California has lost 95 percent of its historic wetlands, more than any other state.

A market for water in the West might spare the federal government the unpleasant task of refereeing an interminable grudge match between those who have the water and those who want it, but there is little else that anybody can say with certainly about what the market will or will not accomplish. We do know, however, what it is meant to accomplish, and, bearing in mind the way in which the future tends to recapitulate the past, we can ask at least two leading questions. The first pertains to function:

Will the market ensure a fairer distribution of California's water?

Probably not. In southern California, it is a relatively simple matter to sell, with a proselyte's conviction, the idea that there is not enough water to go around, even while El Nino's storms [were] drenching the state. Over time the practice has become a familiar bunco game. Earlier [in 1998] the state's Department of Water Resources announced that by 2020, if more supplies were not found, California would face a shortfall of up to 7 million acre-feet in drought years—nearly as much as all its towns and cities together use today. The department cited a population expected to swell to 50 million by 2020, which is tantamount to the entire current population of New York State moving to California over the next twenty-two years. But California's total developed water supply, 42.6 million acre-feet, is enough, in a world without farmers, for 385 million people—more than seven times the population expected by 2020—to shower every morning, commute to work to make water-intensive silicon chips, then head home to wash their cars in their driveways and take a dip in the pool under the sunset's golden, dying rays. In this sense, the state has never had a water shortage and it likely never will. What it has, in the words of University of California ecologist Garrett Hardin, is a "people longage" in the cities and therefore a distribution problem. This problem is real, but it has typically been exaggerated to the point of prevarication whenever those in a position to profit from real estate development have wanted to change more water into more money. The scams are as old as the state, and as long ago as 1907, Los Angeles Department of Water and Power superintendent William Mulholland and his predecessor, Fred Eaton, manufactured a water crisis to ensure public support of their plan to build the Los Angeles Aqueduct and suck dry the Owens Valley, 250 miles to the northeast. Although L.A.'s population more than doubled in the time it took to finish the aqueduct and rob the Owens Valley farmers of their river and their way of life, at no time was the water actually needed; much of it went instead to the nearby San Fernando Valley, which a syndicate of the city's wealthiest men promptly turned into a subdivision. "Scarcity" has been one of California's favorite motivational tools ever since.

Water has always been relatively inexpensive in California. Some California cities, most notably Sacramento, consider the stuff too cheap to meter. But water from California's State Water Project has generally been 50 percent more expensive than water from the Colorado River, and the big Southern California buyers naturally have looked to take at least as much from the Colorado as the law allows. In a perfectly free market, the prices for water from different sources would achieve an equilibrium; that is, they would seek and equal one another. But price-fixing is something of a tradition in California, especially where water is concerned, and it might be overly optimistic to expect that the state's water buyers will suddenly cease such a lucrative practice for the dubious privilege of participating in a market.

Nor will a market for water in the West impose anything but more chaos on the already chaotic division of California's urban and rural terrain. There is no statewide process for integrating, or even registering, local plans, and, besides a rule that housing developments of over 500 units must state where their water will come from, there is no institutional link between growth and water planning whatsoever. In 1940, the 400-mile-long Central Valley sheltered 1.1 million people. By 1998, the population was 5.4 million, and as much as 12 percent of the valley, the richest farmland in America, has been developed—a process that will continue at an estimated rate of 15,000 acres a year. The state itself has predicted that by 2040 the valley will hold 15.5 million people, with one third of its farmland growing nothing but subdivisions and parking lots. By combining the existing general plans of 100 cities and 27 counties in the valley, one is able to see that by 2080, given business as usual, the valley will be home to 26 to 30 million people, all living in a continuous megacity stretching from Marysville, in Yuba County, 300 miles south to Bakersfield, in Kern County, just shy of the L.A. County line.

Because of the stiff property tax ceilings established by 1978's Proposition 13, local governments are forced to compete with one another for the kinds of development that can produce large amounts of revenue quickly. Wildlife refuges and farms simply will not do the trick; shopping malls and housing developments will. The second question is less a matter of function than of form:

Is it wise to surrender to the market a natural resource that so many depend upon but so few are in a position to control? By way of an answer, California's recent history provides a number of cautionary tales.

Most people in Southern California have no clear idea of where their water comes from, and they consider it no more remarkable that two thirds of the water they use each year should flow south, west, and uphill in giant aqueducts to serve their needs than that it should fall as rain from the (northern) sky. People in the north may not know exactly where it comes from, but they know full well where it goes, and the exporting of their water has long been a cause of resentment toward the more populous, more politically powerful south.

What has brought both the water and the resentment south is a jury-rigged delivery system once described, by Curt Schmutte of the Department of Water Resources, as "the fanciful carpentry of a madman." The system's thousands of component parts—waterways, dams, pipes, ditches, siphons, aqueducts, and pumping stations—are owned and operated in some instances by private companies and in others by local governments, the state, or one of two federal agencies: the Bureau of Reclamation and the Army Corps of Engineers, legendary and bitter rivals. The laws governing the water itself—to which rights were assigned and for which projects were built in vastly different eras under vastly different assumptions—are a litigator's dream, and everywhere the system is overlaid with five generations' worth of acrimonious lawsuits filed by the myriad agricultural, environmental, and urban interests that wage California's never-ending water war.

The system's monstrous sucking sound can be heard far into the northernmost part of the state, at the top of the water-rich Sacramento Valley (the northern section of the Central Valley), an elongate, bucolic plain running 125 miles from 14,162-foot Shasta volcano near the Oregon border down to Sacramento and the San Francisco Bay. The valley is watered by the biggest and most reliable rivers in the state as they tumble out of the sodden Coast Ranges to the west and the storm-scraping Sierra Nevadas to the east: the Sacramento, winding down from Shasta Dam, mother dam of the U.S. Bureau of Reclamation's massive Central Valley Project; and its skein of tributaries, including the Feather, which uncoils from the toe of Oroville Dam, mother dam of the Department of Water Resources State Water Project.[3] As the big rivers flow southward they bring to the valley a priceless gift: water to fill the deep, stratified aquifers that underlie it. Most towns and farms in the region have never diverted much of the surface stream flow. It has always been easy enough to dig a shallow well, and anyone above the aquifer has the right to do so. The rivers roll past largely unmolested, to slake greater thirsts downstream.

As a kid growing up in Santa Barbara in the 1970s, I used to be fond of climbing to the top of the mountains behind the city to look over the other side at the Cachuma and Gibraltar reservoirs, incongruous splashes of blue on a brown canvas of flammable chaparral. I watched them fill in winter and drop in summer, exposing bathtub rings of barren earth, and sometimes I watched brushfires raging in the backcountry, more often than not headed our way. There existed a direct, inverse correlation between water level and fire intensity, the two being visibly linked by drought: the lower the reservoirs, I knew, the worse off we were. Santa Barbara was a closed system then, a pocket, isolated by the ocean to the south and west and the mountains to the north and east, but what most set the city apart was its refusal to connect to the state's vast water grid. As I grew older, I came to understand that this was

---

[3]Together, these two massive projects compose the core of the system. The Central Valley Project authorized in 1935 by Franklin Delano Roosevelt, was conceived in large part to rescue farmers in the valley's dry southern section—the San Joaquin—who had used up nearly all of their groundwater and caused widespread land subsidence, in some areas up to thirty feet. The 602-foot-high Shasta Dam went up on the Sacramento, joined by sister dams on the San Joaquin and the Trinity, complete with canals to send the water south to growers. But this effort didn't slow the wheel of demand; rather, it seemed to hasten its spin. The project, meant to rescue 250,000 acres, actually put twelve times as many new acres under irrigation, much of it with groundwater. The aquifer tumbled further, the farmers wanted more water, and the government obliged, this time with a bizarre, decades-long competition between the Bureau of Reclamation and the U.S. Army Corps of Engineers for the best dam sites, regardless of economic or social consequence. By the late 1950s, only one major river draining the Sierra Nevadas remained free—the Feather. Then-governor Edmund "Pat" Brown helped convince taxpayers of the need for a State Water Project to dam the Feather and send its water to southern California by lying about the project's cost: he rounded down three quarters of a billion dollars or so to $1.75 billion, and forgot to mention the $1 billion price tag for Oroville Dam, the system's linchpin. When the bond issue passed by a mere 174,000 votes statewide, the project delivered only 2.5 millon acre-feet of the 4.2 million promised; Brown also had neglected to mention that the bonds would pay for only half the planned infrastructure and, hence, half the water.

more than a mere symbolic stance: beyond the mountains, connected to the grid and a co-dependent of it, loomed the malignant entity we called simply "L.A.," engulfing everything before it in an unchecked flow of asphalt, metal, and stucco, driving hundreds of thousands to seek haven in Santa Barbara and other communities not directly in the path of, or otherwise beholden to, the Blob. But in those months when the air grew hot and dry, and the brush once again caught fire within sight of our homes, it became more and more difficult to insist that L.A.'s narrative of smog, congestion, poverty, and crime was actually being written by the very hand now held out to us in our season of need—a virtually limitless, government-guaranteed supply of water.

In 1979, a year after Proposition 13 passed and won Californians the right to lower property taxes and more and more neighbors to make up the difference, Santa Barbara County's residents, anxious to preserve their small-town lifestyle, voted three to one against hooking up to the State Water Project. This, as much as anything else, made it a nice place, a quiet place—"like southern California was in its Golden Age," visitors would say. Without the water necessary to explode, the Santa Ynez Valley remained achingly beautiful, an open country of golden, grass-covered hills dotted with majestic valley oaks—a good picture of what the San Fernando Valley looked like before the barons of L.A. brought the Owens River to it. But on a Tuesday in June of 1991, after six years of drought that saw lawns and gardens turn brown—and restrictions imposed on washing cars and, eventually, bodies—a little over half of the voters who turned out cast their ballots for artificial rain, electing to join the State Water Project despite the fact that the drought had ended four months earlier. While the reservoirs and groundwater basins filled back up, life returned to normal: driveways were hosed down, lawns were reseeded, and residents once again sang in their showers. Then the bills from Sacramento began arriving.

The cities of Santa Barbara, Goleta, and Montecito had opted for small amounts of state water; few doubted that they could absorb the added cost. But in the small valley towns north of the mountains, officials realized that they were facing a series of imminent municipal defaults. Santa Maria, a city of 69,326 people in the north of the county, had ordered 17,820 acre-feet—as much as the entire south coast. By 2001, their state water bill would be $14.5 million every year; even after levying a 15 percent water-rate increase every year, the city would be unable to pay $7 million of it. In Solvang, a Danish-theme town of 5,122 known for quaint windmills and stores that sell pastries and wooden sabots, household water bills shot up to $300 a month. These voters learned too late that state water was five times as expensive as the water they formerly pumped from the ground, and that the city would be obliged to pay for it whether or not they actually used a single drop.

The little valley towns now [had] only one choice, and that [was] to grow their way out of debt. Quaint Solvang would have to more than triple the number of its water customers to pay off its debt without significantly raising water bills. Santa Maria, despite having furiously rezoned its farmland for tract housing, [could] not grow fast enough to break even: already on the hook for a $177 million share of the pipeline principal, the city borrowed another $40 million. Montecito, one of the wealthiest towns in America, [scrambled] to cover its $5 million yearly state water bill—for water it [would not] use. To compound the irony, state-water buyers are theoretically exempt from Proposition 13's property-tax ceiling. In other words, the County Board of Supervisors could raise property taxes. [So], with county taxpayers facing a billion-dollar debt they never agreed to, and with the specter of county-wide default looming over their elected leaders, only two outcomes are conceivable: higher taxes or more taxpayers.

Already the little realtors' flags are flapping. Ugly, "Spanish," two-story boxes are appearing on streets with faux-bucolic names cut into the golden grass of the valley. I am reminded, when I see this artificially seeded development, of two quotes. The first is from Christopher Lasch, who wrote, in *The Revolt of the Elites*,

> "[The market] does not easily coexist with institutions that operate according to principles antithetical to itself: schools and universities, newspapers and magazines, charities, families."

The second is from Marc Reisner's *Cadillac Desert*, and it provides a bit of bas relief to a man who devoted the sum of his career to bringing ever more water to Los Angeles, despite what that water cost in human misery: "Mulholland begged the city fathers to end their abject deification of growth. The only way to solve the city's water problem, he grumbled aloud, was to kill the members of the Chamber of Commerce."

One windy recent afternoon, I stood on a beach watching whitecaps race on a blue desert lake. I tossed a rock the size of my fist—a chunk of pumice, spat up thousands of years before by a nearby volcanic vent—and it floated on water more saline than the Pacific Ocean. It floated because the water, like so much of

California's water, was never meant to be there in the first place. This 380-square-mile puddle, the Salton Sea, was inadvertently created in 1905, when an attempt to divert the Colorado River to irrigate the Imperial Valley went hopelessly awry. The water blew out a levee in a channel dug to tap the river, and it headed here, to the low point in the valley, known, until it filled with enough water to be visible from space and began to bring up the desert salt, as the "Salton Sink." In the 1950s, the lake was quite the recreational spot; thousands came for the camping and water sports. Now the area is a wasteland, its exuberant past evident only in the mobile homes rusting by the water's edge.

Shore birds and water fowl still fancy the lake, however, and hundreds of species regularly stop off here during their spring and fall migrations. But over the last few years the water has become a breeding ground for disease, and thousands of birds that land here each season never resume their journeys. Lately among the dead have been endangered brown pelicans. Botulism attacks their nervous systems, weakening them until they cannot lift their heads above the water's surface. Eventually, bobbing on a sea made by man's folly, surrounded by scorching desert, they drown.

## Questions for Discussion

1. What is the relationship of water to growth in the small towns Graham talks about, and why might it be said that things work backwards to what one might think?

2. Several times, the article says that California's problem is not lack of water, but ineffective use, particularly for agricultural purposes. Graham argues, further, that no reasonably foreseeable increase in population will create disaster. What evidence does he provide of this, and why, if this is the case, is there still so much panic about water, according to the article?

3. Many people who talk about water and California say that Los Angeles, particularly, should not exist and would not, except for the water brought there from elsewhere. Where do you see this point of view discussed in this article? What stance does the writer, who says he is from Santa Barbara, take on the "Southland's" consumption habits?

## Ideas for Writing

1. After reading the article, particularly if you live in California, what is your attitude toward the issue of water use and conservation? Research the era in

California when water was rationed. How did rationing change behavior? Is there evidence that the changes outlasted the crisis? Write an essay in which you discuss water policies and politics in the state.

2. Watch the movie *Chinatown*, referenced in the essay. What point of view does it influence you to take on the history of water politics in Southern California? How does this complement what you read in Graham's article? Write an essay in which you discuss the historical aspects of water in California. As you write, explain what you would change if you could step back in time and create a different system for water acquisition and distribution in the state.

---

# Sour Grapes: California Farm Workers' Endless Struggle 40 Years Later

## MARC COOPER

*Marc Cooper is a columnist for the* LA Weekly *whose articles, essays, and interviews have appeared in scores of publications including the* Washington Post, *the* London Times, The Nation, The New Yorker, Harper's Magazine, Playboy, *and* Rolling Stone. *His books include* Roll Over Che Guevara: Travels of A Radical Reporter *(Verso 1996) and* The Last Honest Place in America: Paradise and Perdition in the New Las Vegas. *He teaches journalism at the USC Annenberg School of Communication and also serves as Senior Fellow for Border Justice at Annenberg's Institute for Justice and Journalism.*

---- ✦ ----

Arvin, California—When I knock on the door of the Orange Street address I've been given in this dusty down-at-the-heels agricultural town, I get only a shrug when I ask for Pedro Cruz. Pedro works the same Valpredo bell-pepper farm as did 41-year-old Salud Zamudio-Rodriguez, who passed out and died in 105-degree heat, one of three California farm workers to die last month [summer 2005].

"Never heard of Pedro Cruz," the obviously middle-class Latina woman at the doors says brusquely. "Maybe in the back," she adds, cocking her head toward the backyard. Indeed, there, along a rutted alley, are some improvised rental units stacked on top of each other.

I find Pedro and his wife, Felipa, both 45, in the bottom unit—a clean but claustrophobic 350-square-foot apartment with a combination living room/bedroom, a tiny bathroom, and a galley kitchen where an old man, one of their parents, I presume, sits in khaki pants and a T-shirt and swats at flies. An aging window cooler loudly grinds away and reduces the room temperature to an almost bearable level.

Like 75,000 or more of California's field workers, Pedro and Felipa are indigenous Mixtec from Oaxaca, and their Spanish is heavily accented. They are gracious but shy and reticent, and their demeanor is marked by an air of resignation. They live a life in which there is little guesswork.

And having just come back from work, they are bone tired. Pedro drives a tractor on the bell-pepper farm, a relatively skilled job for which he is paid, he says, $6.85 an hour—a dime more than minimum wage. He stumbles over the name of the grower he works for. In fact, he's not exactly sure, because it's really a middle-man labor contractor who employs him. "He's the one who pays us, and he's the one who sets the rules," he says. And now, clearly having said all he wants to, he politely but decidedly turns his gaze to the floor.

Felipa fills the opening. She works grapes for Sun Pacific— which she pronounces soon-pacie—but she says she can imagine how her husband's co-worker Salud died. "To pick the chiles," she says, "you have to run behind the tractor and then be on your knees all day. You are under those vines, bent over in the heat, and you can't breathe. Pobre señor," she says of the deceased, putting her hands over her heart.

"In my work, it is also very hard," Felipa continues. "The foreman demands that each team of three people produce 72 tubs of grapes per day." A tub holds 23 pounds of grapes, sorted, cleaned, bunched and packed in plastic ready for supermarket shelves. "Sometimes it goes up to 96 tubs," Felipa says. "We don't have time to take our breaks. If you turn in less than they ask for, they run you out after three days."

I ask her if she knows that the law requires farm workers be given at least two 10-minute breaks a day, apart from a 30-minute lunch. Unmoving and silent, she merely smiles back at me—as if to say, "What kind of idiot are you?"

**As last month's heat wave peaked** on a sweltering Friday afternoon, the scene unfolding in this farm town on the outskirts of Bakersfield, only an hour and a half, but two worlds, removed from Hollywood Boulevard, might have seemed to many like a sun-induced mirage.

Some 350 people, young and old, many holding the red-and-black flags of the United Farm Workers union, others lofting hand-lettered signs in Spanish reading "No more deaths!" and "Stop the Speed-ups!" braved the thermometer and trudged an hourlong path from a local park to rally on the patio of the historic St. Thomas the Apostle Church.

The crowd sweated and sucked on frozen fruit bars in the oven-hot church courtyard, as a handful of union speakers—including the near-legendary UFW co-founder Dolores Huerta—denounced the recent spate of heat-related deaths, called on the state Legislature to finally enact a long-languishing heat-abatement bill, and kicked off an organizing drive to win a livable field-worker wage of $8 to $10. The assembled hundreds punctuated the oratorical jabs with choruses of "*Sí se puede!*" and "*Viva Chavez!*"

It was a labor-driven political demonstration of enormous proportions for this sleepy village of only 12,000 people where most of the inhabitants' days begin with a silent predawn ride into the unforgiving fields and then melt into the midafternoon, lazing in front of the room fan with a cold beer and some *música ranchera* on the radio. But one, no doubt, fueled by the banner headline in that morning's *Bakersfield Californian*: "Farm worker may be the latest heat victim."

The corpse of 40-year-old fruit picker Augustine Gudino had been found the day before in the triple-digit heat baking the local Giumarra Vineyards. For the previous week, the United Farm Workers had been scrambling to mount the rally to protest the heat-exposure deaths of two other local pickers in the past 10 days. It was by macabre coincidence that the third fatality was reported the day of the protest itself, adding an extra dollop of indignation and stoking the turnout.

"This is the first time in more than 15 years we've seen anything like this," said Fausto Sanchez, a 34-year-old Mixtec community-outreach worker who works at the local office of the California Rural Legal Assistance (CRLA). "I've been around here since 1988 and can't remember any march like this."

For those Californians who live outside the Central Valley, Sanchez's wonderment over the UFW rally might seem a little odd. There's a prevailing popular assumption that superexploitation of the state's farm workers is a closed chapter in some deep, dark past. And that while immigrant fruit pickers and packers might not be getting rich, somehow the struggle of the late Cesar Chavez and his UFW had "solved" the most pressing problems of these workers and forever curbed the worst abuses of the growers.

But exactly 40 years after Chavez's UFW exploded into the national consciousness by leading the great 1965 Delano grape workers' strike and forced America to recognize the plight of those who put our food on the table, nothing could be further from the truth. The golden years of California farm workers lasted barely a decade and then sharply began to fade. "Since the late 1970s, it's all been downhill, it's all been on the defensive," says Oxnard-based CRLA attorney Jeff Ponting.

The landmark 1975 Agricultural Labor Relations Act (ALRA) that passed during the Jerry Brown administration promised a New Deal for farm workers. Today it is little more than a historical asterisk. Wages among California's 700,000 farm workers, 96 percent of whom are Mexican or Central American, more than half of whom are undocumented, are at best stagnant, and by most reckonings are in decline. With almost all workers stuck at the minimum wage of $6.75 an hour, it's rare to find a farm worker whose annual income breaks $10,000 a year. "Twenty-five years ago, a worker made 12, 13, 14 cents for a bin of oranges," says economist Rick Mines, until recently research director at the Davis-based California Institute for Rural Studies. "Today that same bin pays maybe 15 or 16 cents—in spite of 250 percent inflation." Virtually no workers have health insurance or paid vacations. The cyclical nature of the crops throws most out of work for two or more months per year.

In a pattern that one academic calls "ethnic replacement," succeeding waves of ever poorer, more marginal Mexicans, many of them from indigenous communities where Spanish is a foreign language, increasingly constitute the field labor force. The downward-spiraling Mexican economy feverishly churns those waves to the degree that, at any moment, as many as 20 percent of California's agricultural workers have been in the U.S. for less than a year.

Family ranchers and corporate growers have shirked legal and moral responsibilities by outsourcing more and more employment through unscrupulous middleman contractors who feast on the undocumented and the desperate by routinely short-changing them, forcing them to work unpaid overtime, ignoring safety standards, bilking them for rides and rental of tools, and, more frequently than one can imagine, straight-out stiffing them on payday.

The confluence of labor-contracting schemes, hostile Sacramento administrations, historic strategic mistakes by the UFW, and the flood of ever more desperate undocumented workers have, meanwhile, eroded unionization to the minuscule level of less than 2 percent of the work force.

While the 30-year-old pro-worker provisions of the ALRA still look great on paper, field enforcement by the state has become less than lax. Whether through indifference or through sheer lack of resources—including an almost total absence of representatives who can speak the indigenous languages of many workers—the result is grim. "Nowadays, it takes about nine months for a worker to even get a state wage hearing," laments Fresno-based CRLA lawyer Alegria de la Cruz, whose grandparents were key players in the UFW. "By then the contractor is usually out of business. It's basically, 'Fuck you, I'm not going to pay you.'" For that majority of workers who hold no legal immigration status, there are no hearings, no legal remedies whatsoever.

Also defying the stereotypes of the popular imagination, most California farm workers are no longer roving bands of migrants, following the trails of different crops and periodically returning to Mexico. The decade-old U.S. border policy of blockading traditional crossing points and forcing migrant traffic into ever more perilous routes has bottled up California farm workers into more permanent, more settled, more impoverished communities, creating a vast rural underclass that further strains already underserviced Central Valley towns. "Field work is no longer a way to improve your life," Fausto Sanchez said as we stood next to a sprawling grape orchard just west of town and listened to the booms of shotgun blanks fired to scare off the birds. Until seven years ago, when he was hired by CRLA, Sanchez worked these same fields. His wife still works the crops. "In the past, a family could save up three to four thousand dollars from a good season of grapes and then return to Mexico. Now, maybe you can make a thousand dollars, and you're stuck here."

And *stuck* is the right word. One recent survey estimated that nearly a third of farm-worker families lived in "informal dwellings," lacking legal addresses. Cruise the side streets of this town, or nearby Lamont, or virtually any of the hamlets and towns north to Stockton, and you are sure to drift into the unpaved nether neighborhoods in which ramshackle trailers, plywood sheds, collapsing wood-frame shacks, converted garages and out-of-code apartments—many of them managed by slumlord rental agencies—are jam-packed with beds and tenants.

Yes, they are all clichés: The New Grapes of Wrath. The New Harvest of Shame. The Appalachia of the West. And yet, they are all befitting. When journalist Carey McWilliams published his historic exposé of California's treatment of farm laborers in 1939— the same year that *The Grapes of Wrath* appeared—the title of his book decried what he saw as "Factories in the Field." But today, California farm workers would be downright blessed to work with the same wages and conditions that define the average American factory—even with the long-term decline experienced by industrial workers. Instead, today's field workers toil in what are little more than sweatshops in the sun.

**CRLA lawyer Jeff Ponting** takes me on a driving tour of the Arvin-Lamont area, and his default mode is indignation. "Throughout this valley we see the rise of Latino elected political leadership," he says as we pull into the flyspeck settlement of Weedpatch and the car-dashboard thermometer reads 111 degrees. "But because Latinos have so little economic force, they have little real power. The poor people here have no voice."

Founded in 1965 alongside the UFW, the nonprofit CRLA, and its network of ascetic offices stretched through the valley, acts as one-stop no-fee legal defenders of farm workers. A strangely surviving remnant of the Great Society, it continues to receive federal funding—but with increasing begrudgement and limitations (Governor Ronald Reagan terminated its state funding in the early '70s). Under the tutelage of the congressionally created Legal Services Corp., the CRLA can no longer press class-action lawsuits. And it no longer can represent the undocumented.

But along with a private Los Angeles firm, Ponting is currently leading a fight on behalf of locals who got doused in a massive pesticide drift. There's been at least one major drift incident in each of the last four years in this area—most recently last May, when 27 people fell ill. The worst case was in October 2003, when a cloud of the fumigant chloropicrin—the same active ingredient that's used in tear gas—floated off the Yaksitch Farms and enveloped scores, including 165 who are now suing. "People were vomiting, throwing up on the streets, kids were crying and screaming," Ponting says. "It was chaos. And this happens every year. But medical people don't know how to deal with it. They don't speak the language of the workers. The clinics don't know how to recognize the symptoms. They give the workers aspirins and send them back to work."

Ponting walks me from the field across the two-lane state Highway 184. Here are the grotesquely named Spic N' Span apartments, eight small wooden bungalows with peeled paint and warped linoleum floors, lined up on a dirt alley. I pace them off as being about 20 by 15 feet. Though they rent for about $300 a month through a management agency, they wouldn't even qualify for as much as slum status. More like Tobacco Road.

Spic N' Span was ground zero for the 2003 chloropicrin episode. But when we enter one of the units, 19-year-old Rocio Diaz, with her 10-month-old baby, Maire, parked in a basket in front of the window air conditioner, knows nothing of the incident. Freshly arrived from the Mexican state of Guerrero, she begins at zero in California farm-labor history. Rocio's 22-year-old husband is off working at Lucky Farms, she says, earning minimum wage for only six or seven hours of work a day. In the face of the recent farm-worker deaths, his employer is apparently being cautious.

Though the rent is $295, she says, the family will now have to make do on the $700 or so per month that her husband will bring home. She has had to quit working the fields this week because paying a babysitter $10 a day and forking out $5 every day to the "*raitero*," the van driver her contractor was forcing her to use, was eating up most of her take-home pay. "We were living in East Los Angeles, but it got too expensive, so we moved here," she says. "I hope we can make it."

Later that afternoon, Ponting and I randomly come across a nearby group of about 40 laborers, just finishing up a day's worth of picking and packing for El Rancho Farms. At the end of each row of vines, packers, usually wearing straw hats and bandannas across their faces, work standing up at a table under an umbrella. Talking to them, we learn they are paid minimum wage plus a bonus of 30 cents per 23-pound tub of grapes. They can produce about three tubs an hour, adding about $7 a day to their earnings—a grand total of about $60 a day gross.

We also learn that this crew is allowed to take only one break per day, not two. That's one labor-code violation. The workers also say they are forced to take home the grape tubs every night and it is their responsibility to wash them and clean them on their own time. Another violation.

"This may seem like little," says Ponting. "But add it all up and it saves the contractor a lot of money, allowing him to undercut others."

This "layered" structure of contractors and subcontractors has always been present in the farm-labor market, but it has become dominant only since the late 1980s. As immigration, especially illegal immigration, began to soar, California growers were anxious to insulate themselves from legal responsibilities. Farm-labor contractors became a convenient back channel for workers. The FLCs, as they are known, offer the growers not only a package price for labor, but also plausible deniability. It's also a great way to foil union organizing.

"Agribusiness's reliance on contractors as intermediaries in recruiting and maintaining their work force is a disastrously irre-sponsible policy," says Ed Kissam, senior researcher at Aguirre International, a Bay Area consulting firm specializing in farm labor. "The contractors are squeezed by the growers, and the workers are squeezed by the contractors, who often are not very sophisticated business planners. They often figure the easiest way I can make a profit is to cheat my workers," says Kissam.

Some contractors have worked their way up from being fore-men. Others have constructed their niche by mining the fertile recruiting fields of their hometown Mexican villages, opening free-flowing pipelines of cheap cross-border labor. Many are out-of-pocket fly-by-night operations. Yet others have mushroomed into major business enterprises. "Some FLCs issue 15,000 W-2 forms per year," says Don Villarejo, founder and director emeritus of the California Institute for Rural Studies. "They lease not only the workers, but also the tools and equipment to the growers. Some run 140 buses a day."

What a near totality of the contractors have in common is that they were once themselves farm workers. "If you ask me what the single greatest problem is that we face," says CRLA's Fausto Sanchez, "I'd say it's just getting the workers their minimum wage. A lot of contractors just pay cash, a fixed amount, maybe $35 to $40 a day. It's sad how these contractors have forgotten who they once were. They have no shame. They have even less compassion."

Not that workers employed directly by the bigger growers have it any better. Forty-year-old Mixtec Pedro Ramirez has worked the last three years for Giumarra Vineyards, one of the largest grape growers in the world, with 4,000 workers. I meet him on the porch of his dilapidated trailer, which he bought 10 years ago for $6,000. The space he leases in the Arvin-area Buena Vista Trailer Park—a collection of tin that seems taken from a post-hurricane damage report—runs $230 a month. He works a daily nine-hour shift with no overtime, which is perfectly legal in agri-cultural labor. With the standard 30-cents-a-tub bonus, he makes about $70 a day before deductions. "At Giumarra, they don't give

us umbrellas, they don't give us a table, and we have to take home
the tubs and wash them," he says in Spanish.

"They make us do four tubs an hour," Ramirez continues.
"One struggles, but sometimes you can't make that number. If you
don't, you stay after work another half-hour or hour until you do."

"With no pay?" I ask.

He nods his head. "You can't say anything," he continues.
"Raise your voice and the foreman comes right down on you."
Ramirez and his wife have spent the last 18 years working in the
California fields and now have five children—none of whom have
been or will be allowed to work the fields. "I don't want that for
my children," he says. "That's why I have made the sacrifices for
their education. I don't want them to have to do the work I do."

**In 1936, reporter John Steinbeck** came to this same area
and became so engrossed in the lives of Okie farm workers that he
decided to live for a while in Weedpatch—where Jeff Ponting and
I retraced the pesticide drift of two years ago. His eventual *The
Grapes of Wrath* was set, in part, in the federally managed
Weedpatch Camp for migrant farm laborers that opened a few
hundred yards down the road from where he was staying in that
same year of 1936. When the classic Henry Fonda movie version
of the book was filmed, the camp figured prominently as a set.

Now it's called the Arvin Migrant Labor Camp. It's run by
Kern County and not the feds. Its primitive wooden cabins have
been replaced by truly gleaming and modern multibedroom bungalows surrounded by lush green sod. But the camp's 88 units still
house migrant farm workers, who can stay here with their families for up to six months at a time for about $75 a week. There's
also a fully equipped and up-to-date playground for the children.
Altogether it provides a dignified, comfortable and affordable
haven for families who work the fields. It's a reassuring reminder
of what effective government—even local government—can do for
people if there's sufficient political will.

Near the gated entrance to the camp, a couple of thousand
square feet have been fenced off to preserve the original wooden
community center, one of the clapboard migrant cabins and some
rusted farm implements. Local activists are raising money to
build some sort of park and monument to the Dust Bowl refugees
on the fenced-off plot.

When I meet with 48-year-old Gregorio Santiago in Unit 151,
he knows none of this history. Never heard of Steinbeck. Never
heard of *The Grapes of Wrath*. Never heard of Tom Joad. He's
rather excited by all this information I'm giving him, and he

writes down the title of Steinbeck's novel in Spanish so he'll remember to buy a copy.

I'm also struck by the glaring ironies of this situation. Santiago's ignorance is not because he's a stupid or unworldly man. On the contrary, he's an eloquent autodidact, a worker-intellectual with a long history in radical Oaxacan politics. He has two computers and a shelf of books. His grade school daughter possesses a graceful refinement and openness way beyond her years. He's had his own radio show in Baja California. He writes essays about his Mixtec heritage. Apart from working full time in the grape fields, he leads local events that celebrate indigenous culture. Coming back and forth to American fields since 1979, he organized a grassroots political committee in Arvin 20 years ago to take on a hostile local police force.

Now, he and a dozen or so other workers—all Mixtecs—have once again formed a new activist organization, called El Comité de Unidad Popular, the Popular Unity Committee.

Santiago is, in many ways, a Mixtec descendant of Tom Joad, even though he knows nothing of Joad or of his creator. Santiago's world is strictly in the here and now of rapacious contractors, intimidated workers, detestable working conditions and the cultural survival of a people forced to work in an alien world where they are powerless if not just plain invisible. Nostalgia over the Okies is about as relevant to Santiago as would be discussion of Oaxacan farming techniques in the Silver Lake Democratic Club.

Activist groups like his are not at all uncommon in the valley, especially among the Mixtecs, the fastest-growing minority among California farm workers. They have tried, with mixed success, to fill the void left by the shrinking of the UFW. Most prominent among these grassroots groups is the Bi-National Oaxacan Indigenous Front, which has a lot more presence around Fresno than it does here in the Bakersfield area. The Front may have as many as 10,000 members on both sides of the border, and in the Central Valley, it has become the leading Mixtec nonprofit.

Santiago's fledgling group is much more modest. But talk about the ghost of Tom Joad. Sitting in his camp bungalow, just back from the fields, still dressed in a dusty undershirt, jeans and work boots, a black cap on his head, Santiago speaks of his grand vision:

**Maybe even four years ago, things were better here**. The supervisors were more attentive, made sure you have water, more or less respectful of the law. Now it's constant psychological pressure to work faster and pick more. They say if you don't work fast enough, you won't work again. Decent treatment? That's all in the past.

"We need to re-introduce our youth to our culture. Over the long run, we need direct political participation. But before we can think about that, our community needs a deep political education.

"We come from a very different culture, but we live here and we have rights. We have earned our rights and earned our voice through our economic contribution.

"More than anything, we need to organize ourselves, just like other workers do, to achieve our goals. In the long run, we need a union. A real union. But in the short run, we need political consciousness, a real understanding of who we are, how we fit in and how we can achieve what we need.

"We hear a lot about the achievements of Cesar Chavez. But we can't see any of them. Where are they? Truth is, the UFW has no strength here, not among our people. We remember how, when the Mixtecs first began to organize, Cesar called us 'communists.' That's okay, he's gone. We need our own organizations now that speak to our heart, our own union."

When we're finished speaking, I walk out with Santiago to gander once again at the preserved remnants of the original Okie camp. He stares at them a moment and then shakes his head and smiles at me. "That's an incredible story you told me about these people," he said. "They must have been very strong."

In 2004, the daily *Bakersfield Californian* published a devastating multipart investigative series on Cesar Chavez's United Farm Workers that portrayed the union as remote from workers, tiny in numbers and a hotbed of Chavez-family nepotism. The series characterized the union founded by Chavez as nowadays just one part of a $150 million group of interlocking nonprofits, including housing, education and property-management agencies, along with a network of nine radio stations—together providing comfortable employment for the heirs of Chavez, who died in 1993, while simultaneously organizing and unionizing a scant few farm workers.

The *Californian* reports also detailed how staff salaries rose six-fold since 1992. And while public contributions, not union dues, were the primary source of revenue for the farm-worker movement, expenditures on administration and staff were far greater than those spent on charitable projects by the UFW and its allied organizations.

At the same time as the union was claiming 27,000 workers (down from its historic high of 80,000 in the mid-'70s), the newspaper could account for only about 5,000 UFW members under contract.

"If you ask me on the record what I think about the *Californian* series, I will tell you it's all a pack of lies," says a veteran farm-worker advocate who still works in alliance with the UFW. "If you ask me off the record, I will tell you it was absolutely on target."

Perhaps what's most damning about the *Californian* series is how little it resonated, how little attention and reaction it drew. The relative silence didn't reflect so much on the integrity of the reporting (which was rock-solid) but instead suggested that the paper was feverishly punching out a straw man.

Anyone who works among California farm workers, anyone who counts them in the valley, can easily recite and lament the sorry decline of the UFW.

"Go out in the fields and ask today's workers what they think of Cesar Chavez and they will say, 'Oh, you mean Julio Cesar Chavez the boxer,' " says Don Villarejo, founder of the Institute for Rural Studies. "A focus on Cesar and his legacy has much more traction with middle-class liberals than it does with actual farm workers, many of whom have just arrived in the U.S."

UFW influence crested in 1975 with passage of the Agricultural Labor Relations Act, which brought state regulation to the fields, with the union administering scores of contracts up and down the valley. For a brief historic period, farm-worker wages and conditions were visibly and markedly rising.

Within a decade it would all go into reverse. The last time the UFW actually led a strike was in 1979—26 years ago. The Republican Deukmejian and Wilson administrations turned state government away from workers' rights and toward the growers. "But Cesar must also be assigned part of the responsibilities here," says Villarejo. "In the early '80s he abandoned any real notion of organizing and instead poured the union's resources into politics. And if you don't organize, you will die."

There were other strategic mistakes. The UFW's platinum-level legal department fell apart when Chavez tried to force its lawyers to move to the union's remote hillside compound and accept $5-a-week salaries. The marathon grape boycott of the 1980s (and '90s) sucked up union resources, and while it inspired two generations of college students, it failed to obstruct nonunion grape production.

Chavez's union was also deeply inbred with a native Chicano movement, U.S.-born Latinos who populated the fields. Until his death, Chavez opposed illegal immigration, which he saw as little more than an employer gambit to drive down wages. But by the time of Chavez's 1993 passing, the world had shifted under his union's feet. Undocumented immigrants who didn't know what the word *Chicano* meant were already the bulk of field workers.

Writing in *The Nation* magazine on the heels of Chavez's funeral, UFW sympathizer and leftist chronicler Frank Bardacke sharply declared: "[A]t the time of Cesar Chavez's death, the U.F.W. was not primarily a farmworker organization. It was a fund-raising operation, run out of a deserted tuberculosis sanitarium in the Tehachapi Mountains, far from the field of famous Delano, staffed by members of Cesar's extended family and using as its political capital Cesar's legend and the warm memories of millions of aging boycotters."

Chavez died a dozen years ago, and the union has, often erratically, been trying to regroup ever since. Chavez's successor, his son-in-law Arturo Rodriguez—who still heads the union—has made various stabs at restarting La Causa. Ironically, the UFW today has more punch in Sacramento lobbying than it does in the fields. And the mystique of the Chavistas still inspires considerable fear and loathing among the growers and their allies.

On the ground, however, the UFW remains weak. A full-on push to organize strawberry workers in the late '90s, a drive supported with the muscle and millions of the AFL-CIO, failed. The union did have some successes in organizing mushroom workers. And it has a model contract for the 800 workers of the Kern County Bear Creek Corp., a major rose producer owned by a Japanese pharmaceutical company.

UFW leader Rodriguez also reversed the union's anachronistic position on immigration. And a few weeks ago, he allied the UFW with the Change to Win coalition, the dissident unions, some of which departed the AFL-CIO, wanting to put a greater emphasis on organizing.

But in 2005, Cesar Chavez's United Farm Workers doesn't have a single contract with a Central Valley table-grape grower.

Villarejo, and other sympathetic observers, put the current, real UFW membership at about 8,000 to 9,000 members—a tenth of its historic high. Two other unions, the Teamsters and the Food Workers, together represent another 7,000 California field workers. All told, a paltry 2 percent or so of California's field laborers have any union representation.

UFW spokesman Marc Grossman freely admits the obstacles to union organizing. "The only way you can get recognized is to win an election, and nowadays that is very difficult. We know in many areas most of the workers are undocumented, and that makes it very, very hard. As does labor contracting."

What the union can do, Grossman says, is to "help farm workers through what we call direct organizing, getting back to the early 1960s days of the UFW. The old community-service model."

But it remains unclear what leverage can be brought to bear politically, a shortcoming Grossman identifies, since the UFW can't inspire and mobilize significant numbers of farm workers. Even under the Democratic administration of Gray Davis, the UFW had to stage a march on Sacramento and threaten a hunger strike on the steps of the state Capitol to get the governor to sign a bill that imposed labor mediation on recalcitrant growers.

And the UFW has been inordinately lucky under Governor Arnold Schwarzenegger, who has treated the farm-worker issues better than his two Republican predecessors. He has kept a promise not to tilt the Agricultural Labor Relations Board to the right. Last year, Arnold signed a pesticides-drift bill that enraged the growers, and he signed a regulation banning hand weeding for which the UFW had long been lobbying. And last week, after the outrage over the three farm-worker deaths, Schwarzenegger announced emergency heat-abatement regulations requiring employers to provide water and shade for laborers who become sick in the scorching heat.

But in the long term, the viability of the UFW—the union—has to come down to finding some way to organize. One strategy is to adopt a model pioneered by the Service Employees International Union, says UC Davis professor Philip Martin, who has written two books on California farm labor. "You can try and get around the contractor issue by targeting your pressure on the ultimate beneficiary of the work that's performed," he says. And, with some luck, if comprehensive immigration reform now being considered is enacted and significant numbers of agricultural workers are legalized, the balance of forces on the ground might shift.

Some observers argue that the UFW's most significant role at present is, precisely, to continue its lobbying for immigration reform. As to its historic failures, economist Rick Mines perhaps provides the most lucid broader context. "The problems with the conditions of California farm workers are so much bigger than the problems of the UFW," he says. "A head of lettuce costs a dollar in the store, and only 3 or 4 cents go to the farm worker. We could double that to 6 cents, not feel it at all, yet it would make a huge impact in the lives of the workers. There are only a few hundred farm-worker union activists, but there are 34 million Californians. When you see that this society has chosen to have an entire group of people living in very marginal communities—rife with alcoholism, domestic violence, health problems, and leaving women and children abandoned back in the sender areas—then you see something that is so shameful that the problems with the UFW quickly recede."

**Two days after the big UFW rally,** on the third Sunday in July, there is yet another protest march in the Arvin area, again drawing about 300 people. This time it begins at the old Weedpatch crossroads. Two days, two protests—after years of relative inactivity. Something is happening here.

At the head of this protest is 75-year-old UFW co-founder Dolores Huerta. She's not wearing her union hat, however. This demonstration has been planned for months by the Dolores Huerta Foundation. It's a relatively new group that Dolores has set up, recruiting heavily among students and putting its emphasis on community organizing. It's not exactly a rival to the UFW, but there can be little doubt it's a competitor of sorts. At least, that's the way some UFW people see it. Some folks working directly with Dolores tell me the UFW march of the previous Friday was hastily assembled because the union was afraid Dolores' group was getting too far out in front of them. "We knew if we went ahead with this campaign, the union would feel it would have to jump in, and that's good," says one of Huerta's lieutenants.

*"Sueldos Justos"* is the theme of this protest—Just Wages. Though it's only 9 in the morning, the sun is already scalding, and Dolores is sweating profusely as she buzzes around her marching troops. But she seems elated, doing what she likes to do best. Marching up from Weedpatch through the somnolent Sunday sidewalks of Lamont, the bullhorns blazing, the crowd chanting, Dolores is beaming. "This is what it's about," she says to me enthusiastically. "It's about community organizing. It's about house meetings. It's about college kids, it's about bringing the women together. It's about going back to the way we used to do things."

It seems that for better and for worse, 40 years later, it's about finding the strength to start all over again from scratch.

## Questions for Discussion

1. Cooper states more than once that the public's perception of the plight of farm workers has not kept up with their worsening situation. What proofs does the article use to show the dismal situation of the farm workers? Further, what clues do the author's language and approach give to show that he expects sympathy from his readers?

2. One strategy which the large companies take to avoid being responsible for the exploitation of workers is to use farm-labor contractors (FLCs). Explain how this system works and what some of its abuses are, according to the article.
3. Cooper's article takes a guarded viewpoint, at best, when talking about the ability of the United Farm Workers to accomplish change for the laborers. Trace out the argument, explaining the shortfalls that Cooper details. What alternatives does he suggest?

## Ideas for Writing

1. According to the piece, the UFW organization has lost a good deal of strength since its heyday, and now faces questions concerning its effectiveness and the motivations of current leaders. Do some research on the United Farm Workers and write an essay in which you explain whether the group is effective in its efforts or whether another approach, like the one represented by El Comité de Unidad Popular or the Bi-National Oaxacan Indigenous Front, is better suited to the contemporary situation.
2. The "Oakies" mentioned in the article represent another era of disenfranchisement in California farm-labor politics. Research the Dust Bowl Migration during the Great Depression, then write an essay in which you argue *either* that the situation, including both its causes and effects, is much the same now as it was back then *or* that this generation of farm workers represents a different group with a unique set of concerns. You might want to consider how Steinbeck's novel *The Grapes of Wrath* provides historical context for your argument.

---

# Mind Your Language
## HENG L. FOONG

*Heng L. Foong is the Program Director for Pacific Asian Language Services (PALS) for Health. Founded in 1993, the nonprofit agency provides free professional medical interpreting to Asian and Spanish-speaking residents in Los Angeles and Orange Counties.*

—————————— ◆ ——————————

One woman watched helplessly as her physician broke the news about her terminal illness through her dumbfounded twelve year-old daughter; another frantically dialed the cell phone of her truck driver brother so that he could interpret her advanced cancer diagnosis; while another likened it to being deaf and mute saying that it was as if she had "a mouth that could not talk and ears that could not hear." These are just three of thousands of lives affected daily by the lack of a common language and the inability to communicate, not at the grocery store, at the post office, or even at a parent-teacher conference, but at a health care appointment where accurate communication is a fundamental need.

Patient and provider communication is perhaps one of the most important diagnostic tools in a medical interview. The delivery of quality care may not be possible if the patient and provider are not able to express their individual needs and concerns. Without a common language, a physician is unable to ask questions that can assist with diagnosing the illness, and the patient, possibly already stressed, afraid, or in pain, is traumatized further by his or her inability to express symptoms.

Advancements in technology, increased global trade, and travel have all contributed to the growth of a multicultural population in this country. The 2000 United States Census reports that the nation's population is more diverse than ever before; the State of California is home to almost 14 million people who speak a language other than English at home, and of this number, half speak English less than "very well." Some languages spoken include Spanish, Chinese (various dialects), Vietnamese, Korean, Armenian, Persian, and French. California's diversity also brings with it a wide variety and sometimes contrasting perceptions of health care such as the cause of disease, its prevention, treatment, and maintenance, making it additionally vital for health care providers to have unimpeded conversations with their patients. Unfortunately, some providers do not feel adequately prepared to have meaningful interactions with patients from culturally and linguistically diverse backgrounds, and research has demonstrated that providers' biases, stereotyping, and lack of preparedness compounded by the present day health system's pressure to contain cost and limit the time of patient interaction have led to the delivery of inequitable care.

So what can health care providers do to improve meaningful communication with patients who are limited English proficient? The ideal solution is to recruit bicultural and bilingual physicians and nurses who reflect the racial, ethnic, and linguistic make up of the facility's service area population. When the provider and patient share a common language the health care transaction is improved, and trust, the key element of relationship building, is nurtured. A more affordable and commonly used solution is the recruitment of bilingual staff to fill patient contact positions such as in the reception area. These staff members are usually enlisted to act as ad-hoc interpreters during appointments with limited English proficient patients. However, health care communication is sensitive and highly intricate, and should not be left to individuals that are socially conversant, a fact that has been supported by recent research which points to rates of misinterpretation errors with potential clinical consequences when unskilled interpreters are relied upon to convey health care information.

The interpretation of complicated health care communication should be conducted by skilled health care interpreters who are trained to perform at the high level commanded by the health care arena. However, the challenges that confront health care professionals in California when it comes to utilizing trained health care interpreters are varied. The state has few mechanisms to adequately test the language proficiency and train bilingual speakers who want to be health care interpreters in the multitude of languages spoken by its diverse population. Interpreters, many who are certified court interpreters, profess that they are qualified to interpret in health care, but the two fields are vastly different and court certification does not automatically translate into effective and efficient health care interpretation. Also, up until the recent development of standards of practice by the California Healthcare Interpreting Association, little formal guidance has been issued to interpreting professionals who work in the health care field.

Yet the largest hurdle in California remains the lack of reimbursement mechanism to pay for health care interpretation services. According to the National Health Law Program, a national public interest law firm, only 13 states presently draw down federal matching funds to pay for interpreters at least for enrollees of Medicaid and SCHIP (State Children's Health Insurance Programs), known as Healthy Families in California. These states include Hawaii, Texas, Massachusetts, New Hampshire, and Maine. Little progress is expected on this front due to increasingly using untrained bilingual providers and staff, volunteers, family members including minors, contracted interpreters, and telephonic interpretation services. Although this patch work of language brokers can assist in completing health care transactions between a provider and limited English proficient patient, the quality, accuracy, and confidentiality of the communication remains suspect when unqualified interpreters are used, an issue that should not be taken lightly in an era of increased scrutiny on health care quality, patient safety, patient satisfaction, and the dreaded possibility of malpractice claims when egregious errors occur.

However, all is not bleak in the arena of health care interpreting. The State of California has arguably the largest number of health care interpreter training programs in the nation with trainings that last forty hours to several semesters. The California Endowment, a private health foundation, whose mission is to expand access to affordable and quality health care, has played an instrumental role in funding innovative projects on a community and health systems level that examine the importance of linguistically and culturally competent health care. In the previous few years, The California Endowment funded the development of a statewide health care interpreter training curriculum and its accompanying language proficiency exam; the development of statewide interpreting standards by the California Healthcare Interpreting Association; co-funded with The Commonwealth Fund the development of national interpreting standards by the National Council of Interpreting in Health Care; the publication of several resources for health care professionals including a guide to selecting health interpreter training programs; and research, both qualitative and quantitative, that may help collect empirical data or increase awareness of the growing need for culturally and linguistically appropriate health care services.

Resources are increasing for health care professionals working with limited English proficient patients in California yet the awareness level regarding the need for trained interpreters remains frustratingly low. Even with state and federal laws that require the provision of interpretation services by state and federally funded health care facilities, the provider want for quality communication with patients is influenced by many conflicting factors.

Few hospitals have established mechanisms on steps their providers can take to access interpreters in person or by telephone. Fewer have established on-site interpreter programs or full-time interpreting staff, and even less have formal tools to assess language proficiency and train interpreters. Administrators push hospital policies and procedures without having a distinct understanding of their service area population, which can change frequently due to secondary and tertiary migration patterns. Many administrators do not take the time to identify the different levels of needs, challenges, biases, and personal world views held by their front line provider staff. Trainings on culturally competent care, which must be tailored, and methods of effective interpreter utilization are sometimes set aside for 30-minute didactic "brown bag" lunch sessions or less complicated observances of diversity such as Lunar New Year celebration or Latino Heritage Week, which can improve staff morale and satisfy gastronomical interests but sadly do not provide practical lessons which can translate into promoting meaningful hands-on interactions with patients, especially those with differing health beliefs and language needs.

Now a minority majority state, many from around the world, will continue to call California home. To ensure equal access to meaningful health care for everyone in need; to reduce unnecessary health care costs that stem from guess work by physicians when they are unable to communicate effectively with their patients; to protect the safety of all health consumers, improve health outcomes, and preserve public health; and to spare another child from having to broker devastating news to grown family members tipping the fragile balance of family dynamics; those who are limited English proficient must learn to advocate for language assistance in health care settings; health care providers must recognize the difference between trained and untrained interpreters, and refuse to continue a treatment session in the face of unequal communication; health care administrators must lead with conviction, training an eye on positive long term health outcomes instead of focusing consistently on the immediate bottom line; policy makers must be courageous enough to seize the reins of change and guide a much needed overhaul of our health care system; and all of us, should walk a mile in someone else's shoes and lend our voices to those who have "mouths that cannot talk, and ears that cannot hear" to preserve the right of our neighbors, friends, and family members to have access to health care that they can fully understand.

## Questions for Discussion

1. Foong's tone is academic and formal through most of the essay, though not in the opening paragraph, where she presents a couple of brief horror stories to set up the argument. How do you react to these? Does this paragraph effectively prepare you for what is to come?

2. Foong at times assumes the truth of her claims without offering concrete evidence for them or considering the opposition's point of view. For instance, she says that bilingual medical interpretation is a need, but she doesn't talk about the cost, how many interpreters might be needed and in

how many languages, etc. Evaluate the strengths and weaknesses of her argument on this basis.

3. How do you think patients themselves deal with the problem described here? Would hearing more from them throughout the essay sway your opinion on the issue?

## Ideas for Writing

1. Contact a hospital or clinic which serves patients whose first language is not English. Find out what facilities are offered to help these patients. Then contact your local telephone company and a government agency like the Department of Motor Vehicles. How many languages do they offer service in? Depending on what you find, write an essay in which you discuss the disparities you discover, and their ironies, if any.

2. Do some research on the current state of regulation of this issue in California or another US state. Is the situation still as described in this article? Write an essay in which you address a health care provider like a hospital or a health insurance company, or the state itself. Explain the problem of interpretation and suggest the steps needed to create solutions.

---

# The 2% Strategy: A Bold New Approach to Shape the Future of Southern California

## RANDALL LEWIS

*Randall Lewis, Executive VP of the housing and commercial development firm Lewis Corporation, is committed to sustainable development in Southern California, especially on the region's eastern frontier (aka the Inland Empire). A graduate of Claremont McKenna College, Lewis has been President of the Inland Empire Arts Foundation, Secretary of the Los Angeles County Citizens Planning Council, director of the HomeBuilder's Council, and national director of the National Association of HomeBuilders. He serves on boards including the USC School of Policy, Planning and Development and the UCLA School of Public Policy and Social Research. He has written about smart growth for* The Planning Report *and other building industry publications.*

---   ✦   ---

Looking ahead at the housing situation in Southern California, it is not a pretty picture. In fact, it is terrifying! We are facing a crisis of affordability. At the same time we have major challenges with mobility, livability in our communities and, in fact, the prosperity and sustainability of all Southern Californians. This situation will require regional leadership, vision, and courage. The Southern California Association of Government's [SCAG's] Compass 2% Strategy offers a bold new approach and vision. I will discuss why it's needed in Southern California, why it's a good thing, and what steps are necessary for its implementation.

## WHY IT'S NEEDED

The need for fresh thinking is driven by the tremendous population growth that will be coming to Southern California in the next two decades. It is estimated that Southern California will grow by five million people in the next 25 years. Southern California continues to be an attractive place for people, and this attractiveness to newcomers, as well as the natural increase due to births from our existing population, will result in enormous population growth. Our infrastructure is already strained in existing areas, and our scarce resources will not be able to accommodate this growth using old-fashioned patterns of development. Finally, changing demographics and lifestyles also call for new thinking regarding how and where we live. The 2% Strategy offers a fresh approach.

The 2% Strategy has evolved out of the Southern California Compass regional visioning process. It is an approach to optimally accommodate growth in the region. The strategy promotes a concentration of new and infill development along existing and planned transportation corridors and new urban centers. SCAG's current focus is to initiate pilot and voluntary demonstration programs, to target technical assistance to cities containing critical growth opportunity areas as identified in the 2% Strategy, and to provide proper tools and training to encourage participation and cooperation.

## WHY IT'S A GOOD THING

There are many benefits to the 2% Strategy. It can:

- allow for the preservation of valuable open space;
- lessen traffic on our crowded roads and highways;

- help reduce air pollution;
- lessen our dependency on foreign oil;
- increase prosperity in our existing cities and lead to a better business climate;
- create more livable communities that are more walkable and more interesting;
- encourage sustainability for the environment;
- lead to the building of different types of housing that are more appropriate to our changing demographics.

The 2% Strategy is good for cities and counties, offering many resources for implementation. It is also good for providers of housing by encouraging creation of new opportunities for development.

## WHAT STEPS ARE NECESSARY FOR IMPLEMENTATION

Here are some steps needed to implement this strategy. They include, for example, taking the appropriate actions in producing the right mix of housing, using regulatory tools more proactively, and giving more emphasis on design, mixed-use developments, master planned communities, new towns, and public/private partnerships.

First of all, we must understand Southern California's changing demographics, which are more diverse than ever. Southern Californians are living in many different household types, such as singles, couples, retirees, and single heads of households. Many of these household types no longer need or want the traditional big home on a big home site. There are many different lifestyle preferences, such as people seeking recreation-oriented communities, live/work developments, gated communities, homeowner association communities, etc. Often smaller size homes better meet the spatial and financial requirements of these non-traditional households. Common areas such as pools, pocket parks, and gathering spaces can be quite popular. As providers of housing we must be more like a consumer goods industry that has detailed knowledge on the preferences and tastes of our customers. There currently is a real mismatch between much of our supply of housing and this new diversified housing demand. There are estimates that up to 70% of the new households that will be formed in the future will be non-traditional households. Many builders are still providing houses oriented towards the more traditional family market with two parents and two to four children. These homes are often 1,500 to 3,500 square feet, with 6,000- to 7,000-foot home sites. This type of family housing is still valid for many families, but there is not enough smaller lot and condo/townhouse-type housing being built for the smaller households. There is no typical household anymore, and there should not be a typical housing type either.

Next, cities and counties should use incentives to get the types of housing they desire and need. The easiest incentive is speeding up the time it takes to entitle and build housing. This incentive doesn't have to cost anything in terms of dollars or oversight, but it's extremely valuable to providers of housing. It can cut down financing costs, lessen the risk of economic cycles, and lead to less expensive housing in this era of rapidly rising construction costs. A second incentive is the incentive of density. Increased density can significantly lower land costs and lower the costs of infrastructure. In many suburban markets, land now costs upwards of $500,000 per acre. If there are four homes per acre, the raw land cost is $125,000 per home; if there are 10 homes per acre, the raw land cost is $50,000 per home, which can be a significant savings. In addition, there are many fixed costs to a development, such as perimeter walls, traffic signals, and street lights, and greater density dramatically drives down the per-dwelling-unit cost of items like these. Other types of incentives can include lower fees, faster inspections, and reductions in unnecessary standards and requirements.

Building codes and requirements should be examined to make sure they are compatible with the latest trends in higher density housing. All across the country there have been great innovations in architecture and land planning, but it's necessary that local codes be updated to allow for these new patterns of building. Zoning changes should be handled through general plan updates in advance of specific projects being submitted for review. This will save time and potentially avoid controversy.

We must recognize that design is more important than density. It is the quality of the design that truly is important, and good projects with density must integrate architecture, land planning, and landscaping to be good neighbors. While densities definitely need to be higher in the future, unlimited density is not the answer. Each market area has a right density, and a multidiscipline approach is needed to discover the right density. Factors such as surrounding neighborhood housing types, construction costs, sales prices, market acceptance, demographics, and politics all enter into the analysis of the right density. Southern California has many good examples of attractive higher density housing and it also has some not-so-good examples. House tours or visual preference surveys done with photographs are both excellent ways to show both good and bad examples of higher density. We should also remember that with future investments in transit and with the beginning of people using car sharing, there will be increasing interest in housing near good transit.

There will be new providers of housing in the future, and cities and counties must understand who these providers are, what their roles are in the economy, and the best ways of dealing with each type of provider. Examples of these providers are large national homebuilders, regional and smaller homebuilders, planned community developers, not-for-profits, for-profits doing affordable housing, retailers with extra land above or around their shops and stores, office owners with extra parking, corporate and industrial owners with extra land, and redevelopment agencies. Each of these providers has different issues that need to be understood. For example, larger providers of housing will probably not be as interested in small sites and will not be able to devote the proper resources to do them justice. Likewise, smaller developers might not be as appropriate for larger sites because it would strain their resources. When choosing builders, cities should consider their capabilities and expertise to insure the right team for each site.

Rental housing will play an increasing role in housing Southern Californians in the future. Some households will rent because it is all they can afford, but there are also many renters by choice who choose to rent because they enjoy the lifestyle of having someone else do the maintenance or because they're at a period in their lives when renting makes more sense. Most of the rentals going forward will be at the very high-end or at the subsidized end of the market because it's quite difficult to build anything in between. The high costs of land, soaring construction costs, and increasing competition for rental sites make it very difficult to build any housing except at the very high end, which must be expensive enough to cover all of the costs. Currently, for-sale builders are able to outbid rental developers on most sites, which exacerbates the problem of not having enough land for rental housing. Home ownership is an admirable goal, but we must recognize that there will be a strong role for rental housing, and it will be difficult and expensive to provide rental housing.

We must understand that master planned communities will play an increasingly larger role in housing our population in the future. These communities offer many benefits, such as more comprehensive planning; proper placement and financing of infrastructure, such as schools, parks, and public amenities; better segmentation of different housing types to reach all of the markets; and usually stronger standards for design and maintenance.

There will also be new towns developed in Greenfield areas. New town development will be a key part of the growth in the future. These new towns will have the benefit of comprehensive planning starting from the beginning, and can offer an enviable balance of jobs, houses, community amenities, and open space preservation. New town development will require new thinking in terms of financing, infrastructure construction, economic development, and creating a sense of community. Through innovative planning at the regional level, these new towns complement the economic strategy of existing urbanized areas. They also provide opportunities for sustainability and environmental stewardship. New towns offer a fresh opportunity towards a comprehensive approach to community building. Great sustainable communities are about a lot more than just homes. They include physical infrastructure, such as roads and schools and public buildings; natural infrastructure, such as trails, parks and meaningful open space; and social infrastructure, such as systems for safety, for economic development and for community involvement and enhancement. New towns will be built in North Los Angeles County, in North San Bernardino County, and in Eastern Riverside County. New town development must be a part of Southern California's future development. Relying only on in-fill housing is not enough because the supply of housing cannot be built quickly enough and in the right places. I believe new towns should be part of the region's development strategy and that new towns need to be planned properly and smartly.

Planners must study mixed-use developments, integrating residential with other uses, such as office and retail. Mixed-use development, while attractive, has complex issues such as noise, odors, parking, financing, increased construction costs, and many others. In many cases, mixed use is more easily done horizontally with uses next to each other instead of vertically, with uses on top of each other. Our experience is that mixed-use developments have the potential to become great places that not only are attractive but also make the surrounding areas more attractive. These projects may take place in existing urban centers as well as near new transit centers and corridors.

Educating city councils, planning commissions, development staffs, producers of houses, and the general public on the complex issues of growth is critical. City councils need some big picture education on issues of growth and latest thinking on regional solutions to the housing crisis. At the planning commission and city staff level, the education must be more at the "how to do it" level. Cutting edge design and development is complicated, and only through training and education can planning commissioners and development staffs learn the best ways to take their cities' projects into the future. The producers of housing also need to be educated since they often know only what they are comfortable with and may not be as exposed to fresh thinking as they should be. Perhaps the most important group to educate is the general public.

Recently the Executive Director of SCAG gave a presentation to community leaders and members of the public in an Inland Empire community. When they heard his message, they all responded quite favorably to the Southern California Compass program. We have found a very useful tool in educating stakeholders is a tour that starts in their city and then goes to see samples of best practices in other cities. We have done more than a dozen of these tours in the last three years. They typically take three to six hours and allow participants to see and comment on development projects that they like and don't like. The feedback after these tours has always been extremely positive, and it is a tool I recommend heartily.

Only through an education process can community leaders have courage and vision as the dialog regarding the 2% Strategy continues in Southern California. In my opinion, the 2% Strategy is not optional. By showing people how important it is for solving issues of congestion and housing affordability, we can better win public support. The public must also understand that as Southern California competes for jobs and businesses, affordable housing and good transportation for workers are mandatory.

Public/private partnerships can be useful for some projects to leverage the strengths and resources of the public and private sectors. Partnerships can help with joint use projects involving schools, parks, libraries, community centers, and health facilities. In Chino, for example, we are working on a new school that will have a joint use gymnasium and park shared by the city and the school district. We will also have a joint use library shared by the County of San Bernardino and the local school district. The school will also have space for community meetings. In Riverside County we are exploring extra rooms for early childhood education and for limited health services, as well as many other joint use facilities. There currently is a growing awareness of the benefits of child care and early childhood education. In this era of scarce resources, joint use may be an exciting way to provide this much-needed service.

What about the other 98% of land? We must also look at the properties outside of the 2% areas to make sure they are being developed properly. We can't look back and say, "Why did we waste our land in 2006?" We need to recognize appropriate land uses outside of the 2% Strategy areas and be wise about them. In ten years, today's Greenfields may all be infill locations, and we must have proper zoning today to insure proper uses on the other 98% of land. A real side benefit of the 2% Strategy is that it can open the door to smarter thinking on the other 98% of the property. If the other 98% is planned properly, we can insure that sites can be developed appropriately, and those sites which should not be housing can be put to other uses.

Health concerns affect all Southern Californians. There is a growing recognition that how we design communities can impact the health and vitality of an area's residents. By considering design and inclusion of health-promoting infrastructure, we can help our residents lead healthier and longer lives and lower the crushing burden of health-related costs on our society. There are four factors to be considered in designing healthier neighborhoods and developments:

a) The physical plan must promote walkability and safety. Where possible, trails and parks have been proven to increase people's tendencies to walk and get exercise.

b) Physical elements such as exercise rooms, gymnasiums, or community centers also have big impacts. With forethought, all projects—large and small—can incorporate some physical elements to promote health.

c) Partnerships with local organizations, both for-profit and not-for-profit, can be used to leverage resources of knowledge, manpower, and buildings to create programs to promote all elements of health and wellness.

d) Policy changes need to be explored regarding elements such as food at schools, workplace health initiatives, allocation of budgetary resources, and many others. It is at the policy level that the biggest opportunities for change exist.

Finally, demonstration projects are a great tool to encourage good development. These projects can demonstrate best practices in areas such as innovative approaches to high density and new ways of creating learning communities, healthy communities, and communities with a strong social fabric. New changes in technology such as fiber optics or wireless communication or environmental stewardship are other areas where demonstrations are valuable. These demonstration projects need to be fast-tracked through approval processes and, when built, need to be studied to learn what has worked and what hasn't. There is no substitute for being able to see projects in person and take advantage of what's been learned. Targeted demonstration projects have the power to influence dozens of other projects in a very short time.

## CONCLUSION

All of us, the public sector, the private sector, and our communities and citizens have a shared and common future. We also have shared values, wanting a better life for next generations. SCAG's leadership at the regional level is vitally important for Southern California. SCAG has tremendous resources that can guide community leaders with data, technology, and methods for modeling different patterns of development. The staff members and elected leaders of SCAG are well respected and can be used as spokespeople and change agents to help the region through this process. Change is always difficult and scary, but with SCAG's help, we can do what is necessary. The challenges ahead are enormous, but with programs such as the 2% Strategy, I am confident that all of us can have better lives in the years ahead.

### Questions for Discussion

1. Clearly, Lewis speaks from a point of view which supports the solution he discusses. What clues do you find in his tone which give this away? Look for examples throughout the essay.
2. Lewis claims that contemporary homebuyers seek a new style of dwelling, one which better matches their lifestyle than does the traditional single-family house. Does he offer any proof for this assertion? Is it necessarily the case that a non-traditional family would shun the traditional-style house? What could you offer to support your point of view?
3. Where in the piece does Lewis slip from *arguing* the need for a new type of housing to *assuming* it? What sort of rebuttal to the argument could you make if you attacked it on this basis?

## Ideas for Writing

1. Many people react to the problem of growth by giving up the competition for urban space and moving elsewhere. Those who wish to continue their pursuit of the California dream often move to what Kotkin and Frey label the "Third California" (see "The Third California" in Chapter 1). Write an essay in which you support or refute the idea that relocating is a better approach than the 2% Strategy, which presumes that people must—or have the right to—stay in the increasingly crowded urban spaces of California in order to feel they have achieved the dream, and that cities have the obligation to alter their planning in order to accommodate them.

2. Would the ideas Lewis presents work where you live? Is higher-density planned housing needed? Are such ideas already being tried? Find out about local plans for development. Then write an essay in which you evaluate your community's efforts at accommodating growth. Talk about what your city will look like in 5, 10, or 50 years, and what its alternative possibilities might be.

---

# The Paradox of the Hedge—Do Good Fences Really Make Good Neighbors?

## GREG GOLDIN

*Greg Goldin, a freelance journalist, has written hundreds of articles for the* L.A. Weekly, *the* Sacramento News and Review, Los Angeles Magazine, *the* Los Angeles Times, *and many other publications. His topics include politics, media, architecture, and much more.*

---◆---

In the middle of the well-groomed block on South Ridgeley Drive—a self-assured, composed neighborhood in the Miracle Mile district—there is a two-story Monterey-Colonial duplex for sale. The postcard the Realtors mailed out to advertise the property presents an image of half a house. On view are a pair of plantation doors flanked by shutters opening onto a pink-hued second-floor balcony. The first floor is entirely hidden behind an 8-foot hedge. Which, it turns out, is the point of the photograph. No one can see in, or out, for that matter. The postcard makes this clear: "Gated with hedges, intercom entry."

From the vantage of the street—the real, living street—the 8-foot-high, 40-foot-long hedge eclipses everything around it. It crowds the sidewalk and consumes the air. Its mass and scale trigger an instinctive shrinking, and the impulse to move on quickly, to leave. There is an inkling of something watching, perhaps even lurking, beyond the defensive green line.

That hedge is emblematic. Los Angeles is being cordoned off. Neighborhood by neighborhood, street by street, frontyard by frontyard. You can stand in your own frontyard, or idle at your neighbor's, and almost watch it happen. Hedges are growing, everywhere. They're growing tall and they're growing dense. On busy thoroughfares in Hancock Park, on shaded retreats on the steep alluvium of the San Gabriels in Altadena, on communal walk streets in Venice, on innumerable east-west and north-south streets of the Cartesian grid in the flats of L.A. proper, fast-growing trees, usually Ficus nitida but occasionally Ligustrum texanum or Pittosporum undulatum, are planted in a row to close off what previously was open. The clear vista of a manicured lawn, perhaps punctuated with a serpentine boxwood and lined with bedded flowers and pruned shrubs, is being cropped by 6-, 8-, 10- and 12-foot-high hedges. The unpredictable texture of ornamental trees and broad canopies is being replaced by featureless uniformity. Unvaryingly green, thickly foliated and impenetrable, the hedges sprout practically where the sidewalk ends and private property begins. The animated public right of way, scented, colorful, dappled, is being rendered stolid and still.

These new moats both evoke and provoke the divisions between public and private, embrace of the urban spectacle and retreat from it, the creative conflict arising out of proximity and the tranquility born of solitude. It's hard to say which side of the hedge is more besieged. But what is certain is that, in the words of John Chase, "Hedges are the sleeper hot-button issue in civic affairs."

Chase speaks from experience. As the urban designer for West Hollywood, he witnessed firsthand what happens when a city enters its residents' frontyards. West Hollywood, like many of the cities that surround it, had a 42-inch height limit for hedges, which was often flouted. In May 2001, the city drafted a rule that would have permitted taller hedges, with the proviso that homeowners first apply for permission. The idea was to maintain the feeling of an "urban village." It was, in other words, a matter of communitarianism. Or so the city's planners thought. But when word got out, the citizens of West Hollywood were outraged. "I have to get a permit to grow a hedge?" they cried.

"The spaces are as important to people as their pets," Chase says. "It was as though you rang their doorbells and said, 'We're taking your dog.' It's an indicator of how people feel about the city. Does the gaze of passersby defile your space?" The City Council immediately withdrew the height limit and retreated from regulating hedges altogether.

Last year, hedge wars broke out in Santa Monica, where the citizenry continues to skirmish. When residents complained that their neighborhood looked like "an armed camp," the city started to stringently enforce its own 42-inch rule, on the books since 1948. A staff report presented at a June City Council meeting explained: "Open front yards contribute to the neighborhood aesthetic and are enjoyed by the entire community even though they are privately owned. . . . This connection with neighbors creates a sense of community and, in Santa Monica, is one of the factors that make this city a desirable place to live and work."

But homeowners along plummy Adelaide Drive, overlooking Santa Monica Canyon, rebelled after being threatened with fines of $25,000 a day for not trimming their hedges. The ensuing dust-up launched the City Council candidacy of Bobby Shriver, a Kennedy clansman who, until then, hadn't given a thought to public office. Last November, he won. And now hedge height enforcement is on hold while the Santa Monica City Council deliberates on whether streets lined with enclosed private spaces will be enshrined in public policy.

Elsewhere, as in the city of Los Angeles, which also has a 42-inch height limit, which is also routinely flouted, the illegal hedges just keep growing.

Typically, a hedge begins when a swath of grass is yanked out, by pickax and long-nosed spade, leaving a furrow of turned soil a few feet wide. The ground is fertilized, and then a truckload of one-gallon or five-gallon potted trees is unloaded. The trees are spaced about three feet apart, watered generously for the first year, and, if all goes well, overnight, in botanical terms, a hedge will grow. Other than an occasional swipe with power shears, the hedge may be ignored for decades. The Indian laurel, the common name for the ficus used in hedges, is virtually indestructible. You cannot water it too little; you cannot give it too much sun. And although it can be attacked by thrips (one of those pests so prolific that the singular and plural are the same word), it responds happily to being trimmed. In fact, you can trim a ficus into a ball, a lollipop, a football—just about any configuration you can imagine—but usually it's just flattened and topped into a living wall. Ficus is also a thoroughly generic plant type, and thus calls no attention to itself. So it grows, ubiquitous as grass, and just as solidly unremarkable.

What invariably springs to mind when talking to people who live behind hedges is the line from Robert Frost's poem "Mending Wall." "Good fences make good neighbors," the great New Englander wrote of a stone wall that has begun to crumble. Those five words resonate with almost perfect pitch among hedge-growers, who say, simply, "It's another wall." That's what Michelle Sy said one recent spring morning while standing on the sidewalk in front of her modest stucco home on South Ogden Drive, near Fairfax and Venice. "It gives you a little bit more privacy."

Or as Roger Sherman, director of Fresh Urbs, one of SCI-Arc's postgraduate urban studies programs, puts it, "Hedges are a symptom of the fact that people would like to maintain the front porch, but only if they can maintain it behind a veil. They are advancing where the front door used to be."

The advancing front door reflects an urban paradox. As Witold Rybczynski wrote in "City Life," "We need both dispersal and concentration in cities—places to get away from each other, and places to gather. . . ." The problem is that, more and more, the places we gather are being diminished by the forces of the marketplace, in the form of a mock piazza such as the Grove at Farmers Market, or yet another Starbucks replacing the formerly ramshackle hot dog stand at the beach. At the same time, our private lives have invaded these places, with the constant bleat and blather of cellphones and laptops. It is true, as a result of shrinking public spaces, that we long even more ardently for places where we may be genuinely free to pursue our wonts and cultivate our interests. Where else can we go, other than behind our front door?

But Frost also wrote in "Mending Wall": "Before I built a wall I'd ask to know/What I was walling in or walling out." Here is an expression of the countercurrent: The urge for privacy always runs up against the urge for openness. Until recently, there was a broad social consensus about where public space ended and private space began. The open frontyard—perhaps with a white picket fence, perhaps with a trailing rose—although private, was an offering to the community. It also was an acknowledgment that each homeowner was a citizen among citizens. There was a tacit agreement, imported from Frost's New England, that this kind of right of way stood for the democratic impulse, that everyone had a willing stake in the commonweal. Putting up a hedge signals, in

John Chase's words, "that you don't want to be involved in human activity outside what you and your family generate."

Michelle Sy instinctively grasps the difficulties her hedge poses. Among other things, her frontyard is the only one on the block wrapped in a veil. "When we first came to this neighborhood," she says, "we wondered, 'Are we closing other people off by having this hedge?' But now I like having it. All these houses have big front windows, picture windows. If you look around, you'll see that they all have drapes. We don't have anything. It's nice looking out at your own yard and not have [sic] to worry about anyone seeing in."

Coincidentally, Sy's next-door neighbor, Athena Jackson, has a frontyard that is all about seeing in. She has planted a boisterous garden, a work-in-progress that in late April is a riot of color and scent. Seersucker, lemon basil and pineapple sage are mixed with peppers, lilacs and chrysanthemums. Her garden is an outdoor gallery of surprises and unabashed dabbling. Jackson says "people just come by to stand and talk." Here, the exterior and interior worlds are free to collide. In this zone you might conceivably trespass, but an invitation to enter isn't required either.

Sy's frontyard is powerfully indwelling and sedate—moods, in fact, that Sy says attracted her to the home in the first place. The small space, adorned with papyrus and variegated flax, is perhaps 12 feet deep from the interior line of the hedge. It is a tiny cloister, keeping the intrusions of the street—noisome traffic, prying pedestrians, visual clutter in neighbors' yards—out. On the other side of the hedge, in a wide bed, fountain grass spills freely onto the sidewalk. Here, at least, you don't have that feeling of imposition, as you do with the 40 feet of ficus on South Ridgeley. And the layers and changing scales provide visual interest that is missing from most of the grass-and-shrub frontyards up and down the block.

Still, as Chase says, "when someone comes along and puts up Fort Ficus, there is a jarring interruption." The facade of Sy's house, a 1920s Spanish-Colonial Revival, has largely disappeared from the streetscape, along with the unifying sense of place, and spaciousness, that characterized the block for decades. And the same is true almost anywhere a hedge goes in. Several blocks north, for instance, someone planted a ficus hedgerow to hide a black tubular steel fence enclosing the frontyard of a duplex near Pico. A featureless hedge hiding a featureless fence, but behind them stands an architectural gem: a 1940s building reminiscent of a Gregory Ain.

Jim Eserts, the architect who laid out Michelle Sy's frontyard and sold her the home, is something of a pied piper of hedges. He is quick to point out, and rightly so, that "there are plenty of frontyards with no hedges that are disasters too." His clients, he says, want them for "privacy, security, privacy." But there are beneficial "side effects"—aesthetic and pecuniary—of converting "the frontyard into the front room."

Eserts' new home is on South Orange Grove, just around the block from Ogden. The street looks today as it did, perhaps, 50 years ago. From the corner of Airdrome, looking north, the view is unobstructed. You can stand there and count the front doors on both sides of the street. As you walk up the block, on a day like this, when the wind has scrubbed the sky blue, you can read the Hollywood sign. Eserts takes in this broad vista and says, "From a purely pragmatic perspective, a quarter of your property is completely underused. If you're spending $750,000 on a house, why dispose of almost $200,000?"

On Ogden, standing on the sidewalk in front of Sy's house—his former residence—he had explained how hedges ought to work. The ficus hedge there is deliberately set back from the sidewalk to "provide a sidewalk-scape. Otherwise it would have been unfriendly, unneighborly. The idea is to give something back to your neighbors."

Now, pointing at a drawing of his latest conversion, he adds, "the real benefit of capturing the frontyard as another room is that your arrival gets pushed out. Portals define a level of privacy." The blueprints show a series of entries before you reach the front door, which is roughly 25 feet from the sidewalk: the hedge, the front gate, the yard itself (divided into two "rooms," one for entertaining and one for lounging), the original porch and, finally, the front door. "It's arrival, arrival again, arrival still again, and arrival again-again after that." What Eserts has designed is a ceremonial, choreographed entrance to guide you through deepening levels of privacy, the way a Mexican courtyard draws you from the zocalo to the bedroom.

Indeed, one of the ironies of the changing cityscape is that hedges are doing what walls would have done had Los Angeles remained part of the Mexican Republic: pushing homes directly onto the street. That urban imprint, typical of North Africa and the Middle East and perfectly adapted to a hot, dry climate, did not take hold here because the Midwestern speculators and homesteaders who dreamed up Los Angeles borrowed their ideal of the free-standing home floating on a patch of greenery from the suburban English countryside, via Chicago and Omaha.

Across town, Doug Suisman, one of L.A.'s preeminent urbanists, lives behind a fence screening his frontyard, his wife's studio and his own office. Most of the houses on the block, a sliver of concrete clinging to a ridge above Santa Monica Canyon, are fenced or hedged. In fact, beach traffic—on foot and by car—got the street a special zoning variance, permitting hedges and fences to go as high as 6 feet. Suisman's street is in hiding, which he defends. "A hedge is a friendly way to get privacy," he says.

"The old idea of the street as the public room, and everybody gives a piece to that room, is, culturally, an anachronism. Nobody uses their front lawns. It's gotten way too expensive; it's gone way beyond the tithe. A hedge can be a gift to the street too—more than a lawn," he says, echoing Eserts. "Besides, I don't see how a hedge precludes the gregarious person from having a lawn."

This is tough stuff from an architect and planner who has devoted himself to finding ways to make places such as downtown L.A. more urban, by, among other things, coaxing office workers onto their feet. His 1997 "Ten-Minute Diamond" plan is widely recognized as a landmark effort to make the civic center more humane, walkable and vibrant. Yet Suisman announces: "I don't want pedestrians parading on my block." He is speaking in hyberbole, but like most of us, he values his privacy and understands how difficult it is to safeguard nowadays. "I love being in this intimate community, but because it is so intimate, I want to honor the private realm by capturing my open space. People are having to live in denser and denser spaces, and they're responding to that density by modifying their environment. Why shouldn't they?"

Suisman walks out of his gate and wanders next door, where he dissects his neighbor's hedge and fence. "An antisocial wall?" he asks rhetorically. "The double wooden gates are always open. You get a peek into this wonderful garden." Inside is a Provençal parterre defined by low boxwood hedges. An arched, candy-apple-red front door provides visual surprise. The puckered, yellow fruit of a lemon tree hang over the white fence, while twin urns stand guard. The effect is of a veil, which beckons without revealing what it obscures.

At bottom, Suisman is arguing for a clear separation between the civic and the domestic experience. He is looking to produce within the metropolis what suburbia was originally designed to preserve outside it.

According to Robert Fishman, the author of "Bourgeois Utopias," the suburban house was envisioned as a sacred refuge from the "intrusions of the workplace and the city." The home, with its plot of land set on a shaded lane, was exclusively a "world of leisure, family life and union with nature. . . . [T]he modern family [was] freed from the corruption of the city, restored to harmony with nature, endowed with wealth and independence yet protected by a close-knit, stable community." Suburbia was meant to be a community built on "the primacy of private property and the individual family." How better to describe the essential qualities of a single-family Los Angeles home?

We want the public gaze. We want the veil. That is the tension between the two sides of the hedge, perhaps nowhere more pronounced than on the walk streets of Venice. Through nearly 100 years of fortune, misfortune and fortune renewed, the streets in the Millwood and Oakwood sections of Venice—roughly bounded by California, Venice, Lincoln and Electric—remained an enclave of shared space. The homes are on pinkie-sized lots facing public promenades, with the streets tucked behind. The houses peer at one another across a concrete strip no wider than the wheelbase of a Smart car. The front porches nearly kiss.

It is a bit like living on a township square. The tightly spaced frontyards, squeezed together between the tightly spaced houses, inscribe a discrete clearing. This kind of defined, protected aperture invites activity, use. Strolling along one of the walk streets, say, Nowita, you get the sense that you've entered one of those public gardens where everyone has his own plot to cultivate and no horticultural orthodoxy reigns, but where, too, everyone collaborates on tending the larger commons. The space is inclusive, not exclusive. As a pedestrian, you feel welcome. It is easy to strike up a chat with the people out on their porches or digging in their gardens. The interplay of the elements—the flowers, the trees, the low picket fences, the other people ambling by—becomes purely aesthetic. Although assuredly not Broadway in downtown, the walk streets still provide that key to a good jaunt: the spectacle. By design and by habit, these swaths are sociable—gregarious, as Doug Suisman said.

Until someone grows a hedge—which has happened, in a checkerboard fashion, up and down the length of these streets. The twist is: The very fact of openness may be why the hedge goes up. "As they use the property," says Frank Clementi, an architect who lives on Nowita, "they start to see the front as indefensible space. To protect against that exposure, they close it up." Like bars going up on windows, every new 8-foot hedge contributes to the notion that fortifications are necessary.

No one knows this better than Jay Griffith. A landscape designer, Griffith has gained prominence for the gardens he's done for landmark Rudolph Schindler and Richard Neutra houses. His work is sere, and profoundly sculptural, and you can see this when you walk by his house on a double lot in the Millwood section of Venice. Griffith lives behind a dense hedge and a Lucite fence—a conscious dialogue between opaque and translucent. The plastic panels allow a silhouetted glimpse of Griffith's garden, and they permit luminous colors and indistinct forms to radiate out to the street. This lantern effect is a subtle statement about the vagaries of public and private space. Griffith is enclosed, but he isn't entombed—or, as he likes to put it, "inside a bigger womb."

Yet, Griffith confesses, "I have plans to take down my fence. I love what it does for the inside of my yard, and I'm very proud of what it does on the outside. But I don't like the precedent. Venice has more community spirit than many other neighborhoods. The community is falling apart behind the walls and hedges going up."

"Most gardens are not really used," he adds. "They are viewed. They have a calming effect. There is that thing of, 'I can look out my window and I can see greenery. I'm not looking at the hood of a Studebaker, I'm not looking across the way at my neighbor's McMansion.' But the things that are being put up are a lopsided reaction. Soon there'll be shards of glass on the top of them all, like Mexico City."

Even without the broken glass and its exclusionary brutality, most enclosed frontyards simply become dead space. They go unused because they are realms of compression, not expansion; shadow, not light. Which are manifestations of the innermost qualities of hedges themselves, a subject that Pitzer College professor Barry Sanders has been mulling over. Buried deep in the idea of hedges, he says, is a fear of phantoms. "Spooky things happen there," Sanders says, "nefarious stuff. Beginning in the late Middle Ages, all sorts of double-dealings were done on these edges, and the men doing them were called 'hedgemen.' This is where the seamy folks hung out."

As it is to this day. Sanders gives an example: "Just the other day our neighborhood was taped off, helicopters were buzzing overhead, and police officers were shining their flashlights in the shrubbery. A couple of gang kids took shots at cops. The police announced, 'We think they're hiding in the bushes. Watch your hedges.' It isn't that they're hiding in a wall; you can't hide in a wall. But you can hide in the bushes. Hedges have that same connotation. They're horror-producing."

Across the street from the Monterey-Colonial on South Ridgeley Drive is a scene that brings into focus both sides of the hedge—what it walls in and what it walls out. In front of a two-story Normandy-style courtyard, a Chinese elm's lofty, shimmering canopy shades a bronze-colored, stamped-steel bench. A mother, arms stretched, joyously dandles her baby overhead. Mother and baby, too, are made of metal, burnished with the patina of the ages. At first glance, the statue might be mistaken for a Duane Hansen, a deadpan depiction of the quotidian. No. This frozen portrait of filial warmth, set in an urban Eden, is an unintended riposte to the leafy cold shoulder it confronts. Here is a version of the frontyard as it is meant to be, but rarely is.

## Questions for Discussion

1. What threat or imposition are people who grow these hedges to 8, 10, or 12 feet tall responding to? Does Goldin specify it, or does he merely imply it in the piece? What does the presence of hedges suggest about the difference between suburban and urban space?

2. Telling homeowners that they must keep hedges to 42" tall or less is, in effect, telling them that others have the right to peer into their yards. People's reactions to this suggest their discomfort with this understanding of the boundary between private and public space. Explain how Goldin traces the change in values from the time these rules were made up to the present, and evaluate the differences in the approach to public space of two women he mentions, Michelle Sy and Athena Jackson.

3. According to the article, what do people gain when they wall or hedge their houses off from the neighbors, and what do they lose? Use Goldin's citation and discussion of Robert Frost as a way to frame your response.

## Ideas for Writing

1. Research the laws concerning fences or hedges where you live, then walk around and observe people's practice. Do they conform to the regulations? If not, or if there are no rules, what is the practice when it comes to creating barriers? Write an essay in which you speculate on the reasons people construct their space the way they do.

2. Goldin puts the debate over hedges and fences into the context of the larger cultural shift in definition of private and public space. He cites, for example, people living out private moments in public, as when they talk on their cell phones. Find a public place near where you go to school, and observe people's behavior there. Then write an essay defending or criticizing the idea that people need hedges because they create the only relief in a world where little is private any more. Cite Goldin's use of Robert Fishman as you write.

# A Shadow Falls Over the Square
## CHRIS THOMPSON

*Chris Thompson writes for the* East Bay Express *about health care, real estate, politics, education, energy, and other topics of concern.*

◆

**B**ill Harris can get folksy. As the owner of a squat hotel at the edge of the estuary in Oakland's Jack London Square, he makes a point of mentioning that his mother helps out in the kitchen and cooks up a mean waffle. So it may seem odd that Harris recently drafted plans to tear down the four-story Jack London Inn and build a condominium tower that rises at least twenty stories in the air, dominating the waterfront skyline and looming over the patrons of the city's marquee entertainment district. "It's always good to explore all your options," he said. "If we were to go that high, one of the great things is we have some spectacular views here."

Harris is part of an anomalous spurt of overdevelopment that threatens the fragile momentum of Jack London Square, if not the entire Oakland waterfront. In addition to Harris' project, the Las Vegas developer Molasky Pacific Properties has received approval to build an eighteen-story, 135-unit condo tower on Broadway between Second and Third streets, right in the center of the nightlife zone. If these two towers plant their roots here, the neighborhood's entertainment venues could be crippled by noise complaints from the new residents, to say nothing of the overwhelming architecture. The waterfront is a quirky mix of clubs and restaurants, warehouses, and five-story loft apartments, and is just beginning to come into its own. While Jerry Brown felt compelled to offer $60 million bribes to kick-start development in the city's scraggly Uptown district, Jack London Square's magic formula of low-lying buildings, waterfront access, and edgy, post-industrial atmosphere is finally offering the promise of a vibrant downtown neighborhood. But just when Oakland gets a good thing going, someone threatens to screw it up.

Nightlife has always been a little tenuous in Jack London Square. Tensions between revelers and the cops burden restaurateurs, and TGI Friday's, El Torito, and The Old Spaghetti Factory all closed their doors in the last year. Last month, a gang-related shooting sent patrons of the Jack London Cinema running for their lives. But in the last few years, loft condos along Second Street have proven wildly successful, attracting hundreds of middle-class professionals wooed by the neighborhood's funky charm. The developer Ellis Partners is building a $300 million hotel, retail, and cinema complex east of Broadway, which may erode the neighborhood's edgy quality but is an undeniable testament to its potential.

But the partners at Molasky Pacific Properties have taken too big a bite. While the current lofts rise only five or six stories and hover on the outskirts of the entertainment district, Molasky has secured the rights to drive an eighteen-story stake right into the neighborhood's heart. Everett & Jones Barbeque is located across the street from the project, and co-owner John Jernegan worries that his business could suffer a mortal blow. "We don't like it at all," he said. "It's going to be a direct contradiction with our kind of business, where you're going to have an entertainment district, people are out on the streets at night coming and going to entertainment venues. And then you're going to have our barbecue food smell wafting down the street next to $400,000 condominiums. And I'm sure we're going to hear some complaints."

Gary Knect has lived near Jack London Square since 1982 and thinks this could destroy the intimacy and human scale of the district. "You can't really have late-night club activity coexisting with residential activity," he said. "It's always been a marginal success, but this removes the chances of the clubs that are there, or that hope to be there. . . . Big buildings ought to be with other big buildings on the other side of the freeway. When we worked on the estuary policy plan, we thought we were going to have five-story buildings along Broadway. And I thought *that* was going to be tall."

Others see the Broadway tower as a refreshing change from the uniformly squat buildings. "Having an area that is short and tall and medium and wide and thin makes it more interesting," said City Council President Ignacio De La Fuente. "We don't want to be a cookie-cutter copy of anyone, and sometimes the diversity of buildings is more attractive than the normal development you see, either all skyscrapers or all short. . . . I don't think we're gonna have a line of twenty-story buildings along Embarcadero or Broadway. But I think with a few parcels, it will make it look different."

Mark Seiler is a managing partner with the brokerage firm that brought in Yoshi's and Barnes & Noble, and he thinks the Molasky tower is a remarkable leap in imagination. "If you start to fill the street in with those kinds of uses, it could create a very dynamic kind of community," he said. "One of the things about that neighborhood is it's still quiet at night. And by having greater densities, you could attract more retail." But even Seiler thinks Harris' plan for a twenty-story condo building at Jack London Inn may be going too far: "I'd be a little bit concerned about that one."

Seiler is not the only local entrepreneur worried about Harris' plans. "I think he's on crack," exclaimed Joanna Adler, who runs the business Jack London Mail and has lived along the waterfront for a decade, when she heard about the Jack London Inn project. "I don't know how he's ever going to have enough parking there."

The problem is, once you say yes to one high-rise, it's hard to say no to another, particularly if the land values rise so high that building multistory towers is the only way to recoup the cost of acquisition. Molasky Pacific Properties has one last hurdle before it can begin construction: It needs to buy an adjacent restaurant to finalize its plans, and so far, it hasn't been able to close the deal. According to City Councilwoman Nancy Nadel—Molasky officials did not return phone calls seeking comment—company representatives have floated the idea of the city using eminent domain to force the deal through. Although De La Fuente promises that the city would do that only as a last resort, Nadel is worried about the reflexively pro-development mood on the council. "There doesn't seem to be any limit that the council majority and our mayor are interested in," she said.

Opponents of Oakland development are often small-minded, doctrinaire naysayers. People who complain about the lack of affordable housing in the mayor's 10K plan either hope to get a piece of the pie for themselves or are too ideologically rigid to see how desperately downtown needs any kind of housing. Building market-rate condos at the West Oakland BART station is a wonderful idea, but activists with the nonprofit Just Cause are determined to kill it out of a fanatical antipathy to the middle class. The new Wal-Mart is the best thing to happen to East Oakland in years. But Oakland's greatest strength is its rough-hewn authenticity, and the city's waterfront district is where we all rub shoulders. Two towers rising out of the heart of Jack London Square will deform the city's only functioning cabaret district. When Jerry Brown ran for mayor, he promised to deliver an "elegant density" of residents, shops, and nightlife bustling throughout downtown. Down by the water, his vision has spontaneously emerged amid the lofts and hip-hop joints. But two developers have big dreams of inelegant density, and that may ruin the whole thing.

## Questions for Discussion

1. According to this article, what is the character of Jack London Square, and how would this be threatened by the building of the two large condo towers under consideration?

2. Look for language or examples which indicate the writer's point of view on the proposed development. Does he maintain journalistic neutrality, or does he take a side on the issue?

3. This selection seems to suggest that maintaining the status quo in Jack London Square would be desirable. But the place as it is has not been that way forever. Why, then, is further development necessarily a harmful thing?

## Ideas for Writing

1. Do a visual survey of an urban location familiar to you. Try to choose a place which has seen little development for at least a decade or more. What are its charms? What are its negatives? Who lives there? Write an essay in which you either defend or condemn a plan which would bring a Cineplex and restaurant complex to the area.

2. Similar urban "renewal" plans are in place in much of California, from bigger cities like Pasadena and Long Beach to smaller communities like rural Rohnert Park, where a proposed casino is being fought over. Use your library's newspaper index to research one of these, or another place you choose, as a case study. Then write an essay in which you explain the values which both pro- and anti-development interests hold.

# Thinking and Writing about Chapter 4

## Connecting the Essays

1.  Both Didion and Foong write essays which might be put into the category "the downside of the dream." Do they suggest a set of problems which a prospective California dreamer ought to take into account when considering a move to the state? Compare their essays to one of the hopeful selections in Chapter 1. What happens to the dream when it takes on these negative dimensions?

2.  Both Lewis and Thompson talk about development and why it may have negative consequences. But the former speaks in a more general, public-policy voice where the latter talks about life on the ground in a particular locale. Discuss the ways in which their points of view converge despite their different approaches.

3.  Thompson and Goldin are both concerned with how people get along in urban space. Do they ultimately share the same values when it comes to the responsibility of people to one another? Think about ways their essays express similar points of view despite their subject matter being altogether different.

4.  Graham mentions late in his essay an area called the "Salton Sea," giving a little bit of explanation how it came to be and what it now is. Clara Jeffrey takes up this locale at much greater length in Chapter 5. Read Jeffrey's essay, "'Slab City,' from 'Go West, Old Man,'" and write two profiles of the Salton Sea: one which looks at it from the past, as a place which had promise as a vacation spot, and one which looks at it from the present, as a waste land.

5.  Both Cooper and Didion discuss labor issues and the power of union representation. However, they take opposite points of view in their assessments of the success of those who represent the farm workers and the prison guards, respectively. Compare and contrast the ways in which each writer characterizes union power in California. What ironies do you find? Write an essay in which you explain the successes and failures discussed by these writers. If it were up to you, which union would most effectively advocate for its members, and what difference would that make in people's attempts to achieve the California dream?

## Extending the Theme

1.  "Planned" or "Gated" communities, springing up all over California and elsewhere, are unapologetic in their rules-making concerning how homeowners may use their property. Some even specify the colors of paint and type of mailbox. People seem to conform to these demands without qualms. Do some research into the development of one of these neighborhoods. What are its rules? What values are implied in its construction and maintenance, whether they are stated explicitly or not?

2. It's not just prisons which California communities argue over as an economic life-force in communities. On the negative side, many cities in the state have refused "big box" stores (the prime example being Wal-Mart Supercenters) from opening. Research this issue, and write a report which explains how one community of your choosing (examples include Rosemead, Turlock, and Hercules) has waged a battle against giant retail, why, and what the outcome has been. Consider labor aspects, impact on local retail, and any other issues which you find in your research.

3. Cesar Chavez is known by many as the champion of the farm worker. Find out as much as you can about him and about the grape-pickers' strike of 1965, then write an essay which discusses the gains Chavez helped to foster and the importance of his legacy today. Be sure to include discussion of the deliberations and final enactment of the official California state holiday to honor him, which takes place on March 31st.

4. Many people say that Los Angeles as we know it wouldn't exist without "stolen" water. Read up on the issue of Owens Valley water and the aqueduct which brings it to Southern California. (Hint: start by putting "Metropolitan Water District of Southern California" into a search engine.) Then, write about the politics of water in California, discussing either past history or present issues regarding access, cost, use, or conservation. Try to figure out whether the public is tuned in to water issues, and what the various branches of government are doing to make people more aware.

5. Prisons are a huge growth industry in California, but as a fixture in the life of the state, they are nothing new. And over the years, life in prison has provided interesting subject matter for popular culture including music, TV, and film. Find a popular cultural artifact which paints a portrait of California prison culture (classic examples include the song "Folsom Prison Blues" and the film *Birdman of Alcatraz*) and write an essay in which you discuss the myth and the truth about prison life in the Golden State.

# From the Center to the Edges

People who don't live in California, and maybe even some who do reside there, commonly share a perception about the place: that it's got lots of wacky people and ideas floating around. And it's true that a lot of movements that exist outside the mainstream started in California, from the hippy movement of the 1960s to the yoga/wheatgrass juice/vegan trend of more recent times.

As years go by, these ideas are disseminated more broadly in US (and world) culture, sometimes in slightly mutated form. But their inventors and early adherents live on, continuing in the spirit of innovation with which they created their ideas and the lifestyle connected with them. Perhaps because of this, California is seen by many as a place where freedom to be yourself sometimes tips into eccentricity.

But to brand the place as a haven for the counter-cultural is to make two mistakes. One is to see new and different ideas as odd in the first place. The other is to think that everyone who lives in the state somehow exists outside the mainstream. In fact, most Californians live like people in the rest of the country do, going to work in the morning, taking out the trash one night a week, and paying their bills and trying to educate their children with what's left over. Still, whether people take advantage of it or not, in California, there's always the possibility for invention, reinvention, or to drop out of middle-class life altogether, because the California dream, to return to the subject of this book's first chapter, may be lived out in many ways, with no apology to anyone else.

This chapter represents a range of Californias, moving across a number of cultures, subcultures, and geographical areas of the state, not all of which are outside the mainstream. In these readings, you'll meet everyone from a surfer to a writer who lived among the marginalized people who make their home next to a nearly dried-up lake. The geographic range, in addition, spans the two ends of the state and a lot of what lies between. If there's one message here, it's that when you think you know California, you'll discover that it has more facets than you had imagined. And when you think you understand it, it will reveal itself in a new series of complexities.

Gerald Haslam, known as a writer with a knack for describing the unusual or out-of-the-way in California life, starts off the chapter with a description of the many groups populating California's Central Valley. He indicates both their variety and the contributions they have made to life there, and he points up the contradictions and inequalities of this vast middle region of the state.

Matt Warshaw then speaks up for youth culture. He talks about an important part of life for many Californians—surfing. His focus, in particular, is on how one young man on one day lives the dream to capture the world's biggest wave, and the results.

Clara Jeffrey and Stanley Poss range over the geography of the state from the Salton Sea in the south to Humboldt County in the northern reaches of California, but they share a thematic concern as they discuss the ways in which California individuality may be lived out. While Jeffrey portrays people on the far reaches of culture, Poss uses and plays off of the stereotype of California eccentricity, explaining its origins and its positive contributions to life in the state.

Christina Binkley rounds out this chapter by discussing how the Morongo Tribe designed its casino operation for maximum profitability. Indian gaming represents a new facet of life in California, something which has become part of the complexion of the state, influencing both its politics and economics. Binkley's piece surfaces the values that come into play when a community focuses its attention on supporting itself, and it leaves readers to decide for themselves whether the tribe in question is exploiting its origins in pursuit of profit.

In total, these essays represent just a fraction of the diversity of the Golden State, but while they may not include every manifestation of life in California, they do accurately sample the range of beliefs, lifestyles, and values which make California what it is today. This is a place where no limits to lifestyle or self-expression exist, except where the rights of others are infringed upon. The one thing people have always known about California is that you can be whoever you want to be in the state, and that, in a sentence, is the California dream.

# Other Californians
## GERALD W. HASLAM

*Gerald W. Haslam was born in Bakersfield and raised in Oildale in California's Great Central Valley, the setting of most of his books. Much of his writing, starting with a series of pieces for* The Nation *two decades ago, has sought to bring his native state's image more into line with its reality. He has particularly celebrated California's rural and small town areas and its poor and working class people of all colors. Some of his books include* Straight White Male, Workin' Man Blues, *and* Coming of Age in California. *He has won numerous awards for his writing and has been called "the quintessential California writer."*

———————————— ✦ ————————————

It is not a tourist's dream, the daylight journey from San Francisco to Los Angeles down the southwestern edge of the Great Central Valley. Brown hills press from the west, while irrigation rows seeming to flip by like fanned cards pull the eye toward the east, where the San Joaquin Plain stretches. Across it trees and plants sprout in geometric patches, but few people can be seen. This valley is vast, so from Interstate 5 extending eastward into haze toward the unseen Sierra Nevada there is a breathless sense of space: no houses, few trees, frantic whirlwinds dancing across an unplanted tract. Ahead the road shimmers as though flooded.

Night is more revealing and drivers are startled by a multicolored galaxy of lights to the east that seems to extend, in differing densities, hundreds of miles along a plain once dark and bidding. In fact, the Central Valley boasts nearly 6 million residents, as well as the fastest rate of population growth in the state. Those lights cluster mostly along the old route, Highway 99, for it is there that cities and towns have burgeoned: Bakersfield, Fresno, Stockton, Sacramento and Redding; McFarland, Manteca, Live Oak and Los Molinos. The nearby expanse remains void of lights due to corporate ownership: few small family-owned farms here, few communities, just land being tilled.

It is significant that those distant lights are multicolored, because so are the cities and towns and small farms. This Valley is the richest multiethnic rural environment in the nation. Even natives are sometimes unaware of that fact because the Valley's class system and defacto segregation disguise it. There has been a literal right and wrong side of the tracks here, with the affluent—mostly white—traditionally living east of the rail line and Highway 99 in neighborhoods with lawns and sidewalks; the less affluent often residing to the west. Symbolically, the highway has loomed like a local version of the Berlin Wall.

The principal reason for ethnic diversity in the Valley has been the availability of seasonal labor in agriculture, a constant here since the 1870s. People of all backgrounds have performed field work and have, in turn, themselves been viewed by growers as an indispensable resource. That reality has formed the basis of much of this rural society's social churning. An editorial appearing in the *San Francisco Morning Chronicle* September 5, 1875, said in part, "The farm labor problem of California is undoubtedly the worst in the United States. It is bad for the farmers themselves, and worse, if possible, for those whom they employ. In many respects, it is even worse than old-time slavery."

Because this has long been a place to start at the bottom—and, for some, to remain there—many seeking a foothold in American society have migrated here. A recent study revealed more than ninety distinct ethnic groups in present-day Sacramento alone. There have developed many ethnic enclaves in the Valley, towns with large concentrations of this group or that: Chinese in Locke, Basques in Bakersfield, Sikhs in Marysville, Swedes in Kingsburg. Woodville was originally called Irishtown because it was settled by a group from Northern Ireland. A Portuguese colony formed near Hanford and another one developed in the Delta. Alabama Colony outside Madera was settled by white migrants from the Old South. Allensworth, a community of Blacks in Tulare County, was founded in 1908 by an ex-slave, Lt. Colonel Allen Allensworth; it is now a state historical park.

Today there is a new, unofficial colony in the Valley, among the largest ever established here: 25,000 Hmongs, members of one of Southeast Asia's major groups, have settled in the region between Fresno and Merced. The Hmongs have faced resistance both passive and active from the sons and daughters of earlier migrants who find them strange, as Okies and Japanese and Russians were once considered strange. These newcomers from Asia actually fit the Valley's pattern: "What brings the Hmong to Fresno is a peculiar vision," explains Frank Viviano, "composed equally of hope for a better tomorrow and nostalgic longing for the lost agricultural past"—shades of John Steinbeck's Joads.

"Foreigners," which usually means newcomers, have provided far more than labor here. An immigrant from China shipped the first load of potatoes from this region. The Chinese, in fact, have contributed at virtually every level to Valley farming, and they have not been alone. Crops such as dwarf milo maize from Japan, alfalfa from Chile, and flax from India have been brought by migrants, and at least twenty different nationalities have contributed to the wine industry. As historian Anne Loftis has written, the Valley became "a laboratory of races," where groups often brought and practiced agricultural skills honed in their native lands.

For some, of course, their native land was here, the Valley itself, which once boasted one of the richest concentrations of American Indians on the continent—over 100,000 according to most estimates. "Three hundred tribelets of California's five hundred or more belong to this area," write anthropologists Theodora Kroeber and Robert F. Heizer. "Here were to be found most of her Indians, the predominant physical type, and carriers of the most idiosyncratic culture."

Today the Wintun, Maidu, Miwok and Yokuts remain the Valley's least acknowledged ethnic groups—the long shadow of nineteenth-century abuses still seeming to hide them from those who usurped their land. They, who provided the state's first agricultural labor force, now tend to dwell on rancherias along the dominant society's edges, consigned to poverty.

Stereotypically confused with Mexican nationals (many of whom are themselves Indians), disguised by Spanish surnames, or assimilated by intermarriage, California Indians remain hidden in this their own land. But there is something deeper and darker at the core of the invisibility of this state's natives, some festering from the American past that extends far beyond the Valley's boundaries. Indifference, especially studied indifference, may be the greatest evil of all.

Ironically, East Indians have been more prominent in Valley agriculture than have American Indians. Enduring taunts of "raghead" from local nativists when they originally migrated from the Punjab in 1905, East Indians turned out to be experts in irrigation, a skill vital to local agriculture. The Yuba City-Marysville area today boasts the largest concentration of Sikhs in the United States, more than 10,000, with new migrants arriving each day. It is a cultural center complete with a large temple, and Dadar Singh Bains, a local farmer, has become America's biggest grower of cling peaches. "The Hindu," proclaimed a commissioner of the State Bureau of Labor Statistics early in this century, "is the most undesirable immigrant in the state . . . unfit for association with American people." Today, "the Hindus" *are* American people.

The pejorative use of terms like "Raghead" and "Hindu," or "Slope" and "Gook" for Hmongs, is unfortunately also an old Valley tradition. Even more common has been scorn with which the term "Mexican" has been uttered by some, conjuring up images of stoop labor, knife fights, the ubiquitous, dark *them*. A ruddy-faced field foreman near Edison points toward a crew slowly working its way through a field that shimmers in heat and says, "Hell, they don't feel it the way a white guy does." A Tejon Ranch shop supervisor praises a tractor for its simplicity: it's "Mexican-proof." The term "Okie" was for years a fighting word unless uttered with something close to reverence. Now, with the progeny of Southwestern migrants well established, it—like "Spic" and "Hindu," "Wop," and "Portugee"—may be used with perverse pride by the grandchildren of early migrants, nativists and racists be damned.

Nativists and racists—especially those who, paradoxically, are themselves newcomers—consistently ignore the historical importance of immigrant cultures in the Valley. The San Joaquin Valley's most famous grower has arguably been Sicilian-born Joseph DiGiorgio. Coming west in 1915 with money earned wholesaling fruit on the East Coast, he had the capital necessary to dig deeper wells and pump groundwater from aquifers unavailable to those less wealthy. DiGiorgio also discovered that figs and grapes thrived near Arvin in the Valley's southern end. He acquired some 20,000 acres there, and took advantage of modern techniques to improve his harvest. Eventually, his holdings included some thirty farm properties in California, a dozen packing sheds, the Klamath Lumber and Box Company, three wineries, fruit auction houses in major eastern cities, plus ownership of the Baltimore Fruit Exchange—the list could be much longer—a considerable "farm" even by Californian standards. The *San Francisco Chronicle* once said that "DiGiorgio is to farming what Tiffany's is to jewelry."

And DiGiorgio was only one of a host of prominent Italo-American citizens in the Valley, citizens who despite their accomplishments remained "Wops" to some neighbors. Ernest and Julio Gallo became and remain the most productive wine producers in the nation, although they were challenged by Louis Petri. The Giumarra family of Kern County has dominated table grapes, and the influence of Michael Fontana's California Fruit Packing Corporation, the famous Del Monte label, has been profound. Although he did not live here, A.P. Giannini exerted great influence in the Valley through branches of his San Francisco-based Bank of America. Seeing the prominent positions achieved by many Italo-Americans, it is easy to forget that most of their families entered this Valley as laborers, that they too toiled and suffered under that faded sky, that they too faced discrimination. Like others who have succeeded, American Italians did so by dint of hard work, determination, and sharpness; nothing was given to them.

Without "Wops," the Valley would be a different and a lesser place. Racial epithets are still employed by some people who know better yet retain the habit; others, unaccomplished mostly, suffering poverty of mind if not poverty of means, still take solace in hoary illusions of racial superiority. Rough edges remain when varied cultures come together, especially when they are fighting one another for survival near the bottom of the barrel. Racism has been a problem hereabouts, though not an overwhelming one, and it emerges from a situation that also offers one of the region's great potentials: people recognizing shared goals and learning to live together in a class system that borders on a caste system. Intermarriages are increasing as commonality of experience and fate obviates ancient taboos.

Class looms larger than ethnicity in this Valley dominated by huge corporate agribusinesses. The same system that has produced such abundant farm yields has other consequences. The established model of ownership—vast tracts of land concentrated in the hands of a few—plus the need for seasonal labor, have social effects that are far from abstract.

Society here might be divided arbitrarily into five classes: the non-resident rich, corporate owners and executives; the resident rich, a group that includes family farmers, corporate managers, and successful professionals, along with those owning firms that serve agribusiness; a complicated and increasingly multiethnic middle class that includes many owners of small farms, many professionals, as well as those wearing both blue and white collars and providing services to the wealthy and impecunious alike; the upwardly mobile poor, some of them small farmers too, but most providing blue-collar work and frequently in the process of escaping the cycle of migrant labor; finally, a considerable underclass composed in large measure of recent arrivals, along with those who have never managed to escape poverty's grip. In general, each level is larger than the one above it, and less white.

There remains a dramatic and visible gap between haves and have nots in this region where, as historian W. H. Hutchinson points out, the annual value of crops exceeds the total value of all gold mined in the Golden State since 1848. Ostentatious wealth is not uncommon, nor is horrid poverty, and those things too mingle ethnicity and class: explains political scientist George Zaninovich, the son of Slavic immigrants who farmed near Delano, "Wealth is viewed as racial, the proper domain of whites."

In 1980 *The New York Times* announced that six of the ten metropolitan regions with the highest percentage of population on public assistance in the entire nation were located in the Central Valley. It is true that nonresident poor come here seeking work, but it is also true that the economic system here has required that some people remain hungry enough to accept tough work in the fields. Labor, like land and sunlight and water, has been viewed as a natural resource by growers in the Valley. Some people raised here since World War II have come to equate field labor with Mexicans—they *were* that inexpensive resource until Larry Itliong and Cesar Chavez, the latter still a favorite target of local agribusiness, upset the system by organizing the United Farm Workers.

In this place that neither Spain nor Mexico ever effectively settled or controlled, the so-called Anglo majority is now becoming a minority, and Spanish is the second language. Mexican America is, of course, culturally complex because, while other migrant groups have tended to arrive in waves, and settle, the proximity of Mexico and the fluidity of shared history combine to produce a constantly renewed first-generation of migrants from below the border.

Dolores Huerta was raised in Stockton. She has become, arguably, this state's best known Chicana, first vice president of the United Farm Workers and the union's fiery spokesperson. "The pattern here has been *not* to recognize and acknowledge the contributions of nonwhites, like the Chinese who drained the Delta, for example, or the Blacks who contributed so much to cotton culture," she asserts. "Don't be fooled, it is still extremely difficult for nonwhites to escape poverty in this state. The odds remain against us."

There was no large population of Hispanics in the Valley until the period between 1910 and 1920, when large numbers of Mexican *campesinos* joined Filipinos in the farm labor force here. Today there are Mexicans of all colors residing in the Valley, a few whose great-grandparents were born here and others who arrived this morning. Many Americans of Mexican descent have moved into the middle class and above, but many more have not. Some are well-educated professionals, while others have never escaped poverty's icy grasp, and still others—frustrated by Mexico's lack of opportunity—are on their way here right now.

Says Manuel Alderette, whose grandparents migrated north in the 1920s, "The hard thing is to decide you're going to play by

American rules. If you don't—if you avoid learning English and formal education and pretend you're still in Mexico, you might as well go back because you're going to be poor forever. I guess it's natural to want the best of both worlds: the old, familiar culture and America's wealth. But the most you can really hope for is what's happening here. In this Valley, there's a kind of compromise, a lot of Anglo culture, but more and more Mexican too."

Khatchik "Archie" Minasian was raised in Fresno County, and he started life working in agriculture, "picking grapes, turning grapes, making boxes, doing all kinds of menial labor long hours into the heat. This is what life was in the Valley for most of the Armenians—in fact, for most of the people who were willing to work."

Fresno received its first Armenian immigrants in 1885 and today [1990s] is considered one of the world's most populous Armenian cities, for they settled on their own terms and have contributed mightily to the community as it now exits. "The Armenians, who were a proud people," points out historian Loftis, "had the temerity to ignore the suggestions that they were not the equals of their American-born neighbors. They were competitive in business affairs and refused to be segregated to a special neighborhood."

One anonymous Fresnan was quoted as saying during the early period of Armenian settlement, "They are the only foreigners . . . who think they are as good as we are." As it turned out, they were indeed as good, and by the time Minasian and his cousin "Willie" Saroyan were boys early in this century, their parents' immigrant culture already constituted a major cultural presence in the Valley.

In fact, all the Valley's residents—except the Maidu, Wintun, Miwok, and Yokuts—are foreigners, and generally all have considered themselves as good as anyone else. That is why the society in this rural region remains dynamic despite constraints of economics, class and lingering racism. Tough people from varied backgrounds, people willing to toil, have settled here and built satisfying lives—especially for their children.

As a result, those apparently empty fields shimmering east of Interstate 5 are arenas where the flawed but hopeful drama of the California Dream is performed. Buzzing south, travelers see the patches of fields, occasional houses, and hawks riding wind; they see to the dark groves where small towns dot the plain. In those communities, class and ethnicity cannot be hidden or denied, and old prejudices die hard, but they are nonetheless cauldrons of change.

Kids of various colors wander barefoot over this rich soil, over these shaded streets, frequently together, with an easy multi-ethnicity uncomfortable to some of their elders. Those youngsters laughingly throw clods at one another, gaze silently at writhing dust devils, plunge naked into irrigation canals. And many of them, in their very assumptions about what is possible, in their determination to attend college or to marry one another or to see that this or that ethnic tradition is not allowed to disappear, challenge this state to live up to its promise, for the Valley *is* California, and so are they.

## Questions for Discussion

1. What are some innovations which Haslam credits to newcomers who populate the Central Valley? Find examples from throughout the article.
2. Where in the article does Haslam signal problems between the various groups he discusses? Do these examples offset the overall positive tone of the piece? Why or why not?
3. One dark aspect of the Valley is the class distinction and poverty which characterize it, according to this article. Find places where Haslam discusses this in the piece. What solutions does he offer to these problems?

## Ideas for Writing

1. Focus on one cultural group mentioned by Haslam. Learn about their immigration history and current status. Write an essay in which you explain their past and/or present roles in Central Valley life. Is this group living the California dream? What evidence can you provide to indicate this?
2. Choose one town in the Central Valley—perhaps one Haslam mentions. Use your library's research tools—such as a periodical index—to research local newspapers to find out what's going on there now. Write a "state of the town (or city)" speech which profiles the place today and discusses its strengths and challenges.

---

# Surfacing

## Matt Warshaw

*Matt Warshaw grew up surfing, edited* Surfer *magazine in his twenties, then quit to return to UC Berkeley, graduating with a BA in history in 1992. Degree in hand, he returned to writing, producing several books on the sport and compiling* The Encyclopedia of Surfing *(Harcourt 2003). Warshaw was ranked #43 on the world professional surfing tour in 1982 and has surfed in Brazil, Hawaii, Australia, and elsewhere. He is now based in San Francisco.*

———————————— ✦ ————————————

Sixteen-year-old Jay Moriarity from Santa Cruz was so intent on paddling into his first wave of the day and pushing up into the correct stance—and he nailed it, feet spread wide across the deck of his board, head tucked, weight forward and low—that he didn't at first realize he'd lifted off the water and was now surfing through air, just ahead of the curl, thirty feet above sea level.

Moriarity, as the big-wave expression goes, didn't penetrate. The wave had pulsed and expanded as it rolled over Maverick's reef, passing quickly from canted to vertical to concave, at which point Moriarity should have been two-thirds of the way down the face, driving like a javelin for flat water. But a draft of wind had slipped under the nose of Moriarity's surfboard—and instead here he was, still in his best big-wave crouch, levitating near the wave's apex. Now the nose of his board lifted up and backward onto a near-perfect vertical axis, its brightly airbrushed underbelly exposed and sharply limned in the morning light. The crest hooked forward, and Moriarity's arms came up and spread out from either side of his board, creating a Maverick's tableau that couldn't be taken as anything other than a kind of crucifixion.

The religious metaphor is an easy one to make—since big-wave surfers themselves so often use spiritual terms to characterize and illustrate their sport—but it makes you wonder how God, or Lono, or any such divine presence, could have decided to flick Jay Moriarity, Maverick's youngest and sweetest surfer, into the abyss. He was Jay, no nickname, friendly, wholesome, and unjaded—as compared to Flea, Ratboy, Skindog, and a few of the other red-hot and moderately profane Santa Cruz surfers known collectively as the Vermin.

The previous evening, at about 9 P.M., halfway through his evening shift in the kitchen at Pleasure Point Pizza in Santa Cruz, Moriarity phoned the National Weather Service for the updated buoy and weather report. For the past few days, he'd been tracking a North Pacific storm, and his eyebrows went up in stages as he discovered that the surf was going to be bigger than he'd thought, and it was due to arrive in just a few hours.

At 5 A.M. the next morning, Moriarity steered his mother's Datsun pickup north on Highway 1 out of Santa Cruz, a pair of ten-foot, eight-inch surfboards stacked diagonally in the truck bed. An hour later he pulled off the highway near Pillar Point Harbor, just a few hundred yards north of the Half Moon Bay city limit. Maverick's wasn't visible, but out past the harbor jetty, Moriarity could see smooth, wide-spaced ribbons of swell moving toward shore. Big for sure. Maybe bigger than he'd ever seen it.

Another two dozen people—surfers from San Francisco, Santa Cruz, Half Moon Bay, and Pacifica, along with a few surf photographers and spectators—also were driving toward Maverick's in the predawn light. Moriarity parked near the harbor, where he was going to catch a ride on *Lizzie-Lynn*, a twenty-six-foot fishing boat hired by one of the photographers. Moriarity jogged toward the dock, a surfboard under each arm. The weather was dry and brittle, in the upper 40s, but a steady east wind made it seem colder as Moriarity stepped aboard *Lizzie-Lynn*. The boat began to pitch and roll as it cleared the harbor entrance, but it was a short ride, and ten minutes later *Lizzie-Lynn* pulled into a deepwater channel adjacent to Maverick's, about seventy-five yards south of the breaking surf.

It was just past 7 A.M. Ten riders were already in the water, loosely clustered and sitting on their boards, alert but casual as they watched the ocean and waited. The surf had been relatively calm during the boat's approach. Now, almost on cue, a set of waves shifted through the water about a half-mile past the surfers—all of whom snapped to attention like pointers.

Moriarity watched the first wave track across the distant part of the reef, which served as a kind of anteroom for Maverick's-bound swells. The wave, shaped like a broad-based pyramid, grew steadily, then fringed along the crest as it intersected with the group of surfers, their arms like pinwheels as they clambered up the face and dropped, safe, down the back slope. No takers. Not even an exploratory side-long look.

Jay Moriarity stood like a tuning fork on the deck of *Lizzie-Lynn*, staring, almost vibrating with nervous anticipation, three words looping through his mind—*huge and perfect, huge and perfect*. Then a pragmatic thought: *too much wind*.

As he ran down his tactical checklist and got ready to slip over the edge of *Lizzie-Lynn*, Moriarity watched Evan Slater wheel his board around and paddle into the second wave of the set. Slater got to his feet smoothly, but the wind flicked him sideways—just like that. He landed midway down the face on the small of his back, skipped once, twice, then disappeared as the tube threw out around him like a giant blown-glass bubble and collapsed. "Oh my God!" someone on the boat yelled. Everyone scanned the wave's white-foaming aftermath until Slater's head popped up about a hundred feet shoreward from where he'd gone down. More wild shrieks of amazement—"That was *insane!*"—voices tinged with nervous relief. *Lizzie-Lynn* had been in the channel less than two minutes.

Moriarity squatted down, unzipped his nylon backpack, and pulled out a full-length hood-to-ankle neoprene wetsuit, black with blue accents, plus a long-sleeve polypropylene undershirt, a pair of wetsuit booties, and a pair of webbed gloves. The ocean temperature was a skin-tightening fifty-two degrees, but with this layered outfit he might stay in the water for hours.

As Moriarity paddled toward the Maverick's lineup, Half Moon Bay's twelve thousand residents were getting showered and dressed, pouring coffee, reviewing the Monday morning headlines, and glancing outside to take note of the ongoing stretch of temperate weather. Commuters moved onto the highways, driving north to San Francisco, south to San Jose, east to Silicon Valley. Most of Half Moon Bay High's students were still sleeping through their first few hours of Christmas vacation.

What Half Moon Bay locals were not doing was paying any attention to the fact that Moriarity, Slater and the rest were at that moment tilting against waves bigger than anything surfers had ever faced anywhere in the world outside of Hawaii. Maverick's would in the days ahead produce international headlines. It would eventually produce bigger surf. But that morning, December 19, 1994, the huge wind-sculpted waves were changing the big-wave surfing landscape—and doing so in showy, dramatic style.

That it was happening in near-seclusion was partly a matter of geography, as Maverick's is hidden from view behind Pillar Point's silt and sandstone headland and the adjacent boat harbor breakwater. But Maverick's was also relatively unknown: It had publicly debuted to the surf world just eighteen months earlier, in a six-page *Surfer* magazine feature story. For two years before that, it had been something of a shared secret among twenty-five or so northern California surfers.

In addition, Half Moon Bay wasn't a hard-core surf town, and never had been. San Francisco, twenty-five miles north, had long occupied a special niche in the surf world—partly due to the incredibly photogenic wave that breaks under the southern span of the Golden Gate Bridge, but more so because of the curious and pleasing fact that surfing could take root and flourish on the perimeter of such a famous, sophisticated urban center. Santa Cruz, meanwhile, fifty-eight miles south of Half Moon Bay, had a strong claim as the world's greatest surf city. High-quality surf breaks are strung together like beads along the Santa Cruz coastline and the near-Homeric scope of local surf history goes back to 1885, when Edward, David and Cupid Kawananakoa, three blue-blooded Hawaiian teenagers attending a local military school, crafted boards for themselves from redwood planks and tested the shorebreak near the San Lorenzo rivermouth—becoming not just the first surfers in Santa Cruz but the first surfers in America. Wetsuit magnate Jack O'Neill opened his first shop here in 1959. Tom Curren, three-time world champion and American surfing icon, opened his 1990 world title run with a contest win at Steamer Lane, Santa Cruz's best-known break. A few years later, Darryl Virostko, Josh Loya, Chris Gallagher, Peter Mel, Kenny Collins, Jay Moriarity and other young Santa Cruz locals had collectively become the hottest regionally connected troupe of surfers in California.

Half Moon Bay wasn't off the surfing map entirely in 1994. Some of the reefs north of town occasionally produced good, powerful waves, and the long crescent-shaped beach south of the harbor was a fallback when the surf was small. Local surf history, though, was thin and mostly unrecorded. Just a few people, for instance, knew the story of Maverick, the white-haired German shepherd who, one winter's day in 1961, tore into the water behind three Half Moon Bay surfers as they paddled out to try the distant waves off Pillar Point. One of the surfers, Alex Matienzo, who lived with Maverick's owner, thought the surf looked too rough for the dog. Matienzo paddled back to the beach, whistled Maverick in, and tied him to the car bumper. The waves ended up being too rough for the surfers as well; they soon returned to the beach without having done much riding, and left Pillar Point alone after that. Because Maverick the dog had obviously gotten the most out of the experience, Matienzo and his friends called the intriguing but vaguely sinister Pillar Point surf break "Maverick's Point"—or just Maverick's.

Surfing and surf culture hadn't yet made any real impression in Half Moon Bay, which by 1994 was known more for its weathered rows of cut-flower greenhouses and its neatly groomed acres of brussels sprouts, broccoli, and artichokes, for the horse stables, the stately Beaux-Arts city hall building, the sublime foothill views along Highway 92, and an elaborate and well-attended annual pumpkin festival appropriate for a city billing itself as "The

Pumpkin Capital of the World." Strip malls had gone up near downtown and touristy seafood restaurants and nautical-themed gift shops were clustered by the harbor, but local slow-growth advocates had been masterful at keeping large-scale commercialization at bay. They had shut down all attempts to widen Highway 1 and expand the Half Moon Bay airport. Residents, for the most part, were happy to be at a friendly but distinct remove from San Francisco.

Half Moon Bay, the oldest city in San Mateo County, nonetheless has a long and interesting mercantile connection to the sea. Portuguese whalers, in the late nineteenth century, dragged California grays and humpbacks onto the sandy hook of beach just inside Pillar Point, where they rendered slabs of blubber in enormous iron cook pots. Wooden ships were often gutted on the nearby reefs, some producing horrible scenes of splintered planks and floating corpses, others bringing sudden windfall.

During Prohibition, Half Moon Bay bootleggers filled their customized shallow-hulled boats with cases of Canadian-made scotch, rum, gin, and champagne, darted through the surf at night, and made their prearranged drops in the shadowy coves south of Pillar Point. Federal authorities were for the most part outgeneralled by the bootleggers, but in 1932 a midnight skirmish between a Coast Guard patrol boat and a local rumrunner in high seas off Moss Beach resulted in rifle fire, machine gun fire, *cannon* fire, a kidnapped government agent, some hypothermic open-ocean swimming, two separate chases and four hundred cases of high-quality booze being tossed overboard.

Big fines and the prospect of serious prison time may have forced bootleggers to run this kind of no-surrender gauntlet. But it must have been fantastic open-ocean sport, too. "You experience a thrill and fear at the same time," big-wave surfing pioneer Buzzy Trent wrote in 1965, in a passage that might apply equally to Prohibition bootleggers and Maverick's surfers. "You hear that crack and thunder, you feel the wet spray . . . you just power through, hoping you won't get the ax. And then if you do make it, you get a wonderful feeling inside."

Jay Moriarity had a different feeling inside—not so wonderful—as he lifted off the face of his giant wave, spread his arms, and hung like a marionette just ahead of the crest. Thirty feet above the trough, he levitated for a little more than a second. The wind then flipped his board back over the top of the wave, and the curl, distended and grossly thick, pitched forward and blotted Moriarity from view. For a half-beat the wave poured forward, untouched and unmarked. Then Moriarity's surfboard reappeared from the wave's back slope and was swiftly pulled forward "over the falls" into the growing thundercloud of whitewater—a bad sign. Moriarity's board was tethered to his ankle by a fifteen-foot, nearly half-inch-thick urethane leash, and the only way it could have been brought back into play was if Moriarity himself, deep and unseen inside the wave, had been dragged down into Maverick's aptly named Pit.

The wave was now a thirty-foot levee of whitewater, crowned by fifty feet of swirling mist and vapor. Below the surface, energy and mass burst downward, creating a field of vertical-flushing gyratory columns, and Moriarity, trapped inside one of these columns, spun end over end until his back and shoulders were fixed against the ocean floor. He clenched, and a bubble of oxygen rushed past his teeth. Maverick's was a deepwater break, he'd been told; nobody ever hit bottom. The next wave would be overhead in another ten or twelve seconds, and Moriarity wondered if, from this depth, he could get to the surface—to air—before it arrived.

Moriarity pushed off and took a huge, sweeping breast-stroke. He opened his eyes to near-opaque blackness. Four more strokes, five, legs in a flutter kick, exhaling slowly, eyes staring upward, stroke, the light becoming a diffuse gray-green, stroke, throat clamped shut, then one last thrust to break the surface—and he threw his head back, mouth stretched open. He'd been down for just over twenty seconds, but he'd beat the second wave—barely. Two quick breaths, and he hunched over defensively as the whitewater roared over, sending him on another underwater loop, shorter but just as violent. Pinpoints of light were zipping across his field of vision by the time he resurfaced.

Moriarity's breath was deep and ragged. There was no third wave. His respiratory rate eased, and as his eyes refocused, he saw that his surfboard was broken in half: the smaller piece—the tail section—was still attached to his leash; the nose section floated nearby. Evan Slater suddenly appeared, looking concerned. Did he need any help? Moriarity shook his head. No, he'd be okay. He swam over to the front half of his surfboard, hoisted himself on deck, and began slowly paddling back to *Lizzie-Lynn*.

In the late eighties, a surf magazine writer theorized that the essential requirement for big-wave riding is not courage, or daring, or fitness, but a placid imagination. Where an ordinary surfer taking full measure of a wave like Maverick's will lose himself in one of a near-endless number of death-by-misadventure scenarios, the big-wave surfer, fantasy-free, paddles out with some degree of aplomb. And as the untroubled imagination reduces fear and anxiety beforehand, it may also smooth things out afterward. Jay Moriarity, a week later, couldn't do much more than sketch out in the most obvious terms the big-wave vignette—generally described at that point as the worst wipeout, or at least the worst looking wipeout, in surfing history—that soon appeared on the cover of *Surfer* and the front section of the *New York Times Magazine.* "I started to stand up," he told *Surfer,* "and thought, 'This will be a cool wave.' Then the whole thing ledged out and I had time to think, 'Oh, shit. This is not good.'"

Go to http://www.healthebay.org/brc/statemap.asp and click a box to see the beach condition for today.

**Beach Condition Report Card Online (healthebay.org)**

*Source:* http://www.healthebay.org/brc/statemap.asp

But maybe that's unfair. Moriarity's banal reaction may have had less to do with a deficient imagination than with the general inarticulateness of sixteen-year-olds. Or perhaps he was just following the form of big-wave protocol that says, play it down, play it cool.

Either way, there was nothing banal about what Moriarity did for an encore that morning. After tossing the pieces of his broken board onto the deck of *Lizzie-Lynn*, he took a short breather, grabbed his reserve board, ran a bar of sticky wax across the top for traction, and paddled back into the lineup.

Forty-five minutes later he caught another wave, nearly as big as the first one, and made it. In the next five hours he caught eight more waves and made them all.

## Questions for Discussion

1. The writer of this piece is heavily involved in the surfing subculture. Where do you sense his tone or language becoming almost mystical as he discusses surfing? If his intention is to make his audience curious about the lure of the sport, how does his language foster this feeling?

2. The article spends considerable time providing contexts for the Jay Moriarity story by discussing the town and the history of smuggling there. What does this information do to enrich the theme of the article?

3. What happened to Jay Moriarity almost killed him. The article, however, downplays the danger as it discusses his wipeout. What do you think Warshaw wants you to believe about surfing from reading this piece? How does he reinforce this theme?

## Ideas for Writing

1. Do some research into the problem of "localism" amongst surfers. Find a particular example to use as you write an essay in which you discuss how localism goes against the stereotype of the laidback surfer as described in "Surfacing" and elsewhere.

2. Read through a copy of a monthly surfing magazine. Do a content analysis on both the text and the images you find there: What audience is in view? What is assumed about who's in, who's out, and what their values are? How do text and graphics, including ads, complement each other? Write about your findings in an essay in which you explain the insider elements of the subculture you find there and critique the magazine for its biases.

# "Slab City," from "Go West, Old Man"
## CLARA JEFFREY

*Clara Jeffrey served as a senior editor for* Harper's Magazine. *She currently works as deputy editor for* Mother Jones *magazine.* Mother Jones *describes itself as "an independent nonprofit whose roots lie in a commitment to social justice implemented through first-rate investigative reporting." Check it out at www.motherjones.com. Jeffrey lives in San Francisco.*

✦

Entering Niland from the south, I pass the "Chamber of Commerce and RV dump" (a fenced-in dirt lot that hosts a weekly swap meet) and a downtown consisting largely of vacant storefronts. Three miles east of town a small butte marks the old shoreline of Lake Cahuilla, but geology cannot compete with what Leonard Knight has done to it. Using donated paint and mud adobe, Leonard has created an enormous Technicolor landscape—part Pennsylvania Dutch, part Pentecostal—called Salvation Mountain. The work's centerpiece is a giant heart containing the message: JESUS I'M A SINNER PLEASE COME UPON MY BODY AND INTO MY HEART.

Slab City itself is an odd combination of mobility and decay. A gold-rush town without the gold. A pioneer town with satellite TV. Residents turn junk (and junk is everywhere) into shelter, into art. But this is a place where people come not to make something of themselves but to unmake themselves, or at least to leave their pasts so far back in the rearview mirror that it doesn't hurt anymore. Most have fled life's ordinary tragedies, but there are honest-to-God outlaws here, "people whose radar you don't want to be on," one resident warns.

To the casual visitor, the Slabs is a curiosity, one more stop on the see-America-in-your-RV tour. Next will come Yuma, or Quartzsite, or wherever the yen for mobility and a good swap meet takes you. But a lack of resources is the main reason people come to Slab City. A huge gaggle of elderly flock here because their VA and Social Security checks can't cover the cost of a $10-a-night RV park. They come because free is all they can afford, because it's warm, and a short drive to Mexico, where maybe they can buy the medications they need. And they come because although they treasure their independence they're scared of being alone.

During the winter, the population swells to a few thousand residents, the vast majority of whom pack up and leave before summer, when the temperature frequently reaches 110 degrees. Each year a few folks stay on—usually because they're dead broke—and if they survive the heat (I was told that in 2000 nine people did not) they might never leave again. For them, full-time RVing or biking or drifting has become full-time slabbing.

February is the peak season, and all the best spots—known by function, description, or resident—are taken. Driving down Main Street, I pass Poverty Flats and School Bus slab, where the kids who go to school wait for the bus. At the north corner of a dusty intersection Solar Mike sells and repairs the solar panels and batteries that serious RVers depend on. I turn right toward a blue trailer emblazoned with large white wooden letters, WELCOME SLAB CITY SINGLES ("and auxiliary," reads a small caveat).

The Slab City Singles clubhouse is composed of three trailers—a pantry, a library, and a game room—encircling a covered kitchen area; tarps provide a limited wind break. Out front a bunch of raggedy furniture serves as a living room; a fire pit sits out back.

Once inside the dining area, I am approached by a man named Chuck. With a bright blue alpine hat woven from plastic Wal-Mart bags, a cheerful, white-bearded face, a yellow bandanna tied jauntily around his neck, and an Arkansas drawl, Chuck is reminiscent of the benevolent figures found in Disney forests. As is Art, with his elfin ears, stooped shoulders, and a sort of utility belt, cinched not far below his armpits, from which various objects, including a cup, dangle.

"Are you single?" Chuck asks. He's forty years my senior, but I assent.

"Can you cook?"

Before I can answer, a rooster crows from the center of his chest. I jump. He taps a device on his sternum and looks up bashfully. "That's to remind me to take my glaucoma medicine."

Gary wanders in, wearing a poncho. "I'm the token Indian," he says. A former cop in his early fifties, Gary is one of the club's youngest members, as is Wilson, who has an English accent, wears a kepi, and lives in a tent. We all sit out front, shielding our eyes from the sun as David approaches.

"Who've we got here," he says, taking a chair that promptly collapses. After a moment's embarrassment he begins grilling me, cocking a cauliflowered ear to hear the answers to his questions: what am I doing here and where am I from and how old am I and can I cook.

The last question becomes a familiar refrain. The club has about seventy members, mostly unattached men (Chuck and his wife, Peggy Sue, form the "auxiliary"), but new women seem to be valued less as fresh meat than as fresh meat preparers. "Most of these old guys aren't looking for a girlfriend," Wilson later says, "but a mother, I swear to God." There are two other singles clubs in town. The primogenitor is Loners on Wheels, which has chapters all over North America, as does its offspring and rival, the Loners of America (LOAs). Despite the slogan "where singles mingle," the LOWs in Slab City, mostly women, rigorously enforce a no-cohabitation rule to the point of celibacy. They do host the occasional square dance, Wilson says, but "I wound up with some eighty-year-old guy getting all upset because I'm dancing with some old bird who he thinks is his girlfriend. And I need that like a bloody hole in my head." The point of Slab City is to escape that kind of bullshit, those kinds of feuds and rules and conventions, he says, they all say, before detailing the various feuds and rules and conventions currently causing them strife.

In addition to the singles clubs there are annual migrations of Canadians who cluster down by the canal, fortified bunkers scattered here and there, the Apple Dumpling Gang dune-buggy enthusiasts—the endlessly recombining and sometimes squabbling constituencies of Slab City. A central tenet of RV living is: if you don't like your neighbor, just move. But if you have a good spot, with a slab and a gopher hole and maybe even a mesquite tree, and your neighbor is a jerk, why should you move? It's easier, as I would learn, to burn him out.

For the time being I am mercifully ignorant of such territorial remedies, though I know enough to ask where to park my rented RV. After some consideration, they pick a central spot where they can "look out" for me. And for the next two and a half weeks, they do, particularly Wilson, who develops a habit of magically appearing at my side.

Once established, I head to the [local] bird festival. The participants have gathered at a country club where Orvis dealers, wildlife photographers, and environmental groups hawk their wares. In a conference room off to the side, Steve Horvitz, superintendent of the Salton Sea State Park (he has since become chairman of an NGO called Save Our Sea II), regales us with the area's ecological problems. Horvitz talks of the sea's heyday in the early sixties, when the state park received more visitors than Yosemite; when 600,000 boats were launched; when the Salton City 500, called "power boat racing's richest event," was televised on CBS; and residents complained of traffic. Yet at a recent picnic of park employees, he says, everyone paused, forks in midair, to watch a boat go by. "One boat on California's biggest lake and it stopped conversation." He adds that a 1989 survey found that more than half of the people who once visited the sea are now afraid of even being near it.

And who can blame them? Come to the sea and chances are as good as not that you'll be confronted by rafts of dead fish that can stretch on for acres and a stench that seems to combine all the world's worst smells—urine-soaked hallways, skunk, manure, vomit, sulfur dioxide—into one hideous potpourri so malodorous that a Palm Springs attorney who lives forty miles away once demanded Horvitz put an end to it or face a lawsuit.

The smell and the dead fish can be traced back to the problem of nutrient loading. Treated but still phosphate-rich sewage combines with nitrogen-rich runoff to form a kind of MiracleGro that causes algae to bloom. This has several effects. Brown algae is the main staple of the far too abundant tilapia, in turn the main food source of the corvina. Thus, too much brown algae equals too many fish. Worse is the green algae. Its blooms can cover huge portions of the sea, and when they die off the algae decomposes, taking oxygen out of the water and causing a horrible stench. Fish in oxygen-depleted waters surface for air and, failing to get it, die. The death throes of the fish, some of which carry avian botulism, attract birds. In 1997, the disease killed 10,000 endangered brown pelicans. The irony is that the sea has too much life—too many nutrients, too much algae, too many fish.

Fierce debates rage over which is the more dire threat to the sea: the salinity or the nutrient loading. Either one would cost tens of millions, perhaps billions, to address, a tab no one is rushing to pick up, and certainly one that Imperial County, California's poorest, cannot pay alone. This quandary plays right into the hands of the sea's true nemeses: the water managers of Los Angeles, San Diego, and Palm Springs. One water manager told Horvitz that the 1.3 million acre-feet (one acre-foot equaling roughly 326,000 gallons) that flow into the sea each year were "worth a great deal of money to us . . . We want it. We're going to get it. And there's nothing that you can do to stop us."

After Horvitz concludes his talk, I take him aside. His rusty hair and beard are neatly cropped and flecked with gray, and he possesses that solemnity about the planet common to geology majors. Horvitz believes the sea could be saved if the state and federal governments would commit to doing so, but they're "really only good at moving water around. Destroying where it comes from and destroying where it goes." "The sea itself has no rights to the water," he says, so "there's a lot of angling for it," and the metropolitan water authorities would gladly see the ecosystem collapse, because then nothing would stand in their way. California's water rush has lasted for a hundred years, but the more sources that tap out the more valuable are those that remain.

He ticks off a list of examples: In 1993 the billionaire Bass brothers of Texas (and Biosphere 2) bought 42,000 acres of Imperial Valley farmland to sell their allotment of water to San Diego. In 1989 the Imperial Irrigation District cut a deal with Los Angeles whereby the IID conserves 107,000 acre-feet of water a year, and L.A. gets that much more Colorado River water. Now a hotly contested deal is under way in which the IID would "conserve" another 300,000 acre-feet so that it can "transfer" (sell) that "saved" water to San Diego and Coachella Valley (the northern part of the Salton Sink, containing Palm Springs). Although this deal is by no means done, hanging in the balance is a seven-state water treaty, and if California cannot decide the fate of the Salton Sea by December 31 [2002], the Interior Department has threatened to withhold Colorado River water, which would almost certainly lead to rationing in southern California.

The forces aligned against the sea are powerful, which is perhaps why, historically, most environmentalists haven't rushed to its defense. Although California's sprawl problem is at least as attributable to its post-Proposition 13 reliance on commercial development for revenue as to immigration, environmentalists fear that to fight for the sea is to risk accusations of racism, says Horvitz. And Washington is sick of California's disproportionate share of budgetary attention; the state created its natural-resource crises, why should Congress continually bail it out?

I am late for the communal dinner back at Slab City Singles. Four o'clock did not mean, as I had assumed, that the cooking would commence at 4:00 but that the dishes would be done by 4:30. "Some of these guys are really old," explains Wilson. "Look there at Art"—who was shuffling off toward his trailer—"he's going to bed. You'll never see him out past dark." Art, who'd celebrate his eightieth birthday while I was in camp, isn't the oldest. The oldest is Irv, who is eighty-eight and has a great-great-grandson. "He shouldn't be here," someone explained, "but his family doesn't want him, he's too damn mean."

Slab City lacks any kind of medical facility, but in some ways life here isn't that different than at your average retirement community. There are a bewildering array of clubs and activities for those who wish to join. Banter, coffee, tall tales, and card games are also plentiful; only they take place at the fire pit instead of in a cafeteria.

The dean of the fire pit is Frank, a rail-thin World War II veteran who seems cast as the ol' prospector. He pulls off black boots and reveals long thin feet covered in what seem to be ladies' trouser stockings: sheer, navy blue, with vertical piping. He sits back and theorizes about the hidden levers of power, linking King Fahd to the Hudson's Bay Company to Pamela Harriman. Frank is a vegetarian. He practices yoga. He is also referred to by Slabbers as "the local Shylock." "I saw a number of unsavory characters stop at his rig, go in for a moment, and come back out," says a club member. "You didn't hear that from me." And perhaps because of his profession, though others claimed that a feud within the club was the cause, his rig was burned down last year.

"Accidentally?" asks Richard, a community-theater director who resembles the cowardly lion.

"Accidentally on purpose," says Wilson.

Social hour ends a good six hours before my normal bedtime. Back in my rig, hyper-vigilance to potential arsonists makes sleep impossible, so I open Salt Dreams and read about another misbegotten utopia found across the sea, Salton City.

> *Think about the picture you have in mind of the perfect place, and the ideal setting. Wouldn't it be much like this? A place ringed by snow-capped mountains and bathed in warm sunshine winter and summer, and cooled by sea breezes. . . . I have never been able to stand on that rise of land above the Salton Sea without seeing a grand resort city. Now our dream is coming to life.*

-M. PENN PHILLIPS, FIRST DEVELOPER OF SALTON CITY

It is easy, with hindsight, to make a distinction between a dreamer and a liar, a seer and a sucker. But a steady diet of lies can sustain a human being for a long time, especially when the liar believes as well. It's impossible to say whether M. Penn Phillips knew he was running a pyramid scheme, or really believed he was building the pyramids. It doesn't matter now. Salton City functions best as metaphor, the endgame of manifest destiny.

In 1958, Phillips spent $150,000 on 19,600 acres of barren land on the sea's western shore, where the temperature exceeds 100 degrees one day in three. He bulldozed a maze of roads, laid sewer and water lines. He planted 9,000 fan palms along grand boulevards with improbable names like Avon and Acapulco. For as little as $250 down and $29 a month, so went his pitch, ordinary people could enjoy a piece of the "Salton Riviera," which would be "bigger than Capri and Monaco and Palm Beach combined . . . the most valuable piece of resort property on earth." He took prospective buyers on aerial tours, so they could scout property from the clouds. That many buyers would have no equity until the property was entirely paid off did not deter them. On opening day May 21, 1958, Phillips made $4.25 million.

Two years and another $20 million in sales later, Phillips pulled out. He'd drawn back his curtain, but people were too invested to admit that they'd bought into an illusion. The Holly Corporation promptly pursued making Phillips's dream a reality. They built golf courses and marinas and yacht clubs and hotels; they staged their Salton City 500; they lured the Beach Boys, Frank Sinatra, Dean Martin, and President Eisenhower to Salton City, though it is unclear whether Frank and Deano sang or only played golf, like Ike, on the fairways sloping toward the sea. The celebrities were part of the mirage. Around 1971, the Holly developers took their money and ran to Lake Havasu, where they would soon relocate the London Bridge.

Strangely, when the plug was pulled, the waters rose, and soon all that was left of Salton City's ring-a-ding days was the space-age roof of the Yacht Club looking forlornly out over vanished marinas and half-submerged telephone poles. The golf courses have reverted to sand, the palm trees are mostly dead. Sick of being sued for property damage, the IID bought as much waterfront property as it could and razed the Yacht Club and the entire archipelago of sodden aspirations. Today the area boasts one state dump zone for hazardous waste (buried atop ten fault lines), and soon another will receive up to 20,000 tons of L.A.'s trash per day. "Essentially what they are doing to our county is throwing us bones while they're trying to destroy the Salton Sea," says Norm Niver, a community activist and gadfly who wears a Hawaiian shirt and has played music at Merv Griffin's house. We are in the Salton City Chamber of Commerce, which is a step up from that of Niland, but a small step.

Norm's dream for Salton City isn't that different from what Phillips planned, but he has a better idea of what it's up against, starting with a Coolidge Administration law that mandates how much Colorado River water each state in its watershed receives annually. California was allotted 4.4 million acre-feet but has been using 5.2, which nobody minded until Arizona and New Mexico caught the development virus. In 1998, the Clinton Administration brokered a "Quantification Settlement Agreement" whereby California would gradually reduce its take and various water districts would settle their disputes. All provisions have been agreed to, except for the matter of diverting 300,000 acre-feet that now go to the Salton Sea to supply San Diego and Coachella Valley. It's the sea or sprawl. And sprawl has all the clout.

"They're growing a cancer over there," says Norm. "They've got their golf courses going in, their country clubs going in, and all that is 'reasonable, beneficial use' of the water. Everything that's going on in Coachella Valley for the richest 2 percent of people on Earth, maybe 1 percent—101 golf courses, two-mile-long water-skiing lakes where homes start at $1 million . . . the water shopping mall going in at Rancho Mirage because those people 'like to shop around water—that's reasonable and beneficial. Why is this not reasonable and beneficial? We have all these birds and fish, we lose 50 percent of our birds if we keep screwing around with the sea. People say, well, if they don't come here, they'll just go someplace else, but that's not true, because the scientists tell us that they are taxed. They are broken down. They don't have the energy to go find another place."

Norm can rattle off any number of reasons why destroying the sea would be morally wrong and even economically stupid ("it'll cost them a heck of a lot more to do nothing; the dust bowls, the lawsuits, just like Owens Valley"), but he realizes that the plight of property owners doesn't stoke public outrage, and environmental issues do. As a friend put it to him, "It's the birds, not your asses." Unfortunately, the fates of all concerned are in the hands of entities that, seen in the best possible light, are slow to act. Since none of the usual cavalries are coming to the rescue, Norm has, in the best Salton City tradition, pinned his hopes on a quick fix, in this case Terra Organics, a bioremediation company that sketchily claims it can treat the water with microorganisms that will consume the nutrients that feed the algae. These 49 microscopic Pacmans have given a lot of people a lot of hope out here," says Norm.

"Hey, kiddo," Wilson says the next morning. "You want to go visit the Rhinos?" He's been hoarding government issued food to bring to a Slab family. The kids are always hungry; the father—Rhino—is a wild man. There's trouble there, drugs, mental illness, it's hard to say exactly what, but it'll "break your heart." On the way, he and Ron, a big biker who once chaperoned Secretariat around the world, will show me some local attractions.

We load sacks of potatoes and cans of generic food into the back of Ron's minute Datsun pickup and squeeze into the front seat, my feet propped on the dash so that Ron can shift; he grunts an apology with every gear change. First stop is Stab City's home-made desert golf course, eighteen holes, Ron says, "but all you need is a sand wedge." The biggest hazard is an active bombing range that borders the course. Scavengers have been killed or maimed trying to gather artillery casings. Most hail from the Badlands, an outlying area of Slab City full of dealers and crazies who live in compounds fortified by fences, dogs, KEEP OUT signs, and the occasional exchange of gunfire. Wilson points out one such bunker. "Don't ever think you can go over there, luv. I don't go over there."

At the Rhinos' the warning is more profound. Cans and bot-tles and soggy toys are strong to their chain-link fence, which surrounds rotting piles of clothing and refuse and a few dilapi-dated vehicles. "Wait here," says Wilson as we climb out. "They don't know your truck." What looks to be an eighteen-year-old girl approaches. She's wearing a sort of outback hat over coppery skin and dark eyes. Her hands are twitching. "There's Mrs. Rhino." She looks at him foggily. "It's Wilson," he says, but the kids—three boys and a girl, the oldest maybe eight—have already recognized him and grab at his jeans. "What'd you bring, what'd you bring?" they ask. We open the back of the truck and they set upon us like refugees. "What's this?" asks the oldest boy, holding up a can that clearly says corn. Another little boy named Harley gives me a shy smile. His teeth are made of metal.

We carry the food through the compound to the main trailer, also filled with garbage. The kids paw through the offerings and look as if they might eat the potatoes raw. "Thank you, thank you," they cry. Mrs. Rhino thanks us, too, and tells us that Rhino is out trying to sell their pickup. Wilson and Ron express dismay. Loss of mobility, though no one says it, can only spell more disas-ter for this family.

Back near the Singles Club, Wilson spots Rhino leaning over the bed of his truck talking with a few guys. As we climb out, Wilson warns me to keep my mouth shut. Rhino seems at least six four, a big but not fat frame packed into overalls, an outback hat topping a huge black beard and maniacal eyes. His gestures are simultaneously menacing and Falstaffian. He's talking to a white-haired, pockmarked guy in head-to-toe camouflage that matches the netting strung over his camp in the background. The other two guys are filthy, mostly toothless cooter types sunburned a deep pink; their blue eyes glitter from tweaking or poor wiring.

"We've just been out to see Mrs. Rhino. Brought you some food," says Wilson. Rhino thanks him. "Hear you're selling your truck?" "Got to, man," says Rhino, "I gotta file a lawsuit to get my kid back." He tells the tale of one or perhaps two kids being taken by social services. The caseworkers won't visit his place anymore. "They say they're scared. Look at me, am I going to hurt anybody? Government says that my children are in the lower fifth, a 'failure to thrive.' I tell them all my kids start out small, but look at me!" he says, drawing himself up to his full height. He's so animated that he seems to occupy more than three dimensions. "DEA, FBI, HHS, ATF—I got four government agencies with initials that know everything about me. I've been examined, plucked, and prodded. They know how many public hairs I got and how many on my ass."

"You know where this is going," says the vet guy. "Weapons." The cooters nod.

"That's right," says Rhino. He briefly lowers his voice. "I've got it on good authority that in fifty-one days thirty-seven different militias will join forces. Something big will go DOWN." Not that he's in a militia mind you. "They'd either kill me or make me their king!" he shouts.

There should be a certain rhythm to my days, learning about the sea while it's light, returning to the Slabs in the evening, but something's always a little off. Like the way I am awakened abruptly. Yesterday Gary pounded on my door and shouted, "Get your raggedy ass out of bed!" and left a cup of coffee on my steps. Today it is David who knocks. He silently hands me a poem that begins, "Our deepest fear is not that we are inadequate. Our deepest fear is that we are powerful beyond measure."

It's been raining off and on for the last few days, at a rate that elsewhere would be entirely unremarkable but here—where the average annual rainfall is 2.92 inches—is a catastrophe, filling the papers with gloomy harvest prognoses and the ditches with tractor trailers. The weather doesn't bode well for me either. I had arranged for a tour of the Imperial Irrigation District's facilities, but nothing's being pumped now, because the farmers want less water, not more. Instead I meet with Dave Bradshaw, supervisor of the irrigation-management unit. Bradshaw appears drawn by Charles M. Schulz: a bigheaded, genial man who sketches diagram after multicolored diagram of irrigation systems on a giant whiteboard so fast that I feel like I'm witnessing an astrophysics lecture on fast-forward.

Bradshaw creates a flowchart of the water's path from river to field. Of the 3.1 million acre feet the IID transports, 98 percent is used for agriculture. Farmers tell the IID how much water they want a day ahead of time. Using past averages, the IID has already told the U.S. Bureau of Reclamation how much water it will need for the week. Based on the requests of the IID and other water districts in years past, the USBR has sluiced the appropriate amount through the Hoover Dam. Thus a farmer's water order has been en route for seven days before he requests it. Such a prognostic system depends on uniform, reliable weather—as faith in such, the IID lacks large holding reservoirs—but all bets are off "if it rains like this," says Bradshaw.

He whips an eraser across the board and draws a cross section of an imaginary field. The Imperial Valley lacks natural drainage, so six feet under their crops farmers have installed corrugated pipes to collect excess drainage. In the 1989 transfer deal, Los Angeles paid for tailwater-return systems that recycle runoff, known as tailwater, back through cropland. In essence, the sea now gets 100,000 acre-feet less a year, an amount L.A. takes "right out of the Hoover order," says Bradshaw. Revenue was the overwhelming incentive, but the IID also embraced the transfer because, prodded by thirsty constituencies, the state ordered it to "conserve" tailwater. "We had people over here with video cameras taking pictures of the water running off the fields," says Bradshaw.

With a transfer of three times as much water in the works, "now the state's saying [we've got to] keep all that water going to the Salton Sea because if you lower it one inch, there's going to be an environmental problem, so it's a Catch-22 situation," says Bradshaw. "Some were suing when it was going up, some when it was going down . . . At one time there were eighty-six studies [on how to save the sea] going on, so depending on which study you want to believe and which one the state's pushing hardest . . ."

And then there are physical barriers to the agreement, which calls for lining the eighty-two-mile All American Canal, and some of the 16,000 miles of smaller canals, with cement. "It's hard to line something with water in it," Bradshaw notes dryly. The only way to do so is through diversion, which is how we got the Salton Sea to begin with. "Catch-22," he repeats.

That night I take Wilson to Niland for dinner. Over cheeseburgers and beers, we discuss Slab City justice, vigilantism that ranges from relatively mild mischief making—tacks under tires—to homicide. Some years ago, Wilson says, a Slab kid who despite multiple warnings continued to rob other residents was found floating in an IID canal, decapitated. There had been other violent deaths at the Slabs, and suspicious fires like Frank's were fairly common. Theft is epidemic, largely attributable to drifters and, in the case of food and water, illegal aliens. Still, given that it is a basically anarchic community, the place seemed pretty peaceable; most people I met seemed generous and neighborly in a way that's utterly incompatible with the suburban isolation most Americans experience. When a homeowner on the other side of the sea had commented that "you have a group like that and nobody trusts each other because nobody's trustworthy," I had bristled.

Wilson interrupts my train of thought. "I'm on the run, you know," he says. He's scrupulously avoided being photographed, so I'd figured, but I flush anyway. "Don't worry, luv," he says. "I didn't murder anyone."

If people come to Slab City running from anything, it's precisely what I am finding myself immersed in: stories of depression and marital unhappiness, of roads taken and not taken, of regrets and obligation. It is exhausting. In search of a break from two weeks of darkness, I decide to visit Salvation Mountain. Leonard Knight, now seventy-one, arrived here sixteen years ago. He tried to launch a hotair balloon bearing the slogan GOD IS LovE, but it "rotted out" on him. So he thought he'd take a week, build "an eight-foot mountain, but God had another plan."

At about 5:00 nearly every morning, Leonard gets to work, lifting bales of hay—"as I get older, they get heavier"—which, like the paint, his trucks, and his tractor, are donated. The mountain needs constant maintenance, which he does "as often as the paint comes in. Like if a pretty gallon of orange comes in, wow, I paint all the flowers orange. I just play it by ear." In 1990, Salvation Mountain collapsed under the weight of all that paint—Leonard estimates he's applied more than 100,000 gallons—and he rebuilt.

In 1994 county supervisors declared the mountain a "toxic nightmare," to be buried in a hazardous-waste site in Nevada. "The *Los Angeles Times* said that the laws of God and the laws of man are going to collide in Niland, California," recalls Leonard. "And we collided with every museum on my side, because every old painting in the world has lead in it." That, and Leonard is considered an important outsider artist, compared with Grandma Moses. "Gee that thrills me," he says. "I can't believe it. I must be the biggest counterfeit in the whole world."

Later that night, back at the fire pit, Leonard pulls up in his fantastically painted truck and steps out with a battered guitar to serenade us for the evening. As the fire starts to die, he compares his battle with the county to the periodic threats of various developers to turn Slab City into a paid campground. Who, he asks, would pay to be next to a bombing range and to smell the Salton Sea? "I'd almost give a dollar a day not to smell the Salton Sea," he cackles.

A hundred and fifty years ago, Horace Greeley made famous the expression "Go West, young man, and grow up with the country." The trouble is that the country grew faster than anyone could have anticipated, and the flow west has become backwash. We pushed from sea to shining sea, and now our aspirations—sadly diminished as they are to the manicured-lawn variety—have grown too big for the land. We are not living within our means, and at the Salton Sea you can see the bills mount. Here is where the Cadillac desert blows a gasket, where the hucksters go to die, where salvation comes hand in hand with lead poisoning, where the last of the pioneers squat on the last sorry piece of free land, where suburban expansionism and a tidal wave of immigration conspire and collide. That coming bubble of uninsured elderly we keep hearing about? That's here. The speed, crank, and meth that are sweeping through blue collar America? Those drugs are cooked and shipped from here.

The sea itself will probably not survive the seeming necessity of Pizza Huts, of three-car garages and grass in the desert, of our God-given right to golf. Since I left, the urban editorial pages have become increasingly shrill: How dare a bunch of bird lovers and dirt farmers stop progress? When Senator Dianne Feinstein warned that fields could be fallowed voluntarily with compensation, or by force and without, an IID board member called her a "bureaucratic gasbag, pig-eyed sack of crap." In September the state suspended a law that barred the killing of thirty-seven endangered species. The Interior Department is barreling ahead with the transfer, even though it won't release a congressionally mandated environmental-impact statement—a fait accompli that prompted the Sierra Club, the Cabazon Indian tribe, and others to seek a federal injunction in September. The IID hesitantly agreed to limited fallowing, but farmers fear being sued if the sea perishes and the area becomes a dust bowl. Even if a solution to the sea is found, sprawl is like crime: push it out of one neighborhood and it pops up elsewhere.

Yet for all the grinding shortsightedness the valley represents, it is also full of people adept at change, those who shed their skins and start anew. "It's nice to know," someone back in the real world said to me, "that there's a place to go if your life goes to hell."

Slab City is that respite, but it is more. At first glance its residents appear as faded as the fifties landscape they inhabit. But that undervalues their weedy tenacity, their tolerance of eccentricity. Anyway, they don't care what you think. Ideas of conventional success, of anything conventional, they're past that now, if they ever cared to begin with. Whatever combination of adventure and avoidance caused them to hit the road, once a year they gather among the like-minded and together they improvise a meal, a community, a family. One of Leonard Knight's songs puts it best:

> The road treated me so poor, so cold, wet, and damp.
> I came to Slab City, just looking like a tramp.
> Then a family gave me a smile,
> So I think I'll linger here awhile.
> Here in Slab City,
> California, U-S-A.

## Questions for Discussion

1. Despite its somewhat offbeat cast of characters, Slab City has stronger community-based values than those found in the "suburban isolation most Americans experience," according to Jeffrey. What evidence does she use to support this claim? Evaluate the effectiveness of her claim based on this evidence.

2. Choose one of the people Jeffrey profiles. Assess her tone and the details she selects as she talks about that person. Does she present him or her as a refugee from mainstream life, as someone whose ideas ought to be taken seriously, or what?

3. What happens to the Salton Sea area is a reflection of what's going on far from it—in suburbs being developed near distant cities, in political discussions where water is wrangled over, and so on. Explain how the essay relates the cause-and-effect relationship of these far-off events to life, both human and otherwise, in the area near the Sea.

## Ideas for Writing

1. Slab City is a "respite" but also a place where people live unconventionally, or even reinvent themselves altogether, according to Jeffrey. In that respect, it could either be called an ideal place to live the California dream, or a place that attracts people who are fringe characters, loners, or runaways. Write an essay in which you explain your agreement or disagreement with seeing the area as a dream-place. (Hint: refer to a definition of the dream found in one of the readings in Chapter 1 to help make your case.)

2. Water rights issues and water management seem to be constant themes in California life and politics. Research the current state of the issue as it applies to the Salton Sea. Write an essay in which you explain whether the predictions in Jeffrey's article, which suggests that the Sea will not survive the push for development, have come true, or whether the people interested in saving the Sea are winning the battle.

---

# Spaced Out West
## STANLEY POSS

*Stanley Poss is Professor of English Emeritus at California State University, Fresno. He frequently contributes to the* Sacramento Bee, *and is a member of the board of Fresno Filmworks, the Fresno Free College Association, and several community action groups.*

---------------  ✦  ---------------

Along with other urban blessings, the franchised quick-order food joints such as "Colonel" Sanders, The Big M (McDonald's Hamburgers), Dairy Delite, and their legion of competitors have been taken reasonably enough to signify the end of the American dream of westering, the end of the frontier, the end of the Open Road (which has now been seen to lead to a used car lot). But the peculiarly American felt relationship between space and moral and political simplicities survives in pockets and may even be increasing its appeal. As one might expect, the more isolated areas of the West Coast have become attractive gathering spots for those who believe that if only they can get some land, lotsa land (or even a patch so long as it's sufficiently removed from their neighbors), they will fulfill the Thoreauvian ideal of simplification. No one, I suppose, among these New Agrarians thinks of the West in the old way, that is, as a place where a man's a man, a woman's a woman, and there's none of this modern equivocation. But they do seem to think not only that this land is or can be their land but also that, planted on it, rooted in it, they'll draw sustenance from it that will clarify and make whole their lives. Like Steinbeck's Joads, they're avatars of Antaeus.

Chief among their West Coast bases is Humboldt County, an under-populated and thickly forested area on California's north coast whose southern boundary is two hundred miles above

San Francisco. Named for the German naturalist, who, however, did not include it in his travels, it's about one hundred fifty miles long (it's the next to last county before Oregon) and extends inland between fifty and seventy-five miles. Its 3500 square miles support some 100,000 people, that is, about twenty-nine inhabitants per square mile, as compared with San Francisco County's 15,000 for each of its forty-five miles. Like New Hampshire, it has always seemed to me to mark the line where the real north begins, the mythic north; and passing into it from the infinite extensions of San Francisco and Bay Area urbanization is like passing into, say, scruffy, violent, anarchic Keene from sleek and predictable Amherst.

Humboldt County shares some of its amenities with its Eastern counterpart, others are unique. It has redwoods, unswimmable beaches, rain, headlands, Indians; funny place-names such as Kneeland, Samoa, Manila, Fickle Hill, Trinidad, the Mad River, Petrolia, and Hoopa; a big lumber industry, space, clean air, old houses, incipient urban freeways, a small bay mostly mud flats (the bay was called "Humboldt" before the county), some commercial fishing, the coolest summers south of Juneau, cranes and egrets, a depressed economy, and a powerful attraction for those who define the good life as being spaced way out from urban centers: hippies, hairies, van-dwellers, eco-freaks, and the kids generally. Old America overlaid by The Youth, its centers are Eureka and Arcata. Eureka ("You've Found It," the billboards say) is a bare town of 30,000 with more Victorian houses per inhabitant than one might reasonably expect, including that ultimate specimen of Carpenter Gothic, the Carson House. The much smaller Arcata, ten miles north on highway 101 at the top of the bay, has a pretty plaza, hills, shops and small restaurants in the Grand Funk style, cheap movies, a good bookstore, and Humboldt State University, successively Humboldt Normal, Humboldt State Teachers College, Humboldt State College, California State University, Humboldt (Arcata), Hohum (or Bumhole) Tech, and Dumbo (or Limbo) State, an institution with a hilly campus, popular natural-resources programs, anomie, and political influence.

Though a local columnist has it otherwise, nothing much happened in this dim northern land between, say, 1860 and 1960. (At least it's become traditional to say so.) The woods were clearcut, some Indians were killed, Bret Harte wrote journalism for a local paper, it rained. Even today, according to the latest authoritative survey, most Angelenos and San Franciscans believe it's in Oregon. Traditionally insulated from the rest of the state, more or less untouched by population explosions and the problems of the cities, it went its oblivious way. All the upheavals of the early '60's, civil rights, farm labor, the war, seem to have touched it lightly or not at all. Its political apathy is still almost as intense on campus as off. Gown recently voted against open personnel files while Town was simply puzzled by a few bedraggled Safeway pickets ("Cesar Chavez? Who's he when he's at home?"). But times change and even Humboldt County changes with them, chiefly because it has become the West Coast headquarters for young New Agrarians fleeing the cities.

Believing that their lives are well served to the degree they manage to avoid urban and suburban milieus, these new friends of the earth are reifying a constellation of some of our oldest political and social notions. Pervasive antecedents can be found in Brook Farm, Thoreau, the twin concepts of westering and the frontier, the myths of the village and of Eden itself and the opposing myths of metropolis and the jungle of the cities, in *Faust*, *Candide*, W. B. Yeats, John Synge and his islanders, Ken Kesey, Forster's *Howards End*, you name it. Naturally, the Agrarians recoil from the concept that More Is Better and eschew the dream of success, except on their terms. They favor wild or at least rural areas, handcrafts, small co-ops, Victoriana, camp, unwritten social contracts. As nearly everyone knows by now, their values cluster around a few familiar verities. Progress as it's usually defined operationally is a fraud. ITT and the oil companies run Amerika. War is insane. Social and religious and educational and political institutions exist chiefly to maintain the same snouts in the trough (though as we'll see the Agrarians believe one can affect local political issues). White sugar gives you cancer and kills your sexuality. Processed foods generally are poison. History isn't bunk, it's shit. Everything they tell you is a lie because they hate us youth. On the other hand, as everyone knows who hasn't sold out, movies, rock, sandals, beards, jeans, boots, old clothes generally, vans, pot, open-air sex, and natural foods are good (not that any of these comes as the hottest of news).

One would think them a mobile group by definition, but a fair number stay put long enough to vote. And since they tend to vote in a bloc for the antifreeway, pro-environmental candidates, they've directly affected recent elections. Although the local (Republican) Congressman who's never been known to offend the lumber interests or any other institution for that matter is still on the job, the trend has been Left in city and county races. The Mayor of Arcata (wife of a sociology don) presides over an enterprising, not to say free-swinging, City Council, a car dealer was threatened with removal for building on environmentally hallowed ground, and in general the moldy figs are no longer unquestionably in the ascendant. As one can imagine, these events have distressed many of the indigenes and their representative *The Times-Standard*, a Eureka daily that's no foe of the obvious. Linked with the Thompson chain, it's distinguished by its adherence to received ideas, its infallibly platitudinous editorials, its love affair with the Chamber of Commerce and the giant Louisiana-Pacific Lumber Company, its disinclination to fault any institution, and its fascination with area sports. Well, this distress peaked in a recent Arcata City Council election when two young anti-freeway candidates were elected over a large field, one of whom, a member of the Sheriff's Department, put his defeat in perspective when he informed his constituents that they'd turned the city over to a bunch of Hitlerites and punks and made it a little Berkeley. The references had no real referents, as far as I can see, except that one of the winners was the director of the local recycling enterprise. Since Hitler could be said to have recycled the paper of Versailles into the armaments of the Ruhr, perhaps it makes sense to regard recyclers generally as cryptofascists (or commies, it makes no matter).

A similar division occurred in a recent county election when the voters confronted the issue of whether to dam the Mad River in remote and privately owned Butler Valley some twenty miles upstream. The Army Corps of Engineers was set to go but the voters turned their backs on progress and rejected the proposal. This was by no means a straight Environment vs. Growth issue since Humboldters might have had to accept a considerable tax liability for the dam. Nor was the vote on Town-Gown lines: the Nays carried precincts far removed from the influence of HSU. Nonetheless, the anti-dam position of the University weekly and its special supplements, and the hard work of some of the kids, together with the youth vote, generally ensured a defeat for the dam proponents, though it's fair to say the defeat might well have occurred in any case.

The local ad man who chaired the pro-dam committee made it sound pretty ominous without the dam and pretty good with. "We must have some growth and progress," he said, "or this area will become the most depressed area imaginable. Butler Valley is our opportunity to effect moderate growth, to build payrolls, to encourage tourism, which incidentally is our greatest area of opportunity for economic development. This is a desirable type of development as people visit our area, spend money and leave, not posing an over-population problem." But even though he stressed the benefits and amenities consequent upon the dam, even though he pointed out that the land would become public and that floods would be eliminated, the voters weren't persuaded. My point in raising the issue is to call attention to the rejection here of the boosterism argument. As I've said, part of that rejection was merely self-interest in the form of fear of more taxes. But another part stemmed from a wholesale opposition to the mode of living implied in the language of the boosters. And given the stagnant economy of the county, that opposition is remarkable (remarkably short-sighted, its enemies would say). It's not very risky to say that it would hardly have existed ten years ago, since change has traditionally been identified with growth in Humboldt, and both have been thought good.

I shouldn't imply that the loosely cohesive group I've attempted to describe is more than loose. Whether they're real back-to-the-landers or just college kids who like to hike, their chief article of faith is suspicion of federations of all sorts. But, like anarchists who can sometimes put aside their detestation of organizations, they can be counted on to vote in favor of Letting It Be. They don't know Thoreau but instinctively they feel as he thinks. They see themselves as the real Americans, as he did, and like him they're social revolutionaries mostly by indirection. They endorse his idea that "A town is saved, not more by the righteous men in it, than by the swamps and woods that so surround it." They stand for Old America, they believe, and their radicalism is nowhere so apparent as in their deliberate preference for the old-fashioned. The irony is that they come here as to a last frontier for the true America of their imagining, and, coming, change it, despite their howdies and overalls and boots and grannies and calico dresses and VW covered wagons. This change was dramatized by the Fourth of July celebrations on Two Street in Old Town Eureka, the mainline street of yesterday whose Victorian crazies are now undergoing renewal. Two Street is about as close to Eureka's small commercial waterfront as you can get, and in the old days was the place for the whores and high-rollers. Subsequently it became Northern California's most famous Skid Row. Now, as I said, an urban renewal program is underway to smarten it up and capitalize on its raffish charms by bringing in the tourists.

The Fourth celebrations on the Street were revived last year and blossomed hugely into this year's gala. All the straights go fishing and kids take over with booths, music, street dancing, beer, love-ins, grubby and nutty clothes, makeup. The event really deserves a long and lovingly circumstantial and richly Proustian account only the bare outlines of which I can sketch here in this brief Social Note from All Over (Humboldt County). It's a saturnalia, a frolic, a rite of spring, a licensed folly, a carnival (though no one is thinking of giving up meat) in which bikers, Agrarians, children, aging hippies, students straight and emeriti, freaks, and some bourgeoisie mingle as the great Carson House at the top of the street broods inscrutably on the odd goings-on. One has fish and chips, shouts Wow at ten-minute intervals, digs the hairy and colorful Children of Paradise, and drinks beer with the Two Street Poet whose pad lies in an alley just off the Street and thus smack in the center of the pulsing heart of the Great City. Author of the observation that "The fly is on the lip of the Vinegar Jug" and a boyo on whom there are absolutely no flies, the Poet is a translator of Spanish and Mayan literature and a mud man ("without strength, runny vision, mind of mud, can't turn his head to look behind") who reads frequently in local pubs and occasionally works packing fish or teaching an extension course. Never daunted, he is said to have reassured his friends on emerging from a vasectomy by observing dispassionately, "Urethra, I've lost it." His pad was the scene of a large-scale tostada operation in behalf of a local free school whose booth was selling them like, well, hotcakes. Then back to the street and the Roman license thereof. One expected, in the memorable words of Faulkner's Jason Compson, to find them at it like a couple of dawgs in the middle of the square or under a wagon in front of the courthouse. And (again quoting the misogynist Jason) damme if they don't dress so's to make every man they pass want to reach out and clap his hand on it.

And yet for all the gaiety of a Two Street Fourth and the ostensible small-town friendliness of Humboldt County, alienation and anomie abound. Fog hangs on for much of the summer while the winters are mild but the rain almost never stops. The social atomization in parts of the University is pervasive and extreme. You tire of seeing the same people and they you, with the result that everyone tends to clam up (appropriately, I suppose, in view of the Hoopa creation myth that ascribes the curious behavior of the whites in the area to an original union between their progenitors, an ancient fisherman, first of his race to settle here, and an especially succulent *saxidomus* for which he conceived a passion). A lot of not knowing and not wanting to know goes on. In fact, a Cloud of Unknowing blankets the place for months at a time. Friends go by default, paranoia thrives. Shaky marriages fail. The ramshackle and Middle Eastern quality about North Coast life that seemed rather winning initially begins to drive you around the bend. (An English teacher said you have to get over the idea that you're in California because really you're in a wet Cairo.) Phone calls don't get through, memos aren't answered, secretaries disappear. One feels a long way from anywhere by February. Two Street can seem the end of the road instead of Fat City to many of its regulars on the fifth consecutive wet gray Thursday morning. The houses and yards have a Puritan austerity; where once their Sartrean bareness and fragility seemed moving and appropriate and symbolized unaccommodated man, the very image of America, as in *The Last Picture Show*, now they're simply dull. Huddled between sea and hill, crouched under the low sky, the houses are oppressed, spiritless, mean, while their typically treeless yards signify the provincial isolation and smugness of the place as one forgets the real reasons for this North Coast trademark, which are partly economic, partly esthetic, and partly a matter of climate ("With all those redwoods and all that fog who needs trees? We want sun"). The continued existence of the dark forests on Fickle Hill and endlessly beyond is merely pointless. You don't really want to make another trip to Ferndale, the pretty Victorian village down the road, and San Francisco's too far. The local arts are zilch except for a few ceramicists, the music third rate. Morris Graves lives nearby but, while not the recluse Salinger is, almost never shows his work. Life in the hills where some hard-core environmentalists *cum* recyclers are rumored to be living—in redwood stumps or on the reservations or the Samoa Peninsula, a subsistence-level collection of beaten little houses, or in the vans students live in—doesn't bear thinking on. The converted Mother's Cookies truck that seemed so funky in October looks now merely raunchy and the old Corvair van with the jaunty orange Popsicle decal has a flat and looks unsafe at no speed at all. You long for splendid redwood and stone and glass multilevel "Sunset" houses of the sort you might reasonably expect to see in an area like this but almost never do. (Two of the most elegant, both by architect owners, lie off the coast south of the old fishing town of Trinidad but are quite invisible from the road.) You want the frankly sybaritic instead of the everlasting wafflestompers and jeans and minicampers and vans. Swish and posh never seemed so desirable; you find yourself spending more time with *The New Yorker* than is healthy. Away with Volkswagens and Datsuns! Begone, universal ferns and colei! Out, cozy little short-order spots with camp decor and carefully negligent charm! Down with all drift-wood mobiles! Back where you came from, great rusty bolts, shells, stones, and other sea treasures! Nobody comes to visit, the winds keep drilling the rain into you, you've just seen Jennifer Jones as Mme. Bovary, you feel the redwood curtain descending for good, you're in the ultimate provinces.

Money of course is the root but the money doesn't live here, it's in San Francisco, Portland, Chicago. That's why there is no economic base to support the local arts. You can't have an active sponsorship of the arts in a capitalist order without some form of salon system, it appears; you can't have salons without *grandes dames*; you can't have *grandes dames* without money. With money you'd see fewer of the ephemeral houses and more redwood and glass ones. With money you'd have swish villages like Amherst or Williams or some of those other fantastic Western Massachusetts towns that rival those of Kent and Sussex in their happy harmony of trees and houses, fields and farms. With money you could comb and groom the landscape as it is in southern England. But these raw North Coast towns that we believe and die in have their own powerful appeal as they are, if one has a bit of money, that is. There's no question but that Humboldt County gets in your blood if you're at all susceptible to its charms of forest and shore together with a town life notable for its conspicuously undizzying pace and sense of community. In common with other exurbanites, I love the place immoderately, and also, in common with them, feel more native than the natives, like the Anglo-Irish whose assimilation has come to be total, at least from their point of view. Possibly we need a term for this acculturation such as "San Francisco Eurekans" or "Urban Humboldters" or "Angeleno Arcatans," possibly not. In any case, as I mentioned, I and other newcomers change the place by our presence, no matter how great our sense of instinctive rapport with it. But the change is reciprocal as well, so it's a question of who changes first and most. I hope it wins, that is, changes least, this dim northern land, this remote Western Slope, this afterthought of California, this great empire of trees, this garden of earthly delights, this other Eden, this cloudy gem set on a steel-gray sea, this blessed plot, this realm, this Humboldt.

[1977]

## Questions for Discussion

1. What dreams do people harbor when they move to Humboldt County? How could these be understood as fitting in with or contrasting with the California dream, as for instance it is described by the writers in Chapter 1 of this book?

2. What politics do the people in Humboldt County espouse, according to the article? How do these fit with what actually happens in debates over local political issues?

3. At some point, living in this place starts to wear on people, making them long for all that it cannot offer, according to Poss. What does a person start to hate about the place, and what antidote does the article offer to this problem?

## Ideas for Writing

1. Go online or use your library's newspaper index to find out what has happened in Humboldt County in the thirty years or so since this piece was written. (You might want to check real estate prices and population data, to start.) Write a report on the changes, and assess whether the place still has the charms that Poss claims for it.

2. The piece mentions Thoreau several times. Read his *Walden*, then write an essay which explains why he would do well as a resident of Humboldt County.

---

# Morongo Tribe's New Casino Aims to Be a Hipster Magnet

## CHRISTINA BINKLEY

*Christina Binkley is a staff writer with the* The Wall Street Journal *in Los Angeles, where she writes about leisure, culture, and childhood, among other topics. She spent 10 years covering casinos and hotels for the newspaper. She recently completed a book on the rivalry between two Las Vegas gambling moguls, Steve Wynn and Kirk Kerkorian (Hyperion, 2007). Binkley is a graduate of the Columbia University Graduate School of Journalism and lives in the Hollywood Hills.*

---- ✦ ----

Morongo Reservation, Calif.—When the Morongo Band of Mission Indians decided to pour $250 million into a new casino and hotel outside Palm Springs, some members of the tribe pushed to incorporate proud references to their culture—desert themes, local basketry, maybe even a museum.

But tribal elders had something else in mind: a hip, Hollywood-oriented hotel designed to attract young gamblers from Los Angeles who normally flock to Las Vegas. Taking aim at the Paris Hilton crowd, the tribe gave the Morongo casino a Sunset Strip-style nightclub with darkly lit VIP party rooms. A restaurant, called Belly, serves crudo, the Italian version of sashimi, while a gift shop, Stuff, sells clingy tees from the trendy House of Bimbo label.

What's lacking are the Native American touches and the mainstream glitzy decor that characterize many of California's more than 50 other tribal casino operations, which cater for the most part to local gamblers, seniors and middle-age folks. So while the Barona Valley Ranch Indian casino, outside San Diego, has gray-haired country singer Kenny Rogers for a spokesman, the Morongo hired pop music act Destiny's Child to headline its opening celebration in December.

It's all an aggressive bid on the Morongo's part to siphon off some of the growing number of L.A. gamblers, who have recently rediscovered Vegas as a hip weekend destination and helped send casino profits there soaring. "Like anything else, you start with the young people," says Maurice Lyons, the Morongo tribal counsel's 55-year-old chairman, who grew up on the reservation with dirt floors and paper stuffed in windows to prevent drafts. "When they walk in that door, they're going to think they're in Las Vegas. That's where the money's at."

It isn't clear yet whether the strategy will pay off. The tribe doesn't reveal financial results. Mr. Lyons says the first weeks have been "packed" with customers. But Michael Morton, co-owner of N9NE Group, a closely held company that operates the restaurants and clubs at the Morongo, says they haven't done as well as expected initially. It can take a while for word to get out, says Mr. Morton, whose company also operates trendy nightclubs and restaurants in Las Vegas and Chicago. And heavy rains in Southern California have hurt business.

The Morongo casino sits on the tribe's 32,000-acre reservation two hours outside of Los Angeles on Interstate 5, the well-traveled freeway to Palm Springs. Las Vegas, by comparison, is four or five hours from L.A. by car, depending on traffic. The 1,100-member tribe is hoping to benefit from the resurgence in popularity of Palm Springs, Hollywood's longtime resort getaway, as well as their casino's location next to a designer outlet mall with shops selling merchandise from Zegna, Versace, and Escada.

The casino's ultramodern design—the hotel rooms have a silhouette-revealing opaque glass window between the shower and the bedroom—sets it apart from other tribal casinos in California, which are growing faster than anywhere else in the nation. Other Indian casinos often opt to promote their native heritage: In Connecticut, the Mashantucket Pequots' Foxwoods casino calls its loyalty club "Wampum Rewards."

When the Bishop Paiute tribe in California last year considered expanding its casino, some tribal leaders pressed for a themed Native American resort. "We have to put our culture out there where we can. That's how we preserve it," said Paul Chavez, a former tribal official, during a debate last March [2004]. The tribe hasn't reached a decision.

Mr. Lyons says many members of the Morongo tribe similarly wanted to see their culture showcased in the resort. He talked them out of the idea. "When I explained it to them, they understood that this is a profit-making enterprise so we can spend the money elsewhere," he says.

The Morongo, actually a band of several small clans that have occupied the reservation since 1876, have been running gambling operations since opening a bingo hall in 1983. For decades, the tribe was better known for owning Hadley Fruit Orchards, selling dates and other produce at a roadside stand.

The tribe expanded their bingo hall into a casino and added a cavernous wing in 2000. The old casino—smoke-filled, warehouse-like and with chandeliers in the shape of arrowheads—was the cash cow that paid for the new casino next door and has enabled the tribe to buy up more land to expand its reservation around Palm Springs. Mr. Morton says the tribe told him the old casino brought in $360 million in revenue last year, putting it on par with major Las Vegas casinos such as Treasure Island.

The tribe's plan to boost revenue even more involves imitating the strategy of the Palms Casino, the Las Vegas hipster-hangout famous for parties attended by the likes of Britney Spears. The Morongo tribe brought in the N9NE Group because it runs Palms venues such as N9NE steakhouse and GhostBar, whose equivalent at the Morongo casino is called SpaceBar.

In fact, tribal counsel members, most of them with graying hair, studied the Palms closely over the past few years. They visited the edgy Las Vegas resort "repeatedly," says Scott DeGraff, Mr. Morton's partner at the N9NE Group. "They really did their homework."

The tribe also hired the Jerde Partnership, the Venice, Calif., architecture firm that designed the Palms. Thinking the tribe would lean toward Indian themes, Jerde initially offered the tribal

**Map of Indian Casinos**
*Source:* California Official Visitor's Guide

counsel two designs. The first was "more earthy" with wicker and baskets, says Sharmila Tankha, lead architect on the project. The other option had ultramodern lighting effects and a glass-beaded water curtain surrounding a pit bar. The counsel chose the second after considering the options for about five minutes, she says.

To draw 25- to 40-year-olds, about 70% of the casino's slot machines uses video technology rather than the spinning-reel look of most Las Vegas slot machines. "We believe that [our] customer is the gambler of the future," says Bill Davis, the Morongo casino's general manager. "They're younger—they're used to playing videogames."

To avoid offending its loyal gamblers, the casino uses low walls and pathways to segregate slot machines that appeal to older locals but might turn off young partiers from Hollywood. "Our customers don't have to wander past the 'Jeopardy' and the 'Beverly Hillbillies'" slot machines, Mr. Morton says.

Still, the gap between the tribe and its hoped-for customers was clear at the casino's two-night opening event. Performing for tribal members on the first night's Indian-sovereignty celebration were Jay Leno and rock elder Carlos Santana. Afterward, tribal members straggled into the casino's clubs, while at least one young band member frowned and left to hunt for action that, on that night at least, was absent.

Casino officials say the opening event wasn't for the hipsters they expect to draw going forward, but instead was for tribal members and their friends. "That isn't our crowd," says N9NE Group's Mr. DeGraff. Indeed, nearby that evening members of Destiny's Child were holed up in the casino's luxurious VIP suites. They appeared the next night at a glitzy celebrity event to which most tribal members weren't invited.

Still, the tribal counsel plans to cater to demands that their culture be showcased somewhere. Mr. Lyons says plans will soon be drawn up for a museum on the reservation, to be located about a mile behind the casino.

## Questions for Discussion

1. The marketing approach the Tribe chose for their casino has left a "gap between the Tribe and its hoped-for customers." What arguments does the essay use to justify the approach the Tribe took? Look for both stated and unstated arguments.

2. What do you find out about the business of casino gambling which surprises you? Are your beliefs about tribal gaming challenged by what you learn in this article?

3. The Morongo Tribe plans to open a museum to showcase its culture. Does the article present that as being more, or less, effective than building tribal design into the casino itself? What reasons could you offer to defend their decision, based on what you learn through the article?

## Ideas for Writing

1. The attempt to build new tribal casinos has created hot debate among citizens in many California communities. Select an example of this phenomenon, and write an essay in which you explain the strengths and weaknesses of each side's point of view. For one example, put "Graton Rancheria and gaming" into a search engine or your library's newspaper index.
2. For many people in California and elsewhere, the argument about the proliferation of Indian gaming comes down to tribal sovereignty versus the negative effects of gambling on communities. Imagine that a tribe is trying to build a large casino near where you live. Would you support the effort, or would you be against the growth of gambling operations? Write an essay arguing your point of view and taking into account the other side's case.

## Thinking and Writing about Chapter 5

### Connecting the Essays

1. Jeffrey and Poss talk about the more out-of-the-way places in California. These might be described as alternate venues in which to enact the dream. What similarities do you detect between the Salton Sea area and Humboldt County as described in the pieces? Do they seem to attract the same type of people? What are the values of those who live there?
2. Both Binkley and Haslam talk about Native Americans, though the focus of their articles is altogether different. How might you contrast Haslam's characterization of the Native Americans who live in the Central Valley with Binkley's portrayal of the contemporary Morongo Tribe? Where might there be value clashes between them if they were to dialogue about what's important to them?
3. Warshaw talks about young Californians practicing their favorite means of self-expression, and Binkley talks about a tribal casino as attempting to attract people with a defined sense of style—the "hipsters," in her parlance. Do these writers assume that young (or "younger") people in California are sold out to the idea of having a defined lifestyle—surfer, hipster (or, for sake of discussion, something else)? Is this a California phenomenon, or one which is generally true of youth culture, without regard to geography?
4. Haslam talks about an "other" California—the scattered small towns in the Central Valley. Jeffrey shares this focus on the obscure, the out-of-the-way, the overlooked. What about each place is worthy of preservation, according to the articles? Discuss how each might be said to be creating history about places and people who might otherwise be obscured or forgotten.
5. Each of the writers in this chapter could be seen as discussing an alternate culture, depending, of course, on how the "mainstream" is defined. Take any

two not paired above and figure out how they share a set of values, beliefs, or cultural practices, and how these fit with or clash with the California dream as you define it from other sources. (Hint: review Chapter 1 on the dream.)

### Extending the Theme

1. The attempt to develop Salton City has overtones of the big dreams and hype people often equate with California. Write an essay in which you explain how M. Penn Phillips fits into the profile of the typical California dreamer, and what happens to such dreamers in the end. You might strengthen your essay by contrasting another person to Phillips, either someone you know, or someone you've read about. (Hint: William Willmore, who founded Willmore City in the 1880s, is one such dreamer.)

2. Tribal gaming issues have played a large role in recent California politics. Several ballot propositions on gaming have been contested in the past decade or so. Research one of them, and make an argument about whether you would have voted yes or no on it. You can find a list of them by looking at www.ss.ca.gov/elections, or search for 1998 Proposition 29, 1998 Proposition 5, or 2000 Proposition 1A.

3. Many subcultures have either been invented in California or popularized there. Some might include the gang subculture, the car culture and particularly hot rodding and low riding, and the New Age movement. Choose one of these or another one that you identify. Read up on it, then write an essay in which you talk about the origins and values of this subculture and how it fits with the spirit of the state.

4. Watch some old beach movies from the sixties (*Beach Blanket Bingo* is one such film), or listen to some surf music (such as that of the Beach Boys). Write an essay in which you talk about the lifestyle portrayed in the examples you choose. What's not said about life in California which might change the viewpoint of the watcher or listener?

5. Read further in the works of Gerald Haslam. Write an essay in which you describe his overarching vision of the state of California, or his portrayal of one aspect of its culture. How does Haslam's presentation of the state help to give a more complete picture of the subcultures present in the state but often not thought of when California is discussed? (Find out, for instance, what he says about "Oildale" or the "Oakies.")

Barbour, Heather. "Slice 'N Dice: Smaller Legislative Districts Will Yield More Lawmakers, More Accountability, and Better Decision Making," *California Journal*, January 2005.

Binkley, Christina. "Morongo Tribe's New Casino Aims to Be a Hipster Magnet," *Wall Street Journal*, March 2, 2005, p. B1. *Wall Street Journal*, Eastern Edition by Christina Binkley. Copyright 2005 by Dow Jones & Company, Inc. Reproduced with permission of Dow Jones & Company, Inc. in the format Textbook via Copyright Clearance Center.

Burt, Kenneth C. "Fighting for Fair Employment," Jewish Labor Committee 64th Annual Recognition Awards Brunch, June 1999. Used by permission of Kenneth C. Burt.

Cooper, Marc. "Sour Grapes: California Farm Workers' Endless Struggle 40 Years Later," *LA Weekly*, August 12–18, 2005.

Darling-Hammond, Linda. "Lesson One: Training Counts," *Los Angeles Times*, September 1, 2002, p. M2. Reprinted by permission of Linda Darling-Hammond.

Davis, Mike. "The Third Border," in *Magical Urbanism: Latinos Reinvent the US City*, Verso, 2000, pp. 59–65. Used by permission of Verso.

Didion, Joan. "The Promise of the Prisions," in *Where I Was From*, Knopf, 2003, pp. 182–188. From *Where I Was From* by Joan Didion, copyright © 2003 by Joan Didion. Used by permission of Alfred A. Knopf, a division of Random House, Inc.

Fischer, Douglas. "You See Gridlock, I See Heaven," *Oakland Tribune*, January 2, 2006, p. 1. Reprinted by permission of Douglas Fischer and the *Oakland Tribune*.

Foong, Heng L. "Mind Your Language," SSG/PALS for Health Program. For more information about health care interpreting contact the National Council on interpreting in Health Care at www.ncihc.org or PALS for Health at www.palsforhealth.org. Used by permission of Heng L. Foong.

Glass, John and Judith Glass, "Unprotected Californians: Health Care as the new Civil Rights Issue," 2006. Reprinted by permission of John F. Glass and Judith Glass. Their thanks and appreciation to Doris Isolini Nelson for her unflagging devotion to universal health care and for sparking their interest and involvement.

Goldin, Greg. "The Paradox of the Hedge—Do Fences Really Make Good Neighbors?," *Los Angeles Times*, May 22, 2005. Used by permission of Greg Goldin.

Graham, Wade. "A Hundred Rivers Run Through It," *Harper's Magazine*, June 1998, Vol. 296, Issue 1777, p. 51. Copyright © 1998 by *Harper's Magazine*. All rights reserved. Reproduced from the June issue by special permission.

Haslam, Gerald W. "Other Californians," in *The Other California: The Great Central Valley in Life and Letters*, Capra Press, 1990, pp. 164–173. Reprinted by permission of Gerald W. Haslam.

Hodson, Timothy A. "History, Myth, and Political Instability in California". Reprinted by permission of Timothy A. Hodson, Center for California Studies, California State University, Sacramento.

Jeffrey, Clara. Excerpt from "Go West, Old Man," *Harper's Magazine*, November 2002, Vol. 305, Issue 1830, p. 52. Copyright © 2002 by *Harper's Magazine*. All rights reserved. Reproduced from the November issue by special permission.

Kotkin, Joel and William Frey, "The Third California," *Los Angeles Times*, January 29, 2006, p. M1+. Reprinted by permission of the authors.

Lapham, Lewis. "The Way West," *Harper's Magazine*, January 2000, Vol. 300, Issue 1796, pp. 6–9. Coyright © 1999 by *Harper's Magazine*. All rights reserved. Reproduced from the January issue by special permission.

Lees, Robert. Statement to the House Un-American Activities Committee. April 1951.

lê thi diem thúy, excerpt from *The Gangster We Are All Looking For*, in *California Uncovered: Stories for the 21st Century*, edited by Chitra Banerjee Divakaruni, et al., Heyday Books, 2005, pp. 150–156. *The Gangster We Are All Looking For* by lê thi diem thúy, copyright © 2003 by lê thi diem thúy. Used by permission of Alfred A. Knopf, a division of Random House, Inc.

Lewis, Randall. "The 2% Strategy: A Bold New Approach to Shape the Future of Southern California," SCAG State of the Region Report 2005. Reprinted by permission of Southern California Association of Governments. The complete State of the Region Report is available at www.scag.ca.gov/ sort.

McWilliams, Carey. "Population Whirligig," in *California: The Great Exception*, University of California Press, 1998, pp. 83–88.

Mills, Michael. "Blacklist: A Different Look at the 1947 HUAC Hearings." www.moderntimes.com/blacklist. Used by permission of Michael Mills.

Moran, Chris. "Graduation Marks Triumph for Homeless Woman," *The San Diego Union-Tribune*, May 30, 2004, p. B4. Reprinted by permission of *The San Diego Union-Tribune*.

Mungen, Donna. "The Anti-Heros: The LA4," in *Geography of Rage*, Really Great Books, 2002, pp. 97–99. Donna Mungen, "The Anti-Heros: The LA4," previously published in *LA Weekly*. Used by permission of Donna Mungen.

Piland, William E. "Sabotaging the California Dream," *Change*, July/August 2004, Vol. 36, Issue 4, pp. 20–25. Reprinted with permission of the Helen Dwight Reid Educational Foundation. Published by Heldref Publications, 1319 Eighteenth St., NW, Washington, DC 20036-1802. Copyright © 2004.

Poss, Stanley. "Spaced Out West," *The Yale Review*, 1977.

Reed, Ishmael. "My Oakland: There Is A There There," in *Writin' is Fightin'*, Atheneum Publishers 1998.

Rieff, David. Excerpt from *Los Angeles, Capital of the Third World*, Simon & Schuster, 1991, pp. 154–162. Reprinted with the permission of Simon & Schuster Adult Publishing Group from *Los Angeles: Capital of the Third World* by David Rieff. Copyright © 1991 by David Rieff.

Salario, Alizah. "Kids and Gangs: Seeking Solutions," *Eagle Rock Post*, June 2005, pp. 4, 13. Used by permission of *Eagle Rock Post*.

Schrag, Peter. "California Here We Come," *Atlantic Monthly*, March 1998, Vol. 281, Issue 3, p. 20, 22+. © Peter Schrag (1998)

Starr, Kevin. "A Nation-State," in *California: A History*, Random House, 2005, pp. ix–xiv, copyright © 2005 by Kevin Starr. Used by permission of Modern Library, a division of Random House, Inc.

Thompson, Chris. "A Shadow Falls Over the Square," *East Bay Express*, November 9–15, 2005. Reprinted by permission of *East Bay Express*.

Waldie, DJ. "My Place in Califonia," in *Where We Are Now: Notes from Los Angeles*, Angel City Press, 2004, pp. 47–50. © 2004 Donald J. Waldie from the book *Where We Are Now: Notes from Los Angeles*, Angel City Press. Used by permission.

Warshaw, Matt. "Surfacing," excerpted from *Maverick's*, Chronicle Books, 2000. From *Maverick's*, © 2000 by Matt Warshaw. Used with permission of Chronicle Books LLC, San Francisco. Visit ChronicleBooks.com.

Yasuda, Machiko. "Being Japanese is Pretty Cool After All," *L.A. Youth*, 2005. Reprinted with permission by *L.A. Youth*, the newspaper by and about teens. By Machico Yasuda.

Map 2.6 Number Hispanic, California Counties, 1990, UC Data and California Policy Research Center. (http://ucdata.berkeley.edu:7101/new_web/ldb/map2_6.jpg). Map 2.6 Number Hispanic, California Counties, 1990, UC Data and California Policy Research Center. (http://ucdata.berkeley.edu:7101/new_web/ldb/map2_6.jpg) Used by permission.

Map of CSU campus locations, www.calstate.edu/datastore/campus_map. Map of CSU campus locations, www.calstate.edu/datastore/campus_map. Used by permission.

Map of Beach Health Conditions, Heal the Bay online at www.healthebay.org/brc/statemap.asp. Map by Heal the Bay. Used by permission.

Map of Indian casinos, California Official Visitors Guide. Map by Eureka Cartography, Berkeley, CA. Used by permission.